How to

DOMINATE

$1 and $2 Blinds
No Limit Hold 'em

Secrets the pros don't tell you

by Sam O'Connor
Las Vegas' old man of poker

Bloomington, IN Milton Keynes, UK
authorHOUSE®

AuthorHouse™
1663 Liberty Drive, Suite 200
Bloomington, IN 47403
www.authorhouse.com
Phone: 1-800-839-8640

AuthorHouse™ UK Ltd.
500 Avebury Boulevard
Central Milton Keynes, MK9 2BE
www.authorhouse.co.uk
Phone: 08001974150

First published by AuthorHouse 6/01/2007

ISBN: 978-1-4343-0289-2

Printed in the United States of America
Bloomington, Indiana

This book is printed on acid-free paper.

This book is dedicated to
all the Pilgrims who have
wanted to make the Sacred
Journey to the Summit of
the Holy Game of Poker.

A special dedication to
Carolyn who continues to
make life worthwhile.
And to Mike who made it
all possible.

Apology

I write this apology in deference to the movement to give women the same rights and recognition as men. I'm all for it.

The astute reader will note that I use the words "he", "him" and "his" in this book when referring to all poker players. But, if the female gender for that player has been established, I use the female pronouns "she", "her" and "hers".

Many writers, in order to be politically correct, have taken the word "their" to be used generically in the singular. I view this as feeble political overture and a grammatical disgrace. The plural word, "their", was never intended to be used in the singular and no new pronoun has been invented to refer simultaneously to both genders in the singular, however badly needed.

In deciding whether to be politically correct by modern standards or grammatically correct by traditional utility, I have fallen on the traditional side of grammar.

Understand, I do hold the female of our species as an equal part of all humanity. They are not the women and we the men. *Au contraire.* We are, together, humans and in the good world we hold each other in respect and as one.

Parenthetically, it's interesting that the women of poker have yet to blend completely with the poker community. But some of us are working on it. Where we find nicknames among the men, such as "the mouth", "the professor", "the ice man", "the preacher" and "the grinder", we don't find those kinds of names among the women. We do, however, find respectable names like Jennifer Harmon, Annie Duke, Clonie Gowen, Jennifer Tilly, Evelyn Ng and Susie Isaacs, without any trace of a scurrilous nickname. Nor, to their credit, do they seek such nonsense.

Additionally, the tournaments, in my opinion, continue to insult female players with "ladies tournaments" and "ladies events". While these decidedly sexist promotions are endured by the many, I prefer to view all participants in all tournaments as collective "poker players".

The most recently liberated half of our species continues to play wonderful poker and, I hope, will someday find they are in the noble game without a trace of prejudice or innuendo. May it come together soon.

Meanwhile, I'm looking forward to the day when new pronouns are invented for generic gender referral in the singular, something that will replace my admitted bad use of "he", "him", and "his".

When the new pronouns arrive, I will do more than gladly use those new words; I will herald their arrival and champion their cause.   -   Sam O'Connor

How to Dominate $1 and $2 Blinds - No Limit Hold Em

Table of Contents

Discussion 101

Do You Want to Win?

Do you really want to win? Or do you just like to see the cards and to gamble?

The secrets of winning are in understanding the people and the cards, and applying the power of knowing how to play. When we understand the complete game of poker, we are ready to dominate the game.

We must understand the cards and the people and we must be decisive. In turn, when we are decisive, we put our money where our belief is. This is the basic power of the game. It is a simple concept, but we are constantly surprised at how many people play poker and don't understand it.

What you don't know, WILL hurt you in poker. But the readers of this book will understand the power and will win over those who do not understand the power.

In this section, over the next few days, we're going to establish one true thing:

Poker is not a card game played by people.

Poker is a people game played with cards.

Over many years, the game of poker has grown from a three card game to a seven card game. But the power in the game has remained the same.

Ever talk to a Porsche enthusiast? Mr. Enthusiast, why do you like the Porsche? It has no plush seat, little luggage space, and practically no bells and whistles. It's a lot of money for not much luxury.

Mr. Enthusiast will tell you he likes the Porsche <u>because</u> there are no bells and whistles.

The automobile is small; it is basically engine, transmission, steering and wheels. But it is precisely engineered. It truly is the basic driving machine. The pure, the uncomplicated, the true. Mr. Enthusiast doesn't depend on automatic anything. He leaves little to chance. All things that are done in the car's driving, he does with his own hands. <u>He has control.</u>

1

Control.

The professional poker player wants control. He needs control. When he loses control, he loses his money. When he has control, he wins the opponents' money.

By exercising some control over the opponents, he gains information about what kind of hidden cards they are playing. By knowing the players, he can learn when they are bluffing. By manipulating the players, he finds the areas where he can bluff. When he can Dominate the players, he can Dominate the game.

Anything left to chance? Of course, that's why it's called a gambling game. But, if the power player has control of the game, he leaves less to chance than others do. In taking fewer chances, the dominating player knows how to win.

The cards can't be manipulated, at least not within the rules (see Cheaters' Glossary), but action taken on cards can be controlled, and the opponents can be influenced and made to reveal many things.

Power and Image.

Power in poker is perception. It is the perception by the other players that we have the power.

We have to earn that image. It begins very early, earlier than sitting at the table. It begins with the manner in which we approach the table. It continues as we take our seat. Next comes the manner in which we arrange our players' checks. Be it the eagerness, or resolve, or calm objectivity we convey, we're being sized up. We haven't played yet and we already have an image.

If we give in and play a weak starting hand, that first impression of weakness will be the image we will have for a long time at that table; maybe we will never be rid of it at all that day.

When beginning play, we'll make the first hand we play a strong hand. Everyone at the table is watching. Everyone is paying special attention, even if it doesn't seem so. We need to appear to be strong. It may take a while to get that strong starting hand, but that's okay, we'll wait for it.

Now, in following this advice, what will we establish? We will play power hands to project a power image. That means we play strong hands. Then, when we have the power, we'll use it to dominate and to win some hands that the cards say we're not entitled to. Even if the weaker player often has better cards. Who had the best pocket cards? Who knows? The Dominator won the money.

What made it possible? The winner correctly perceived that his image was powerful in the eyes of the loser. And it was. Some players are in the habit of calling the opponents' attitude toward the dominant player "respect". The correct word is "fear".

Of course, it's nice to win many hands with overwhelming cards and that is called good luck. But, here's the huge dominating advantage: The Dominator can actually receive less than his share of good cards - and win big money.

The Shih Tzu.

An ordinary Shih Tzu is a small dog, but my girlfriend had one even littler; he weighed only five pounds. He knew he was small, but he was a player.

One day when he was on daily patrol, guarding the top of his driveway, two black labs dared to enter his domain. He watched them for awhile. Then, suddenly, his hackles went up and, with the ferocity of a miniature grizzly bear, he charged the black labs. The two labs looked at each other as if to say, "Can we be bothered with this?" and trotted off toward uncontested territory. The Shih Tzu strutted back to the house, head held high, and was much too proud and accomplished to be approached by humankind for at least twenty minutes.

On another occasion, he charged the tom cat down the street. The cat viewed the onrushing little dog and sat waiting. The little dog made a four skid stop just six inches away from the calmly prepared cat. In that instant, the Shih Tzu decided he had better choose his opponents wisely. He made friends with the cat.

Power poker and picking the right spot for confrontation is what winning is about.

Theoretically, if all players at a table played only the card odds, and played them correctly, over the long haul they'd all break even in a home game, and all lose in a casino game because of the rake.

In reality, if we are as diligent as my girlfriend's Shih Tzu, we will win more than our share of pots. To win more than our share, we need information.

Poker is a game of incomplete information. We never know enough about the hand our opponent holds. Even when we have the nuts, it pays to know about our opponent's hand and our opponent so that we can play our hand to win the most money. And when we have a marginal hand, we need all the information we can garner.

Bear Skin Betting.

It is easy to imagine how gambling and the art of playing the players got started.

A small boy wearing a bear skin for warmth picks up a pebble and places both hands behind his back. He then moves his hands in front him and asks his companion which hand he thinks the pebble is in. After his friend guesses, the boy then repeats the procedure and asks the companion to guess again. Has he moved the pebble to the other hand? Or, anticipating the guess of his companion, would he keep the pebble in the same hand?

Whether he switches the pebble to the other hand depends on how well he knows his companion. The more the guessing game continues, the more complicated it gets. And the outcome depends on how well the two boys know each other.

Then, of course, when the wager has escalated, the boy drops the pebble behind his back and offers two empty hands for his marked companion's choice. No. Wait. That's Three Card Monte.

Which would you rather be, the boy switching the pebble or the boy doing the guessing? Would you rather be the power player representing the power hand, or the opponent having to make the call? It's all about control.

Once again, the game is not about pebbles – it is about how well the two boys know each other and can anticipate which hand the pebble is in.

It's time to conjure up the old adage: Poker is not a card game; it is a people game. We can learn the mechanics of the poker cards, almost as well as boys know pebbles. But we will win when we know people.

Say it again, Sam: When we have learned the cards and the power bets, we can establish power. When we learn about the opponents and how to play them, we will usually win.

Do you have the power yet?

Minnesota Fats.

Fast Eddie and Minnesota Fats are dueling with cue sticks. The stake horse is there on behalf of Fats and on behalf of himself because he has a few wagers on the game. The contest is for money and for the street reputation of who is the best pool player.

Each player runs several racks before relinquishing action to the other player. The smoke is thick and the contest is exciting to the small gallery. So far, the players, tops in their field, are playing excellently and are fairly even.

After long play, Fast Eddie breaks loose with a series of brilliant shots and he is, so far, the winner of the day. But Eddie wants to play Fats some more pool.

Fast Eddie says, "I'm the best, Fats. Even if you beat me, I'm the best player."

Fats' mentor and stake horse immediately says, "Stay with this kid. He's a loser."

"EVEN IF YOU BEAT ME", expressed enough doubt in the mind of Fast Eddie for the stake horse to see weakness and to signal to Minnesota Fats that now was the time for the cavalry to charge and take the win.

"The Hustler" movie is good and the book, by Walter Tevis, is even better. The film, an Academy Award nominee, features Paul Newman as Fast Eddie, Jackie Gleason as Minnesota Fats, and George C. Scott as the stake horse. The movie deals satisfactorily with the thin line between winning and losing, but the book underscores that valuable message even better than the movie: A winner must adopt and maintain a winner's attitude.

5

Every player who sits at the table wants to win. But is he willing to lose? The consistent winner is never willing to lose. He is, by definition, a winner.

We're examining the types of players at the table. We'll start with our favorite player, one of us, the power player.

The power player does not doubt his ability to win. Moreover, he isn't interested in whether he is the best player. He isn't interested in putting on the best show. He is interested in winning. Never, ever, will he walk away from the table a loser who says, no matter how lowly or loudly, "I may have lost but, anyway, I was the best player". The power player is there only to win.

In being winners, we learn the skills we need. We keep improving ourselves and our skills, and apply our knowledge with a winning confidence. Because that's what a winner does.

Winning is something the power player not only knows, it is so deep inside him and is a part of him (hypostasized) that it is the foundation of his success. He knows his tools for a winning record at the poker table and he uses them.

Power Player Tenets.

The power player's stake is the money he has set aside for his poker venture. The amount is not money that will affect his every day living. It is, therefore, money that brings no additional pressure on the power player when he plays; the stake is his to continually build. He does not enter a game where his stake is not enough for the betting level of the game. His total bankroll is sufficient that, if he has a bad run of cards, the bankroll lives to be played many times again.

The power player knows today's game is not the whole picture; it is just one more day in a much larger poker game. At the end of a reasonable period, the power player knows he will show a profit.

The power player makes bets that count. Nearly all bets are at least the size of the pot, sometimes larger.

With few exceptions, the power player does not call. He checks when he needs information. He is not afraid to throw away a hand, because he knows there is power in throwing away a hand.

The power player does not chase money with a second best hand because he knows his power diminishes along with his money when he makes a second best play; he makes only power plays.

If the power player is getting small cards, he doesn't play, because he knows there is power in not playing. If he can find no cards to play, he leaves the table because he not only has lost his blinds and some beginning bets, he has never established his power image and he won't play without it.

When the power player is not in a hand, he studies his opponents' actions and their play. He frequently reviews the table in his mind, recounting what he knows about each player, in turn, to the last seat.

The power player does not look away from his opponents during a hand he is playing because he now will apply what he has learned about those opponents. The power player is confident that knowing his opponents is the most important part of winning. It makes it possible for him to win more than his share of pots.

In the following pages we will get more specific about these tenets and winning as a Dominator. We'll learn a few rules which we will practice until they are second nature. Then, in the final pages of this book, we'll learn when and how to make exception to those rules and Dominate the game.

It's all in these pages. For best results, read them in the order in which they are written.

Enjoy the ride.

The Hold 'Em Game

Poker – Understanding the Power

Hold 'Em – The Beginning

The reader should start this tutorial with Discussion 101.

Poker is not a card game played by people.

Poker is a people game played with cards.

Bill Boyd had a talent for the management of poker and a vision for its future that far surpassed his legendary playing skills. Bill was a good five card stud player but, beyond that, some would say his playing skills are a little exaggerated, even though he was very good.

Bill's long suit was managing a card room and his insightful contributions to casino poker are many. He introduced the center deal to Las Vegas which is now in every casino. He replaced Bee poker decks with the plastic bridge decks that are now used everywhere. (In the 1950s, you could hear the dealers in Las Vegas scream about the small plastic decks, all the way from downtown to the Hacienda.) He also introduced the "snatch and grab" five card stud game which proliferated, much to the shame of the Las Vegas history of poker.

Living in the gambling business in the 1960s was a gas, in the Sinatra vernacular of the day. The town was alive and pulsing. There was the surface entertainment that the weekend visitor knew and enjoyed exploring. But those of us who lived there were smug in the knowledge that it was an insider's playground, a familiar turf that was fun to know and to move around in.

But it was fun for tourist and resident alike. Even the visitor knew something deliciously sinister was not only constantly lurking in Las Vegas' dark underbelly but some nefarious deed could be taking place at the very moment. There was mystery and excitement for everybody, visitor and native alike, every day in Glitter City.

The 1960 Las Vegas atmosphere was particularly heady and magical. It was the era of The Rat Pack and Ocean's Eleven – the original. Dean Martin was dealing "21" at the Sands, giving the money away and driving the pit bosses crazy. Frank Sinatra was getting in fist fights and driving his dentist crazy. Those were the days when $5.00 for the captain could get

9

you into almost any main show in town, but a $500.00 bill couldn't get the mayor in to see Frank, Dean and Sammy at the Sands because there simply was no more room.

In those days, you could drive the entire Strip without slowing down and conveniently time the only traffic light, the one in front of the Stardust.

In 1960, lounge shows were a bargain. There were Vicki Carr, Della Reese, and others. Revelers were entertained in lounge shows just for the price of a drink. You could drop in on Don Rickles at the Sahara without a reservation or an admission fee.

I was at the Sahara for the 3:00 a.m. Rickles show, nursing my scotch rocks, the famous night Sinatra arrived with his entourage. Rickles stopped dead in mid sentence when he spotted Sinatra coming down the aisle: "Frank! Come on in! Make yourself at home – hit somebody!"

There were only five card rooms in Las Vegas in those days and one of them wasn't even a poker room; the Sahara had a pan card room for the ladies and gentlemen from LA. And there was Faro, the game that built the west, dealt at the Stardust on the Strip and at the Las Vegas Club downtown.

In the sixties, poker dealers were paid almost the same dollar amount in sixties dollars as poker dealers are paid today in inflated dollars. That means today's poker wages have greatly deteriorated from the days of yore. And tokes were just as good in the old days, sometimes better, depending on the game. So we poker dealers made more money back then and we deserved it because, on balance, we were much better dealers than the run-of-the-mill, deck-waving, card fumbling, get-on-your-nerves dealers that often confront us today. We had to be good in those days; the customers were more sophisticated and were often tough. We had to please them and, at the same time, we had to operate and protect the game.

Dealers had their own games. That is to say, we were assigned a certain table and game and it was ours to develop by cultivating a local following. The better dealers we were, the better games we were assigned and, consequently, we had incentive to strive for perfection and the games became even more successful. Dealing skills and people handling skills were rewarded in those days.

10

So, -- Once Upon a Time, in the "old west" town of Las Vegas, on a very slow day in 1960, there were only two poker games spread at the Golden Nugget, a dollar limit five card stud game for the tourists and a two and four low ball game for the locals. Half the dealers and shills were standing idle, reluctantly getting to know each other better. On that particular day, payroll was not cost effective and Bill Boyd was pacing. It was time for innovation. It was time to expand. It was time for Texas Hold 'Em.

Some years before, Bill had introduced Razzle Dazzle (later known simply as Razz) and he found it to be good for the house. It was low ball stud and it easily leveled the playing field. Ordinary players liked it because it was simple to play and they didn't have to fear the hustlers. It was hard to find a way to play it well and it was easy to play it badly. The game could coast all day with a steady rake and without any player taking serious money out of the game. Now Bill Boyd was looking for another great house game and he was to come close to finding it in Texas Hold 'Em.

Slim Johnson was from Texas and was one of the shills at Boyd's poker emporium. At the time, Texas Hold 'Em was being played around Texas and a few of the neighboring states such as Louisiana and Oklahoma, but it had not yet reached Las Vegas.

Slim asked Bill on this particularly slow day in 1960 if he would like to offer a new game to the public.

Sure Bill would. Idle dealers and spare shills were seated promptly at an empty table and Slim taught Bill Boyd and his employees, including me, the rules of Texas Hold 'Em. We, the idle dealers, took turns behind the rack. Slim didn't teach us how to win – no one in Vegas knew how to play the game, including Slim – but he taught us the rules.

Soon, two men from Texas joined us and the dealer took fifty cents a hand from the pot.

We were playing $2 and $4 limit and Bill Boyd immediately saw, with seven cards, five of them shared by all the players, it was hard to protect a hand with four dollars. It placed the players on more equal footing than seven card stud. Therefore, not much money was likely to leave the game, especially the way we were playing that particular day, and Bill Boyd immediately declared it a winner for the house.

I was a dealer in my middle twenties, working my way up the apprenticeship ladder, hoping someday to be assigned my own game. I dealt the Hold 'Em game that fateful day at the Golden Nugget in 1960, a day that unwittingly will be celebrated every day in poker arenas, on the internet, and every year in championship poker tournaments around the world.

It was from the Golden Nugget that the game eventually made its way across the street to Binion's Horseshoe where it was ably promoted to its deserved realm of fame and fortune.

In 1960, we were all used to five card games and Hold 'Em didn't seem much like real poker by the day's standards. It was easy to see, in our Nugget practice game, that many of the winning hands were draw-out hands. I couldn't fathom how players, in real play, could ever be attracted to so little protection and to so many draw outs. Little did I know that odds would be calculated, play would become sophisticated and the limit game would escalate to no limit.

Texas Hold 'Em would be developed by expert players to systematically separate weak players from their money.

At the end of the first day of Hold 'Em, Bill Boyd shouted to me, "Hey, Kid. It's time you had a game to deal and you can have this one if you want it."

I shouted back. "No, thanks, Boss. I'll wait for another one. This game isn't going to amount to anything. NOBODY'S EVER GOING TO PLAY IT."

Discussion 200

Hold 'Em – Preparation

The reader should start this tutorial with Discussion 101.

Poker is not a card game played by people.

Poker is a people game played with cards.

Freddie Ivans was Bill Boyd's swing shift manager at the Golden Nugget. Freddie was the old fashioned, quiet kind of shift boss. He expected professionalism and spoke up when he didn't get it. Usually, he didn't have much to say. So, when Freddie spoke, everybody listened.

Then there was the other Freddie Ivans. He was the Freddie who was a drinker and a player. Sometimes, after work, Reticent Freddie would sit in the Razz game and become Garrulous Freddie, and it could happen after only a couple of drinks. Actually, he showed no favoritism in the games he'd play; when he was ready, he was willing to play in any poker game.

When Freddie was playing, strangers would come by and want to get in the game, so they could take a shot at the drinking, gambling man. But the locals knew about their talkative friend. They had a saying. "Freddie gets drunk, but Freddie's checks never do."

Fred Ivans, no matter what he was playing, no matter what his condition, always played to win. He had a discipline and a will to win that most everyday poker players could only envy.

We don't condone excessive drinking, of course, but we admire a high level of poker winning discipline when we see it.

Discipline will be the watch word as we look at the game of hold 'em. There will be many temptations to leave the rules and regimen that are part of the power player. We must resist each and every one of those temptations. We will discuss them again later in this book in a new light. Meanwhile, we never hear those siren calls because we are winners. We are the power players.

In hold 'em, we are entering a new version of poker. Yes, it's been played awhile and, through promotions, movies, TV and the internet, it is presently the most popular poker game. Nevertheless, it is the newest poker in more than two centuries of the holy game. And there are many and varied differences between hold 'em and its forerunners.

In five card stud, we were limited to five cards. The game was streamlined and, therefore, extremely manageable. There was a wide margin of opportunity for the serious player.

In draw poker, we got more than five cards to play with. We had to throw some away before we got new ones. Nevertheless, for the first time, we had more than five cards to choose from. But only two bets. Straights and flushes became a major factor. But the game was still quite manageable.

In seven card stud we, for the first time, were able to keep more than five cards and choose the five we wanted to play. Possibilities opened for players of all types. And, because of the seven cards, the quality of risk management was invaded by more opportunity to gamble.

Now, in hold 'em, we are not only able to use the best five of seven cards, we are playing an entirely different poker game. It has plenty of opportunities and, at the same time, it is full of pitfalls.

In our following Discussions, risk management will be the prevailing beginning strategy. Probabilities will figure more prominently. Excuses to play bad hands will raise their ugly heads more often. The weak will succumb to the excuses. The power playing Dominator will be disciplined and remain strong.

In playing hold 'em, plays of short duration at the table will be diminished. There will be more pots, more hands and more play. More time at the table will often be needed to determine a decisive win. We will log more losing days than the old style poker, but we will win more money on the winning days.

In hold 'em, tells and opponents' patterns of play will be more important than in any other poker game.

Tournaments will become attractive. And sometimes tournaments will last for the better part of the day; maybe they'll last for several days.

We'll periodically become introspective at the table. If we're playing our B game, we'll bring it up a notch to our A game. If we're playing less than a B game, we'll decide whether we should be playing at all that day.

The secret of maintaining discipline will be in maintaining confidence. When we lose confidence in ourselves, or in the game, when we start feeling sorry for ourselves, for our bad luck, we will lose the discipline and attitude required to win.

So, when we're in a funk, we'll go home. We can't win without confidence and the discipline it fosters. And the power player is there only to dominate and to win.

First, we'll discuss hold 'em in general. That will be followed by types of games in each of the below categories.

In the coming Discussions, we will look at hold 'em in the following categories:

- Low limit hold 'em briefly in order to help place the no limit game into perspective.

- High limit hold 'em briefly for the same reasons.

- No limit cash hold 'em, the Dominator's reason for this book, although we'll mention tournament poker now and then.

We'll find the best way to dominate the small blinds no limit hold 'em. We'll be the conqueror of $1 and $2 no limit games and, perhaps, we'll be able to ascend to the big blinds games, if we wish, and if we have the ability.

We won't discuss Omaha, Utah, D-Day, Timbuktu, or any of those other gambling type card games. Those games are for those who are interested only in the action. Those games mostly are for gamblers.

The power playing Dominator isn't looking for the best gamble; he is looking for the least gamble. He is there to win.

We WILL dominate the small blinds no limit games.

Discussion 201

The Power Player Attitude

The reader should start this tutorial with Discussion 101.

Poker is not a card game played by people.

Poker is a people game played with cards.

Texas Hold 'Em is the most convoluted of poker games. It is, therefore, considered by some to be the pinnacle of poker playing opportunity. And, as far as variety in strategy is concerned, there can be no arguing with the statement that it is the most complicated. Texas Hold 'Em deserves a lot of study.

While hold 'em is the most involved game of poker, it is also the easiest for the run-of-the-mill poker player to become addicted to – and it is the game in which the run-of-the-mill player can easily lose.

The action is fast. There are many excuses to play in many hands. There seems, nearly always, to be something to draw to. In other words, it is an invitation for the weak player to have some fun; it is an invitation for the weak player to gamble. It also makes the game an opportunity for calculated risk, and an opportunity to win for the power player.

We will see many types of players arrive at our hold 'em table.

- The "scientific" player will be there. There are many of these types who come to the table and know all the odds in every situation. They are not unlike the engineers I used to play duplicate bridge with. They came to the table with slide rules and analyzed every hand after it was played. They seldom won because they didn't account for the people factor. Happily, the people factor in hold 'em is very much larger than in bridge.

- The "serious" players will be there. They'll play the game with determination, but we'll find they just haven't quite put it together.

- The players who play just for the excitement will be there. They'll win occasionally, when their luck peaks. On the many days they lose, they will say they are "unlucky". They'll be intent on winning as many pots as they can, which means they'll play a lot of hands.

- The players, who have calculated their tolerance level of loss for the day, will be there. We'll be glad to see them.

- The power players will be there as Dominators. That's us. We'll be interested, not in winning the most pots, but in winning the most money.

While hold 'em was born of seven card stud, the differences are so many and varied that we must place hold 'em in its own category. We will NOT be comparing hold 'em to seven card stud.

We will assume, for these purposes, that the reader has read, explored, and understands the Discussions on poker that we have made to this point. The learning evolution of poker from five card stud is necessary in order to understand the methods and advantages of playing power poker.

We are going to discuss hold 'em in limit, pot limit, and no limit. Each will be discussed in its turn, but the ultimate target will be no limit and the domination of that game.

We'll start with limit cash games, which are the games for most people. The strategies for every limit level, $10 and $20 to $1,000 and $2,000, will be the same. The quality of player company may move upward as the limits increase, but the game remains a limit game and the strategies remain the same. Only the color of the players' checks change.

Even though we have the advantage of knowing the techniques of power poker, we can't win every day. No one can; there are too many hand possibilities and too many draw-outs in hold 'em. But we do know that yesterday, today and tomorrow are all one poker game and, at the end of the month, we should be in the winners' column, certainly at the end of the year.

On the following page are some general rules for playing for the day.

- Play when you feel like a winner. An optimistic attitude is paramount to winning.

- Don't play when you're feeling badly. This rule covers physical illness, stress, fatigue or any such related maladies. And don't play if you are feeling emotionally down.

- Bring your best game to the table. Your second rate game just won't do. Others will be playing their A game.

- Play the power game as set out in these Discussions. If you establish a power image at the table, you are playing your best game.

- If things don't go right (expect it to happen) don't lose any more than you can win the next day.

- Stay to win more. If things are going right, the game is still good, you feel good, stay to play well and to win more. If you stay in control, it could be your biggest day.

- Any time you realize all you're doing is just waiting for good cards, you've been there too long. And you definitely have no power image.

- Systematically, go around the table reviewing what you know about each player.

- If the game doesn't suit you and you still feel optimistic, change tables.

- Be patient. The best way to be patient is to take an intellectual view of the game. Eventually, we all get our share of good cards. A bad beat or loss for the day is only a small part of the big game.

- Don't let a loss get you down; you can win on another day. And don't let a win make you careless.

- At all times, be a power player who plays by the power player standards.

Discussion 202

The Chart and the *Playable* Hand

The reader should start this tutorial with Discussion 101.

Poker is not a card game played by people.

Poker is a people game played with cards.

The following is a list of ranked two card starters for hold 'em. It is easy to find this kind of list on the net and in books, and most anywhere. Almost never will two of the lists agree. However, the exact ranking is not important. It is only important to know that some two card starters are better than others, and to know the approximate relative value of the two pocket cards.

The margin of *play* is so important in hold 'em that the exact ranking pales in importance to position and the playability of the hands.

We do know, however, pocket aces are the best way to start and that pocket kings are the next best, and so on. The following are the fifty best pocket cards for starting a hand in hold 'em. In the following chart, "T" stands for ten and "s" means suited.

rank		rank		rank		rank		rank	
1	AA	11	JTs	21	J9s	31	76s	41	QT
2	KK	12	QJs	22	AJ	32	97s	42	54s
3	QQ	13	KJs	23	KTs	33	A2s	43	K9s
4	JJ	14	ATs	24	87s	34	65s	44	J8s
5	AKs	15	AQ	25	Q9s	35	77	45	75s
6	TT	16	T9s	26	T8s	36	66	46	J9
7	AQs	17	KQ	27	88	37	AT	47	44
8	AJs	18	QTs	28	KJ	38	55	48	T9
9	KQs	19	98s	29	QJ	39	86s	49	33
10	AK	20	99	30	JT	40	KT	50	98

Although fifty pocket card combinations are listed, normally we will not be playing cards past number 31, depending on our position, the players involved, our power image in the last ten minutes, and whether or not we must mix our play. More on that later.

19

The reader may have come upon computer analyses that rank the probability of winning hands. The above chart will stray from those probabilities.

The reason the above chart is different is that it represents the hands that will win the most money, not the ones most likely to win. The hands listed are the most *playable*. We're interested in the play and the money.

The pocket cards shown are the beginning hands that not only have the possibility of winning, but can be stronger in *play*, thereby creating more action and winning bigger pots, or winning pots sooner. For instance: Queen / Ten, suited, will win more hands than King / Queen, unsuited. But the smaller Queen / Ten suited hand cannot be bet as strongly in the opening betting and after the flop as the unsuited King / Queen. Therefore, the King / Queen is junior in probability but it wins more money and therefore gains a higher rank on our chart. It is more *playable*. Likewise, Ten / Ten will win a lot of pots, but Ace / King will win more money because it can be bet with more confidence and generate larger pots or quicker, safer winners more often – it, therefore, is more *playable*. In short, the chart ranks the hole cards that have the best chance to make us the most profit.

As we have learned in all other poker games discussed here, poker is a game of big cards. We can *play* the big cards; the small cards, more often, have to wait for help while we call off our money.

We also know the more combinations we have toward those straights and flushes that we do play, the better the possibilities. If those combinations are additionally *playable* because they are large cards, the outlook is exponentially brighter.

Queen / Jack, suited, has more probabilities than Ace / King for a straight because the ace high is not open ended. Queen / Jack, suited (ranked 13) can also make a flush. Nevertheless, we'd rather hold and play Ace / King, unsuited (ranked 10) because of the advantage in early play. Remember, we'll soon be talking about no limit here and we'll make the cost dear for an opponent to draw against our Ace / King. It is, therefore, more *playable*.

The suited factor such as Ace / King suited over Ace / King unsuited is an advantage, of course, but it would be a mistake to overrate it. The possibility of making a flush is less than six percent. We won't get too excited about the flush but maybe we'll make it accidentally.

Small pairs are included in our list of fifty and deserve special commentary, now and later. A small pair, for these purposes, is any pair of less value than two tens. We include them mostly because we play them in games where there are six players or more in every hand. (In good company, we throw them away with regularity, depending on position.)

The best expected outcome in loose games with a pocket small pair is to flop a set of three of a kind. But there are other advantages. If a large pair is flopped and no opponent seems excited about it, we may have the top hand with two pair. Naturally, the higher our pocket pair, the better, and the smaller the flopped pair, the better. We may also wind up eventually with the best, or only, full house.

Small pocket pairs are included in our chart because, when they win, they often win large pots. We won't hesitate to throw them away when the flop doesn't help and there is heavy betting; we don't want to risk trying to help them with the two cards yet to come, calling off our money along the way.

In loose games, everybody plays for the price of the big blind. In these limper games, the power player image is almost eroded. A good game can go to the limper type game with the addition of just a couple of new players. The new and weaker game slips in on us gradually.

If the game can't be changed back to a power game, we must realize the game is not the one we've been playing in, the one where we've established our power and won a few hands. We suddenly find, in this new game, that we're playing the probabilities along with the other players. We're just trying to do it smarter by promptly throwing away the poor probabilities and calmly pushing to the limit, the good probabilities. When this happens, it's no longer possible to establish and maintain the power image and use it to our advantage.

One strategy might be to win just one of these family pots, refuse to put any more into the fray, say good night, and go home. In the world of probabilities for a limper game, our one big pot win might well be our winning peak for the day.

21

Discussion 203

The Basic Categories of Players

It is recommended that the reader begin this series with Part 101.

Poker is not a card game played by people.

Poker is a people game played with cards.

The birth of the Imperial Palace on the Strip in the nineteen sixties brought a new interest in Las Vegas from the Far East. The "Empire" in the title could have been in the Middle East or Austria-Hungary, and the design of the hotel wasn't really Asian, except by mild suggestion. But tourists from the Far East seemed to relate to the Palace and an increasing number of Asians came to Vegas from cities in the United States and across the Pacific Ocean.

The game was a nice little $1 and $2 hold 'em game at the Palace that included two visitors from the Far East.

Also in the game was a familiar Vegas figure, the maladroit Steamboat George. He gained the nickname "Steamboat" because, on those infrequent occasions when he would win a pot, he'd make a "woo woo" sound like the characteristic steamboat whistle most of us can identify from the movies. Someone said, "He sounds like a steamboat," and that's all that is required for a nickname in Las Vegas.

Contrary to our accustomed image of the slim, elegant steamboat gambler, George's wardrobe replaced French shirts and ruffles with worn trousers and a gravy-stained shirt, both of which hung tightly to a soft round belly.

Before every round of betting, George first peered over the wire rims of his glasses to see the table and watch the cards that lay there in front of the other players and then he looked down through water-spotted lenses at his pocket cards. After that, he played the best he could.

On this day, our two visiting friends from the Far East spoke in their native tongue quite a lot. Foreign languages were, and still are, considered bad form in a poker game, but the game was for small stakes, and the two Asians showed only some halting English, so the understanding dealer was cutting them a little slack. He watched their play and found no evidence of collusion. In fact, they seemed to enjoy playing against each other. Moreover, they never spoke to each other during any hand played at the table.

Steamboat George, however, was nervous about the visitors.

The dealer tried, quietly, to assure Steamboat that everything was all right and that, as dealer, he would continue to be watchful. But ol' Steamboat was losing, and he preferred to be concerned. Finally he spoke to the strangers.

"You know, I spent a little time in Japan. I didn't learn to speak the language, but I learned to understand a lot of it. I don't know exactly what you're saying – it's been a while since I was around Japanese - but I can tell what you're talking about."

One of the pair looked up slowly. He took his time, then calmly replied, "That's very interesting, Mister Steamboat, because we are not speaking Japanese, we are speaking our native Mandarin Chinese."

———————

It's important to know all we can about our opponents and be confident in that knowledge before we make any aggressive moves.

We already know that, when first seated, the power player plays only very strong hands. In so doing, he's building the strong image he requires to gain respect in his play, but even more important, he is watching all hands to learn about his opponents. More than that, he watches every movement they make.

When we land in the game, the opponents have only one new player to study but, in the same amount of time, we power players must learn about each and every one of our new opponents. Discipline and awareness are our watch words during this intense learning period.

The power player knows that each player is an individual with a unique style of play. To assume that one player is identical to another is to commit bankroll suicide, but the power player will group his opponents into broad, familiar classifications at first, because it's a good, simple way to divide and study them.

23

As the power player learns more, his opponent groups will fall into sub-groups. Then the sub-groups will, in turn, dissolve into specific knowledge of each opponent at which point the power player is playing against individuals, instead of broad classifications.

If he has learned about his opponents and he has established his power image, our power player is ready for full active play and table domination.

How does the power player automatically categorize the play of opponents as soon as he sits at the table? The broadest categories are easy: "tight" and "loose". As the power player learns who fits into those two broad brush areas, he'll make at least one more division of each category. That second cut will divide the tight group into "tight-aggressive" and "tight passive", and the others into "loose aggressive" and "loose passive". When he does that, he has increased his categories from two to four.

The four categories are fairly well known and have been well treated in other publications. Below is a small review of the categories and a more complete examination follows in the following two Discussions.

The tight aggressive player plays tight until he thinks he has the best hand and then plays hard making big bets and doing what is necessary to protect his winning hand. (Actually, that is what we do while we're learning about the table.)

The tight passive player merely waits for the strong hand and calls bets, hoping his hand won't be drawn out on.

The loose aggressive player plays loose and hard. Table bullies fall into this category. When they are lucky, they win big. But the big ones can sink like a stone.

The loose passive player plays many hands and makes many calls. "Calling stations" are loose passive players.

Please note we have commented on both types of aggressive players sometimes winning but we declined to say that passive players sometimes win. I suppose they do sometimes, but certainly not enough to remark about it. Certainly, the key to winning in no limit is aggression.

The power playing Dominator falls into none of the four categories for any length of time and is all of these at one time or other. He plays the roll of shifting gears to each category according to the nature of the game and the nature of the situations and the nature of the opponents in the hand.

The Dominator, then, can't be classified among the familiar four. He remains an enigma to his opponents. He mixes his play, making him hard to play against.

Now, here's what this book is about: Just saying we'll mix our play won't make us winners. We must know all the safe and powerful rules of play and, when I say that, I mean know them deeply. After we learn them deeply, we can play the dominating game that selectively mixes our play in the right way and at the right time. It has to be learned, practiced and executed with a lot of experience.

The reader must slowly digest in correct order what is contained in these pages. When he has completed the Discussions and applied them with diligence and he has acquired the needed experience, he will find himself in the fifth category of player – The Dominator.

Discussion 204

Loose Players

It is recommended that the reader begin this series with Part 101.

Poker is not a card game played by people.

Poker is a people game played with cards.

Everybody looked forward to Burt Taylor visiting Las Vegas and coming to the poker table. He was a small time movie producer by entertainment industry standards, but he made enough money to be a bit showy. Maybe he was a small fish in the big Hollywood pond but, at a Las Vegas poker table, he had the opportunity to be a big fish in a small pond.

Burt would arrive at the poker room dressed in what used to be called "casual elegance". He wore an imported silk shirt, open collar, with the kind of pants and jacket that would go with it. He'd leave his six-foot-six chauffeur/bodyguard standing just outside the boundaries of the card room, ever watchful over his boss's safety.

The floor person would greet Burt effusively and usher him to his favorite poker game. Burt would buy a rack of checks and greet everyone at the table in a loud but courteous manner. He was there to make an impression.

Burt had little strategy when he played poker, but he played the best he could. He'd play a little tight at first, until he lost the first rack and then he'd immediately buy another and play a little looser. Then he'd buy another rack. The longer he stayed, the looser he played and the empty racks quickly multiplied.

Everybody gave Burt the conversation he wanted and those that got the good cards got his money. Finally, he would announce, "Floor man! One more rack. And this is the last one." Alas, the feeding frenzy soon would be over as all feasts must eventually end.

Burt was not a mark, or a sucker, or a pigeon. Burt was a pleasure player, the antithesis of the power player. He knew what he was doing. He was there to lose, yet be in charge of his losing. He'd be losing his way. If he wasn't the biggest producer in Hollywood, he could be the biggest producer at the poker table. And he was; he knew how to do that.

26

A winning day for Burt Taylor was in making contact with the minions, noting what he perceived to be their envy and admiration, and not having it cost him any more than he had planned. Burt always had a good day at the table. Burt Taylor was happy.

Thank god for pleasure players.

Burt was the epitome of the loose player because he was both aggressive and passive. He just hated to be out of a hand. If he had a good hand, he was aggressive. If he had a bad hand, he called it through to the end. Now, that's not too hard to read. He was two types of loose players and we'll examine them both.

Loose Aggressive.

The LA (loose aggressive) player is the most difficult for the power player to deal with because it's hard for the power player to find out if the LA has a good hand.

Few of the power player's familiar tools will give him information about the LA. Tells are hard to find. His table talk reveals almost nothing. And, when we think the LA might have a good hand, we can't put him on anything specific. Along with show-off movie producers in this category, are aggressive drunks and anyone, usually loud or at least garrulous, who is at the table for the sport of it.

All poker hustlers, whether power players or not, don't like the LA player to be at the table. The LA player has no respect for a power player and it's hard for the power player to gain control. In other words, the LA is a loose canon and is in the way of power play because he is habitually charging the pot no matter what cards he's holding and, worst of all, he's in a majority of the pots.

We do not chase the loose aggressive player, even though sorely tempted. But, then, power players never chase.

When the other players decide to chase the LA, his lucky streaks move their chips to his side of the table quicker than they thought possible. Or, often the chaser chases the LA to another player's hand that has both the LA and the chaser beat.

The LA isn't playing smart, but that doesn't mean he can't have a good hand. Good hand or not, he can't usually be bluffed, although he will do a lot of bluffing.

When playing this type, we power players must wait for a strong hand and then play cautiously. The LA will do our betting for us; no need to try to raise him out of the pot. (Another exception to our "never call" rule.) It's not exciting, it's not control, but it is survival and, with a few good cards in the right spot, this manner of play against the LA can make us a big winner.

The LA will lose, of course, sooner or later. He'll have a good time while he creates a great source of profit for someone with lucky cards. The pots won against the LA can be much larger than expected because of all the extra money he puts into the pots. But it's a lot like showdown. Those players who have good cards will win his money.

Since the LA is in a lot of pots, he disrupts the game. He turns every thinking player into a tight player. He robs the power player of room to maneuver.

The harm is that the thinking players at the table begin playing like robots, waiting for the nuts against the rogue LA. And meanwhile, thinking players must deal with each other. It's easier when the LA is not in the hand, but, even then, the rhythm of play has been disrupted.

After the LAs have left the table, there will be a short period of adjustment. After adjustment, the power player will be back in control.

Loose Passive.

Unlike the LA, the loose passive player (LP) does not constantly charge the pot and therefore is not as much a threat to the control of the game.

The LP is a calling station. He seldom raises but calls a lot of bets. He loses because he plays many mediocre hands, loses many of them, and he doesn't get value for the hands he wins. Other players lead in the betting for and against him.

The one effect the LP and the LA have, however, is they both tighten up the power player's game. It may sound contradictory, but the loose players, the ones that charge (LA) and the ones that call (LP), make other players have to wait for good tight hands.

But it isn't all that bad. We can play our power game to some degree. Our game will be played against the other players while we wait for the nut hand against the loose player. There are times when we can maneuver a winning hand out of the pot and take the win from the LP, who, with a mediocre hand, just made the last call.

While we're doing some fine power playing with the thinking players, we must remember to keep an eye on the unthinking LP down at the end of the table who is calling everything that's being bet. He's hard to bluff. So, when he's in the pot, we still have to have a good hand.

Discussion 205

Tight Players

It is recommended that the reader begin this series with Part 101.

Poker is not a card game played by people.

Poker is a people game played with cards.

Slim Lewis was a daily poker player in downtown Las Vegas in the 1960s. He wasn't after fame or fortune; he just wanted to pick a few players' poker pockets every day. On occasion, he played at the Boulder Club in its dime ante no limit draw game, but Slim preferred the quarter ante no limit stud game at the Four Queens. He liked the stud game because it was more basic than draw poker and it offered Slim more opportunity to apply his tight strategy. Slim also liked the four bets in stud while there were only two bets in draw. So, with more than twice the ante in the Queens' stud game and twice the number of possible bets, the stud game was a much bigger game. A player could win or lose a thousand dollars in the quarter ante stud game in a very short while. That was significant money in the 1960s.

Slim Lewis was a tight player. In merely observing Slim, the conclusive evidence for tightness was there before play began. She arrived at the same time every morning. He dressed neatly and comfortably; the insurance of a sweater was always handy, just in case. Slim always bought the same amount of players' checks when he sat down. He arranged the checks carefully. He usually sat in the fifth chair because he liked the continuity and familiarity of sitting in the same place, and the fifth seat was usually available. He kept his own thin cushion at the casino to soften his chair.

Slim would keep his seat at the table all day while other players came and went. He kept his checks neatly stacked and made the same slow motions in everything he did, looking at his hole card, reaching for his checks, throwing the hand away. He was pleasant enough, but he didn't like light conversation. He preferred to be quiet. He must have thought he was stealthy in his determination to be in pots where he always had the best hand. He was stealthy enough; Slim nearly always won.

Slim Lewis could have been the poster boy for tight players. He made money playing poker because new players would try to draw out on him and they would eventually pay him off. Slim waited for them and he had the patience of Job.

With only a few pointers, Slim Lewis could have been a power player. But, instead, Slim was tight, usually passive and occasionally aggressive. Meanwhile, while others paid him off, he was beaten by any power player who chanced by because he was easily bluffed.

Tight Aggressive.

The TA (tight aggressive) player very often doesn't find cards to play and is, therefore, not in many pots. When he comes into the hand, he comes in raising and the power player's attention is immediate. "Where did he come from? Haven't heard from him in half an hour." It's an easy decision to get out of his way in the occasional hand he deigns to play and getting out of the way should be done most of the time.

But what if we're holding a pair of aces? When we raise him back and, when we have the power image, he'll usually fold his hand.

We won't violate the power rule. We'll raise him when we think we have the edge. We don't want him to string along and we don't want to wonder what he has. We want his money now and we want him out of the pot. He isn't likely to call but, if he does, we'll be cautious and still play the hand in the power player manner.

We'll try to keep the TA seated on our right, so we're in a position where we are not the player the TA is raising. We'd rather be in a position from which we can gracefully muck our hand.

Seat six would have been a good place to be at Slim's table. When we're on the TA's left and he raises, and we believe we have the superior starting cards, we can re-raise and, by coming over the top, we'll chop his raise. If he then again raises, we have learned early just how good a hand he has. And we know his second raise is always aces; he can be holding nothing but aces.

31

Remember, the TA is tight and he requires a good hand to play at all. It therefore requires a far superior hand for him to re-raise. But if he calls instead of re-raising, he has a good hand he's not quite sure of. We have to make sure we have a very strong starting hand with which we started this raise procedure. We'll take it from there.

When we don't have the aces, we might be able to raise him and take the pot (bluff), but we'll be sure to pick the right time. One criterion for establishing the right time for the bluff is the cool calculation and decision that he isn't tired of us taking his bets.

The easy-to-bluff tight player doesn't think he's a producer. He thinks he's playing the best and smartest possible game and, if he loses, it's because he just didn't get good cards. But he's a producer to the power player who fears him not. He is one of the players who provides the plays that give the power player more than his share of pots.

Summary: We have two good chances to beat the TA because we always know where he is in a hand. He is, after all, no mystery to us. We can:

- Bet and take his money.

- Re-raise and take his raise money. (This is always best, when it happens.)

- Have the best hand and take his money after the next cards or the final cards. (A bigger pot with more risk.)

Tight Passive.

Playing it safe is the most dangerous thing you can do.

The TP is much easier to read and to beat. He is a lot like the Loose Passive except that he nearly always has a good hand. Typically, when he's in the hand, he isn't likely to make a bet, but he'll call anything we put out there. It's hard to tell just how good his hand is, so we check to him a lot. His check along with our check or his bet will give us a ton of information because he's so easy to read. When we have a good hand he's a prime candidate for a check and raise. We'll know the right time.

When the TP wins, he wins small pots. But when he loses, he loses the big ones.

We won't be fooled: The call of a big bet from a Tight Passive player has the same strength, and is as big a statement, as a big bet from a Tight Aggressive player.

If, when we check our hand for information, the TP presumes to make a bet, his hand is very strong. At that time the power player decides whether to raise or to throw his hand away. Those are the power player's only two choices. The decision of whether to raise or fold will rest on the strength of the power player's hand and his specific knowledge of the individual TP.

If, after the check, the TP checks along, we have learned a little and we get a free card. The free card is his too, of course. Now we assess our hand and his, and we either bet or check.

Remember, he's passive, but he's tight, and he started with good cards. But he can, at times, be bluffed. TPs aren't usually thinkers. If they were, they wouldn't just play tight, call their money off and hope their hand holds up.

Naturally, the TP frequently slow plays his hand. Sometimes out of fear, sometimes because it is a trap. Those calls he's making are big indicators.

Tight Passive players are always welcome at the power player's table. We know where they are in their play at all times and they don't complicate things by jamming, or even raising, pots.

With the TP, we can get out of a hand gracefully or, if we have the cards, we can win the TP's money. One nice thing, he loses much faster than the Tight Aggressive player.

Discussion 206

Player Mix

It is recommended that the reader begin this series with Part 101.

Poker is not a card game played by people.

Poker is a people game played with cards.

We've demonstrated in simple terms and examples what power play can do. We've summarized it, added the play mix, and now it seems natural to take one more step.

We'll briefly discuss playing our players a little more before we address the individual types of games. Of course, we will always discuss the application of power in each type of hold 'em game.

We're going to touch briefly on the mix of players in poker games. We will consider all these topics later in greater detail when we examine each type of hold 'em game to be played.

Since there are hundreds of thousands of poker players, there are hundreds of thousands of poker faces. We learn each of the new ones as they appear in our games.

Probably the first poker we played was at home or a friend's house when we were in high school. It's a long way from the games on the kitchen table to the World Series of Poker but many of those WSOP faces are strikingly familiar to us. Yet they are all different.

The game, no matter where it is played, is about people. Grandma was nice but, in the kitchen table poker games, she was hard after your match sticks. She, and the rest of the family, each played in a different way and you played them accordingly.

The game mix at the final table of the WSOP is comprised of ten power players. The power player who gets good cards and maintains his power mode will win the money. The big games are fun to watch and stressful to participate in because they last so long and the rewards are huge.

The power player who is a daily money player is looking for the best mix at a table. He's after a win for the day and isn't interested in encountering another power player at the table. He wants the table to be his. However, it's hard to sit down in a casino game today and not find another experienced player. Sometimes you know him by name and, if you know him, he certainly is familiar with you. In small no limit money games, power players know each other and they generally stay out of each other's way.

Sharing a small no limit table with another power player is manageable and necessary, but as many as four power players can be a little cumbersome. Still, there are four or more other players who will take turns pitching their checks to the three or four power hitters.

In the larger games, especially no limit games, power players or reasonable facsimiles abound. In the smaller blinds games, like $1 and $2 blinds, they are scarcer. The small blinds are the training ground for the fledgling Dominator and those small no limit games best ensure the Dominator's win. And that is what this book is about.

The more variety at the table, the better. It gives us a chance to mix our play and play our players. The opponents that give up their money the easiest are the most welcome.

This isn't a social event for the power player; he's there for the money. Variety is his fodder.

Floor man! At our table, we'd like two TPs, two TAs, two LPs, and two LAs, with an attractive conversationalist on the side. That's a good start. But in twenty minutes or so, the opponents will no longer be categorized by the power player; they will be individuals, each with his own style, habits and tells. They are traditional players and they are welcomed by, and belong to, the power playing Dominator.

For those readers who still haven't picked up the central theme of the power rules, it is this: The power player isn't at the table to gamble. He removes as much of the gambling element as he can from his play. He wants to know what his opponent has. He wants information about everything and everybody at the table. He wants control of the game.

The power player isn't interested in the best gamble; he is interested in the least gamble.

Instead of gambling, the power player strives to know all he can and, thus, to be a paragon of risk management. When the information is diligently obtained, control effectively established, risk management properly implemented, the power player has side stepped the bulk of gambling and has had a good business day. He comes to the table with venture capital, invests it wisely, manages it with power and gets a good return on his time and money. He may not have made many friends, but he has influenced a few people.

Lately, the greatest barrier to risk management has entered the fray. "California Style" hold 'em has arrived and it is being played everywhere, including the East Coast and Las Vegas.

The California Style name comes from the people who now have legal hold 'em in their state and are welcoming, full throttle, the thrill of gambling. The style is industrial strength loose and sometimes we find the entire table playing the new style. It can happen often in our small limit games, but is even more prevalent in the lower limit hold 'em games.

The size of the pots, calculated against the draw, gives almost any loose aggressive or loose passive player an excuse for staying in the pot. Those loose players are drawing optimistically to doubtful hands and they'll often pay maximum money at low limit levels just to see the river. The luckiest draw will win the pot. The power player has no control in this limit gambling game and he cannot gain control. Nor can any player. If you want a good shot at poker money, don't play here.

The no limit game helps reduce the number of pot odds type limping gamblers usually found in limit games and gives the power player more control.

There is no room for us to maneuver in the limper game. If he likes, the power player can elect to stay in the game to see if he can make a pocket pair of aces hold up (with four other players drawing to the river, the odds are against it), or he can go to the craps table.

It is suggested here that, if a game in which we are playing turns into one of these gambling limper fests and we can't bring ourselves to leave, we might try to win one pot and then go to dinner.

Discussion 207

Playing Big Slick

It is recommended that the reader begin this series with Part 101.

Poker is not a card game played by people.

Poker is a people game played with cards.

The following are the fifty best pocket cards for starting a hand in hold 'em. The chart is not calculated on the probability of becoming a winning hand; it is based on the probability of being the most *playable* hand and making the most money. In the following chart, "T" stands for ten and "s" means suited.

rank		rank		rank		rank		rank	
1	AA	11	JTs	21	J9s	31	76s	41	QT
2	KK	12	QJs	22	AJ	32	97s	42	54s
3	QQ	13	KJs	23	KTs	33	A2s	43	K9s
4	JJ	14	ATs	24	87s	34	65s	44	J8s
5	AKs	15	AQ	25	Q9s	35	77	45	75s
6	TT	16	T9s	26	T8s	36	66	46	J9
7	AQs	17	KQ	27	88	37	AT	47	44
8	AJs	18	QTs	28	KJ	38	55	48	T9
9	KQs	19	98s	29	QJ	39	86s	49	33
10	AK	20	99	30	JT	40	KT	50	98

"Big Slick" is a colorful name and the ace / king combination deserves it. The first reason it deserves the name is Big Slick is made of the two biggest cards in the deck. So it's big, not only big, but huge. And it is slick because it can win a lot of pots. It is also slick because it is one of the slipperiest and most misplayed two card starters available to the hold 'em player.

Big Slick should be played aggressively from last position. We should pick our spots and know our image to raise from a middle position. We should be cautious about raising from an early position. There will be much more on positioning in a later Discussion.

Like small and middle pairs, many players can't let go of Big Slick. These players would like to give the ace / king a bad reputation. As long as they have the overcard, they'll hang on trying to pair on the turn and the river, calling off their stacks along the way.

Here's the rule with ace / king: If we don't flop an ace or king, we throw it away. Are there exceptions? Of course. Just make sure they *are* exceptions.

The exceptions lie in our knowledge of the players we're up against.

- There is the player whose play we know well and we know that, even though he bets after the flop, he could have nothing. When we have Big Slick, we will not call this player; we will raise him. But we must be sure of our player. An outstanding tell would be helpful. Our raise may get us a free card on the turn. On the other hand, if he shows true power after our raise, we'll leave the hand gracefully.

- Also, there is the player whose play we know well and we suspect that he may have a drawing hand to a straight or flush. With two big overcards, we'll make him pay to draw to his straight or flush. When he misses, we likely will not have to show Big Slick. If we do have to show our cards down the line, we have a good chance of having received help, or we could have the best hand without any help.

The confidence and feeling of power we have in ace / king, lies in the knowledge that whichever is flopped, ace or king, we have the top pair with the best kicker. When we get our flop, we bet with impunity.

But supposing we are holding ace / king and we get queen, ten, seven on the flop.

Pocket	*Pocket*	*Flop*	*Flop*	**Flop**
A♣	K♦	Q♠	10♥	7♣

This hand must be checked, if we can. If we're bet into, we will usually throw it away. We have only two more cards, turn and river, with which to match our pocket ace or king, and we will have to pay for each draw. We have a 12.7% chance of catching an ace or king on the turn and less chance on the river.

Anybody even thinking about the inside draw to the straight? Then go back to Discussion 101 and start over. We have an 8.5% chance of making the inside straight. Even adding it to our 12.7% chance of catching an ace or king, we're the underdog against a small pair. Since we're getting two draws, want to add all four of them together? If so, jump ahead for a minute and read Gamblers' Fallacy, Discussion 403.

If there is action from the opponent with this hand, we throw it away, with possible departures in the above noted rare exceptions.

Big Slick, suited, is ranked higher than Big Slick, off suit, because of the chance of a flush. We rank it higher, but we don't get too excited about it.

Before the flop, we have a 22% chance of making a flush on or before the river. However, to get there, we might have to pay for the flop, the turn and the river. After the flop, we have a 19% chance of making the flush on the turn and a slightly lesser chance on the river, after paying additional money for the turn.

It's easy to see trying for flushes without the high cards in the pocket makes no mathematical sense. So we draw to the high cards and make the flushes accidentally.

There will be more Discussions on pot odds later in this book.

Suppose we hold ace / king suited and we get two of our suit on the flop. It's important to note, if we make a flush on the turn or the river, we won't have just a flush, we'll have a nut flush and the winning hand.

Pocket	Pocket	Flop	Flop	**Flop**
A♦	K♦	9♦	8♦	6♣

To act, a few good questions must first be answered.

- What's the action like in this hand? How many in the pot; we must figure our pot odds along with our chances of making top pair or the flush.

- Has the pot been raised? Of course it has; we raised it. Was it re-raised? If so, from what kind of player? Is he sitting in front of us or behind us?

- Is one of the blinds in the hand? Those middle cards could have paired him or made him a set.

- Is there a player in the pot who likes to play middle connectors? He could have a straight, or a good draw to one.

One other question, for fun. Do we hope an opponent has pocket queen / jack of diamonds so that we can beat another high flush? The answer is no. It decreases our chances of making a flush by almost 24%. There is a larger matter at hand than just having the best flush; we first have to make the flush.

Moreover, the high cards are more important for value than the flush possibility. Learn it well; a lot of money is lost drawing to just a flush.

Altogether we have an approximate 32% chance of helping the hand by pairing our pocket cards or making the flush. Considering pot odds and only one opponent, we're okay. When we add opponents, overall money odds are better.

But, when we add more opponents to the story, the probability of a pair of aces or kings taking the pot diminishes because of the number of draws by more players who might be holding high cards. In four way action, or better, we may need the flush to win. Because of pot odds in a four way pot, it'll be a good bet.

Lesson learned:

- We start the hand with Big Slick by coming in raising. Suited or off suit makes no difference because we hold the two biggest cards. We play the ace / king cautiously when we don't flop some help. We throw it away early when it isn't working.

Discussion 208

Pockets Pairs to Play

It is recommended that the reader begin this series with Part 101.

Poker is not a card game played by people.

Poker is a people game played with cards.

The following are the fifty best pocket cards for starting a hand in hold 'em. The chart is not calculated on the probability of becoming a winning hand; it is based on the probability of making the most money. In the following chart, "T" stands for ten and "s" means suited.

rank		rank		rank		rank		rank	
1	AA	11	JTs	21	J9s	31	76s	41	QT
2	KK	12	QJs	22	AJ	32	97s	42	54s
3	QQ	13	KJs	23	KTs	33	A2s	43	K9s
4	JJ	14	ATs	24	87s	34	65s	44	J8s
5	AKs	15	AQ	25	Q9s	35	77	45	75s
6	TT	16	T9s	26	T8s	36	66	46	J9
7	AQs	17	KQ	27	88	37	AT	47	44
8	AJs	18	QTs	28	KJ	38	55	48	T9
9	KQs	19	98s	29	QJ	39	86s	49	33
10	AK	20	99	30	JT	40	KT	50	98

Our beginning discussions on pocket pairs will address small limit cash hold 'em games

The beginning two cards in hold 'em in the chart above are played in various type games, in various positions in those games, and with various players at those positions.

- The condition of the game. We're looking for a game mix, some players tight, some loose. But we always want a game in which we can establish our power play. The condition of the game will help decide which of the pocket cards in the above chart will be played. Multiplayer, where-everybody-plays-every-hand, type games will not be discussed here. We don't belong in those games.

41

- The type of players. We will consider tight aggressive players, loose aggressive, tight passive, and loose passive. The above chart of starting pocket cards will be played depending on how many of these players are at the table and where they are seated.

A few days ago Murphy sat in a limit hold 'em game and almost immediately drew a large pocket pair. He was in fourth position and came in raising. One of the players to act looked at Murphy and said, "We haven't been doing that here." Everybody who acted after Murphy glared and folded their hands. He got two grudging calls from the players who were already in the pot. Murphy knew it was the game for him.

Large Pairs.

Advantages. The easy part of large pairs is that we will play them from any position in any game. And, as power players, we raise with a large pocket pair from any position.

Raising in a late position is really nice, but we do raise from any position. The idea is to maximize the pot or take the pot right now if there are no callers to our raise. We raise, even if we're under the gun, or if we're one of the blinds, or if we're first to bet after the blinds, just as long as we have the big pocket pairs, AA, KK, and sometimes QQ. Large pairs are defined as aces, kings, marginally queens and, sometimes, jacks.

Disadvantages. The hard part of large pairs is being willing to throw them away.

Let's say we have pocket kings. The tight player (loose or aggressive, it doesn't matter) hasn't been afraid of our raises. An ace flops and the opponent comes out betting. It doesn't necessarily mean we're beat, but it is decision time. Usually we'll throw the kings away, but let's consider our tight opponent. We have our player sized up and decide a raise will tell us where he is in the hand. An aggressive player will raise us back if he has aces. A passive player will call our raise if he has aces. If he has no aces, the tight player may throw his hand away, again depending on the player.

When there is an ace on the board, our pocket kings usually aren't any better than if they were pocket deuces.

The point is, no matter how long we've waited for the large pair, we must throw them away when we think we are beat.

Playing Pocket Aces. We're raising with the aces because we have the superior hand before the flop. If the flop doesn't help our hand, we usually can still bet with authority. A flop of ten, seven, four, probably leaves us in charge and we can bet aggressively.

But the flop may have hurt our hand. A flop with two or more face cards, accompanied by aggressive betting from the opponent, has probably hurt us. There could now be two pair or even a set for the opponent. Another danger flop is seven, eight, nine, or similar middle connected cards. Aggressive betting from the opponent with this flop could mean we are beaten.

Watch for one of the blinds to become suddenly active; he may have gotten in the pot with middle cards to "protect" his blind and a middle flop may have favored him. And then there is always danger of a flush. We must know our players, assess their positions, and act accordingly. Aces after the flop can be a disadvantage and the earlier we make the decision, the better.

Depending on our players and the level of betting, we throw our aces away when they are threatened. However, if we're still in control with a good or neutral flop, we bet all we can.

Playing Pocket Kings. Pocket kings must be protected! They can be drawn out on at any time. When an ace hits the board, our kings are in danger. It doesn't matter whether the opponent is a loose or tight player, anyone can start a hand with an ace. And many will start anywhere, anytime, with as little as ace / deuce. What happens when the tight player at the end of the table gets his ace and comes out betting? We throw our lame kings away.

When kings don't get help on the flop, they at least need neutrality. An ace indicates extreme danger. An open pair, connected middles, anything that may help an opponent, are things that can threaten our kings.

So we bet our kings aggressively while we can. Kings deserve the pot at any time before an ace hits the board. And we'll take it anytime.

Discussion 209

Playing Queens and Jacks

It is recommended that the reader begin this series with Part 101.

Poker is not a card game played by people.

Poker is a people game played with cards.

The following are the fifty best pocket cards for starting a hand in hold 'em. The chart is not calculated on the probability of becoming a winning hand; it is based on the probability of making the most money. In the following chart, "T" stands for ten and "s" means suited.

rank		rank		rank		rank		rank	
1	AA	11	JTs	21	J9s	31	76s	41	QT
2	KK	12	QJs	22	AJ	32	97s	42	54s
3	QQ	13	KJs	23	KTs	33	A2s	43	K9s
4	JJ	14	ATs	24	87s	34	65s	44	J8s
5	AKs	15	AQ	25	Q9s	35	77	45	75s
6	TT	16	T9s	26	T8s	36	66	46	J9
7	AQs	17	KQ	27	88	37	AT	47	44
8	AJs	18	QTs	28	KJ	38	55	48	T9
9	KQs	19	98s	29	QJ	39	86s	49	33
10	AK	20	99	30	JT	40	KT	50	98

Maverick lived on jacks and queens. He was a legend of the west.

Large Pairs.

While pocket kings are vulnerable to aces, whether pocketed or on the board, queens and jacks are even more vulnerable than kings. The further we get away from aces, the absolute top pair, the more vulnerable our pocket pairs become. We begin decreasing value with kings and vulnerability doubles with queens and then it triples with jacks. Still, queens and jacks are ranked third and fourth on our opportunity chart, above, and we're glad to find them as our pocket cards. We merely have to know how to play them.

Playing Pocket Queens. A general rule is that we can bet or raise with queens in any position. Depending on players, we can even re-raise, but not with the impunity of raising with aces, or even kings.

If our re-raise is re-re-raised over the top, we're probably facing at least kings on the first raise and aces on the second raise. In that case, we throw our worthless queens away.

Let's say there is an opening bet, we raise and our raise is called. When the flop contains an ace or king and a bet is made by an opponent into our power raise, we throw the queens away. That's the power of the pre-flop raise; it makes decisions much easier. We don't get attached to the ladies; we're ready to show them where the door is. They can hold our hand later under better conditions.

When we raise with queens and the flop does not include an ace or king, we're likely still in charge. When the opponents check to our power raise, we'll come out betting and hope to take the pot before the ace or king comes on the turn - or the river. Queens are dangerous and can easily lose with the next card. We want the pot now.

When the flop shows it may have helped someone draw to a straight or flush, we'll be careful. If a player bets into our power, we must decide whether he has made his straight or flush or if he is the type of player who is charging into us with what is still a drawing hand.

One of the great advantages of establishing the power image is in knowing no responsible player is going to bet into us with a weak hand. We only have to judge what that particular player may think is a strong hand or a weak hand. There are those who think four diamonds after the flop is strong. If we have that kind of opponent, and we think he has only four to his straight or flush, we bet all we can; if he wants a made hand, he'll have to pay for it. And that goes for after the turn, too.

If we believe the flop has helped the opponent, either because he is showing strength in the face of our power raise, or because the board now has a king or ace, say goodbye to the queens. Don't worry about being bluffed; good players are bluffed a lot. Catching bluffers is for the larger pots and for the players on whom we have a good tell or a revealing betting pattern. Meanwhile we'll trade a few bluffs involving smaller pots and usually wind up winning more bluffs than the opponents win from us, because of our power image.

<u>Playing Pocket Jacks.</u> Jacks in the pocket, which are three times more vulnerable than kings and much more vulnerable than queens, are often misplayed. Again, it's because the average player gets too attached to them.

Jacks are the fourth best pocket cards to start with. They are valuable. They are raising cards from middle to last position, unless there has been a bet and a raise before our turn to play. In that event, we'll have to judge our players. Sometimes we'll re-raise; we'll never call; we'll usually throw the jacks away.

Two jacks are vulnerable on the flop. Got two jacks? Hold your breath until the flop comes and hope for middle and low cards. If we can get by the flop, we're usually in good shape. If not, we have no use for the lowly knaves.

How about a good, or neutral, flop? (In this case, a neutral flop is very good.) Now we're in business and that's what we like about a pair of jacks. With no overpair, we play them much the same as we did the queens, above. We bet hard. We raise. We want the pot now, before we see paint on the board and things get complicated.

Jacks are more easily thrown away than queens, but the hands are similar. If there are big raises and re-raises by good players before the flop, they are nearly always betting some big cards. And, with all the money that's in the pot, they aren't likely to let the hands go. It'll be showdown time after the river and all they have to do is match a part of big slick or other high card or a connecting combination. In the face of strong betting at any time during the hand, we introduce our jacks to the muck.

We'll win pots with pocket jacks, lots of pots. But we'll be careful. They are the last bastion of solid pocket pairs, are playable mostly from middle to late positions and approach being marginal from anywhere.

46

Discussion 210

Playing Middle Pairs

It is recommended that the reader begin this series with Part 101.

Poker is not a card game played by people.

Poker is a people game played with cards.

The following are the fifty best pocket cards for starting a hand in hold 'em. The chart is not calculated on the probability of becoming a winning hand; it is based on the probability of being the most playable hand and making the most money. In the following chart, "T" stands for ten and "s" means suited.

rank		rank		rank		rank		rank	
1	AA	11	JTs	21	J9s	31	76s	41	QT
2	KK	12	QJs	22	AJ	32	97s	42	54s
3	QQ	13	KJs	23	KTs	33	A2s	43	K9s
4	JJ	14	ATs	24	87s	34	65s	44	J8s
5	AKs	15	AQ	25	Q9s	35	77	45	75s
6	TT	16	T9s	26	T8s	36	66	46	J9
7	AQs	17	KQ	27	88	37	AT	47	44
8	AJs	18	QTs	28	KJ	38	55	48	T9
9	KQs	19	98s	29	QJ	39	86s	49	33
10	AK	20	99	30	JT	40	KT	50	98

Big Slick, suited, is the next in order on our chart for winning money. But, in our discussions, we'll be following hand categories instead of the chart rankings.

We are finished with discussion concerning large pairs, at least for the time being. Large pocket pairs can raise from any position. But, because middle pairs are more vulnerable to overcards, middle pairs must be played more cautiously.

The general rule is to play strong pocket pairs aggressively from any position and play lesser pocket pairs aggressively from middle and later positions. Like the prime directive, "don't ever call", the second directive is to nearly always play aggressively.

Middle Pairs.

Playing Pocket Tens. This section of discussion will apply almost equally to pairs of tens, nines and eights. Positions are now much more important.

Early position is not a good place for pocket tens or less. We have the choice of limping in or throwing away this lousy middle pair. The decision will rest on the type of game we're in and where our tight and loose players are seated. However, limping usually is not part of the power player's image and play; so any decision to limp in anytime with anything will be a departure from the rule.

Perhaps a once-in-a-while limp in will not be noticed, or perhaps the game has moved to loose aggressive and we've had to sacrifice our power image momentarily. (If the table has moved to loose aggressive or loose passive, we also should be thinking about leaving and return on a day when we can avoid massive bankroll fluctuations. We'll be back when we can exercise more control over the game.)

When we call in early position, we are waiting to see what the rest of the players are going to do. If there is a raise, we may call to see the flop. (Again, calling is not our style.) When calling a raise from a good player, we are hoping for help on the flop from a defensive position. So we usually are better off not calling the raise. We might have been better off by not entering the pot at all. (Speaking generally, we throw away early tens with regularity.) If there are two raises behind us, we definitely throw the tens away, no matter where the raises came from. In short, what are we doing in an early position with tens?

In middle position with pocket tens, better yet in late middle position, we can come in raising, which is more our style of power play. If there is another raise behind us from a good player who has jumped the fence to call the second raise, we throw the tens away. If the player is a habitual loose raiser, we could re-raise, but we'll never call.

It is time to play the table. It is time to know the players well. It is time to be diligent. If the flop shows no possibility of an overpair, we are free to take the lead. However, if a good player raises behind us, he's telling us he has large cards, maybe a pair, maybe a set, but at least ace / king, and now it is decision time. Our decision will depend on what we know about the opponent.

If we take the lead and players are calling us after a low flop, we'll watch for the suits and connectors for flush and straight possibilities. If we think opponents are calling on the come, our decision and holy duty is to make them pay to see the turn and the river.

One of the interesting aspects of holding middle pocket pairs in a mild three way or better action, is that the opponents are probably holding large cards that are not yet paired. This means that we have as good a chance of catching a set as those holding most of the large cards do of pairing. Well, maybe not quite, but it's an interesting comparison. However, if we get no help from the board, watch out for the overcard pair. That's the danger. The sooner we take the pot and keep the intruders away, the better.

If we place jacks in their own special category, the middle pairs then are tens, nines, and eights. The higher the middle pair, the less chance of the opponents holding an over pair.

Also, when a large pair is open on the board, it is necessary to have the largest second pair and, again, the higher the pocket pair, the better.

In late position with pocket tens, we've had the opportunity to see what most of the table is doing. If there is heated activity resulting in several raises, we can throw the tens away. If we like the action, or lack of it, we come in raising. Maybe we'll take the blinds and one limping player with them. We'll be glad to. But, at this point, we know we have a hand to play.

General rule: Play middle pocket pairs rarely from early position, cautiously but strongly from middle position, aggressively when the coast is clear from late position. Middle pairs are encouraged only from late positions.

Small Pairs.

The small pairs, anything below an eight, are barely worth discussing in limit poker. Sometimes we're stuck with them when we're the blind. Sometimes, in a multi-way pot we limp in when we're in a late position, just to see if we can flop a set. (If this type of game cannot be corrected by power raises in later hands, we should think about leaving the game.) No small pair is worth a sizeable investment. Some people make a habit of playing small pairs and those players are money behind in that investment.

49

Discussion 211

Playing Large Connectors

It is recommended that the reader begin this series with Part 101.

Poker is not a card game played by people.

Poker is a people game played with cards.

The following are the fifty best pocket cards for starting a hand in hold 'em. The chart is not calculated on the probability of becoming a winning hand; it is based on the probability of being the most playable hand and making the most money. In the following chart, "T" stands for ten and "s" means suited.

rank		rank		rank		rank		rank	
1	AA	11	JTs	21	J9s	31	76s	41	QT
2	KK	12	QJs	22	AJ	32	97s	42	54s
3	QQ	13	KJs	23	KTs	33	A2s	43	K9s
4	JJ	14	ATs	24	87s	34	65s	44	J8s
5	AKs	15	AQ	25	Q9s	35	77	45	75s
6	TT	16	T9s	26	T8s	36	66	46	J9
7	AQs	17	KQ	27	88	37	AT	47	44
8	AJs	18	QTs	28	KJ	38	55	48	T9
9	KQs	19	98s	29	QJ	39	86s	49	33
10	AK	20	99	30	JT	40	KT	50	98

Ace / Queen

Please notice that a pair of tens ranks higher on our chart than ace / queen. Still in the order of discussion, ace / queen naturally follows ace / king. The junior ace / queen are connected, but with a gap. They are referred to as connected "one gappers". But the one gap really won't affect our play much because we'll play only for the big card value.

If we start with two diamonds, we will flop two more diamonds only about 10.5% of the time. And, after flopping the two diamonds, we still won't have a hand. Our chances of making a flush from the four flush are still only 19% on the turn and about the same on the river, and we have to pay for those cards before each draw.

Let's look again. 10.5% to make a four flush flop, 19% to complete the hand on the turn and about the same chance on the river. Clearly, we will be playing the pocket ace / queen of diamonds for the large cards and for the diamonds only incidentally.

It's time to more closely define early, middle and late positions. Early positions, in a ten handed game, are the first three players to act after the blinds. The next three players hold the middle positions. The last two players are in the late positions. The blinds are simply the blinds and we play them according to what we know about those positions.

The blinds, if they are in the hand, will have to act first after the flop. When our opponents are in the blinds, do they "protect" their blinds by playing every blind? If there are many players in the pot, the blinds could hold middle cards since they didn't raise. If they should catch pocket aces, do they slow play them?

Ace / queen can be played from any position somewhat like ace / king and, like ace / king, we're not too enthusiastic about the early positions. Our play from early positions will depend on the type of game we're in.

Like ace / king, ace / queen can raise from middle or late position in some types of games, such as loose passive games, or in late position in tight games where a semi-bluff might be worthwhile. And we play them a little more cautiously than ace / king.

Again, ace / queen ordinarily should not be played from an early position. Also, if there has been a raise from early position from a conservative player, ace / queen should be thrown away no matter where we sit.

King / Queen

Now let's consider king / queen in an early position, whether suited or off suit doesn't matter. We have abandoned being the beneficiary of any ace, and an ace might benefit our opponent. This is a dangerous situation.

There are a lot questions to be answered regarding the play of our king / queen and they all are about the type of game we're in, what our image is, and who is likely to be in the hand against our marginal early pocket cards. Most of the time, we will elect to muck the pocket king / queen when we're in early position.

As we change to middle position, then to late position our king / queen becomes much more valuable and our strategy changes. There are many games in which we can raise in middle position and certainly there are games where we can raise in late position. Watch the position, watch the players. How many in the pot? Look for tells. Is a player behind you eagerly fingering his chips? Is he a good player? Will he raise? We can't stand a re-raise from a good player when we have pocket king / queen.

Except in a multi-player pot, our king / queen must be thrown to the muck when raised by a good player; a mere single ace gives him the advantage. Even with ace / deuce, the raiser has only to catch the ace to bring us down.

In a multi player pot among loose players, we'll call the raise and see the flop. (Are we sure we should be at this multi-pot table? If it doesn't change soon, we'll leave.)

Another king on the flop may not be good enough. We want an extraordinary flop with lots to draw to. That's the nature of the limper style loose game. (Our power player winning strategy is no good here. Let's stop this gambling and either change tables or go home. We'll come back when we have the power player's edge.)

As we descend to queen / jack, then to jack / ten, our strategy is much like king / queen except we are losing value and become more cautious and we tighten up a lot. We play fewer pots. We play them if they are one gappers or no gappers but we play them for their big card value. And, again, it doesn't matter if they are suited or off suit, because we play them for the pictures on the cards. But to play any of these marginal hands, the power player image must be firmly established.

There are arguments made by experienced players on why jack / ten suited is one of their favorite pocket starters. Some will call all the pre-flop raises with this ridiculous hand. The crux of their view is that the high to middle suited connectors can catch more helping cards because the other players hold the high cards. But that assumes there are a lot of players in the pot, a type of game not suited for the power player. In a game where we have established the Dominator image, jack / ten is just another middle connector. There will be more discussion on this subject later in this book in the Dominator chapters.

Discussion 212

Playing Middle Connectors

It is recommended that the reader begin this series with Part 101.

Poker is not a card game played by people.

Poker is a people game played with cards.

The following are the fifty best pocket cards for starting a hand in hold 'em. The chart is not calculated on the probability of becoming a winning hand; it is based on the probability of being the most playable hand and making the most money. In the following chart, "T" stands for ten and "s" means suited.

rank		rank		rank		rank		rank	
1	AA	11	JTs	21	J9s	31	76s	41	QT
2	KK	12	QJs	22	AJ	32	97s	42	54s
3	QQ	13	KJs	23	KTs	33	A2s	43	K9s
4	JJ	14	ATs	24	87s	34	65s	44	J8s
5	AKs	15	AQ	25	Q9s	35	77	45	75s
6	TT	16	T9s	26	T8s	36	66	46	J9
7	AQs	17	KQ	27	88	37	AT	47	44
8	AJs	18	QTs	28	KJ	38	55	48	T9
9	KQs	19	98s	29	QJ	39	86s	49	33
10	AK	20	99	30	JT	40	KT	50	98

Middle suited connectors start on the chart in the second column.

Small connectors begin in the fourth column and continue through the fifth column. We don't make a habit of playing any of the pockets in the fourth and fifth columns. They are on the chart, at this time, to illustrate what we don't play.

Those readers who have compared our chart, above, with other charts have noticed that the above chart has a higher regard for middle and small connectors than it does for small pairs. The reason is connectors are more *playable* than small pairs simply because they can flop a superior pair.
Because they are more *playable*, connectors are higher than small pairs on our money chart than they are on most probability charts.

53

Because the small pair that manages to become a set is usually played in a loose game, our connectors can draw out on the starting small pair in two places. We can draw out frequently with a larger pair. Then, occasionally, our straight will beat the set if the opponent was lucky enough to make one.

We aren't particularly thrilled that our beginning connectors are suited instead of off suit. In those instances when they make a flush, they are baby flushes and can easily be beaten by a larger flush.

Who remembers Chris Moneymaker's 2003 WSOP last hand? He eliminated Sam Farha for the championship by playing five / four off suit (not even on our chart). The flop was five, four and who-cares what else. The two pair, fives and fours, held up and Chris was champion. It was two million dollars for Chris and a bad lesson for everybody else who came to believe it was a good play. When it came to playing poker, Chris Moneymaker would rather be lucky. But, in fairness, he was in a heads up situation.

The suited connectors on our chart are placed higher than off suited connectors. But the difference between suited and off suited isn't much. When we get past rank 15, the importance of determining which two starting cards are best diminishes; we need a lucky flop. Additionally, rankings 16 through 30 tend to swim together without distinction. Rankings 31 through 50 are swimming in even muddier water. It is only important to know which pool these risky starters are swimming in.

So, when do we play these little charmers? Sometimes we play them when we're the blind because we can limp in when there have been no raises. We are not "protecting" our blind; we are simply calling at a discount. We'll see the flop, especially if the action is multi-handed. We'll also muck the hand after the flop, unless we're overwhelmed by flop results and we can bet first with decided authority.

A word about the blind. Once we have placed our players' checks in the middle of the table, before or during a hand, those checks are no longer ours. Those checks are held in abeyance by the dealer until a winner is declared. The money we place in our blinds is no longer ours and, therefore, not ours to protect.

If we play in the blind, it's because we have a very good starting pocket, or it could be because we have a weak, but inexpensive, possibility that could be very profitable if it works. In those instances, we'll sometimes see the flop at our blind's discount price.

A word about mixing play and being a power player. Mixing play for the dominating player is different than mixing play is for most players, even many professional players. Most players will mix their play by changing their playing mode. They'll raise with pocket aces one hand, then call with pocket aces the next hand. The power player doesn't get cute and doesn't do a lot of guessing. We always play with power and make the opponent do the guessing. We mix our play and make him think "Is he there or is he buffing?" Our advantage at the table is in our power bets and our power image, in our ability to make the opponent guess what we're doing with the same power bet.

It's a good day when we can sit down at a table, play conservatively, observe and learn about our fellow contestants, play a few hands and win with power. On those days, we have established our power, we are in the rhythm of the game and everything is going as it should. We are "in the zone".

There is much more on mixing our play later in this book. Please be patient. First, we must absorb the discipline.

Occasionally, we experience a long drought. No hands for half an hour or more, maybe hours. Our image has gradually been relegated from power player to simply tight player. We don't like to hear, "I hope I get the hand he's waiting for." We have to mix our play so that, when we get those good starters, we'll get some action. After all, getting those pocket aces after a long period and not getting value for the hand, is a hollow victory. We don't want too much action, but we do want to win a rewarding pot.

When we, the power players, aren't getting the big cards, or cards in the right position, we have to play lesser valued cards, the kind we find in the third or fourth columns, above. The power player's style is the same. We come in raising, but not nearly as often. We can do this a few times, at intervals, before our power image has eroded and perhaps pick up a few short pots or blinds during this dry period. But, let's say, the good pockets still don't come. Soon, in order to stay active, we must play lesser cards. Or go home, which might be the better choice.

This is important. We, power players, playing lesser cards, try not to show our hand. We are in and out of pots, but not often, until we get a good flop. The opponents must not know that our purpose is simply to stay active as cheaply as we can.

If the drought continues, we play those middle connectors and pairs and soon we will have a drawing hand of some kind. We may have to take it to the river. It's good if we win this hand after the river but, for purposes of this discussion, we must recognize that we have shown we started weak. We have shown, to those who care to notice, we will play an occasional weak pocket. This means our image has changed a little. But the image can be repaired if we get some good starting cards. And, when we get that good hand, we'll likely get some good action.

This also is important. The power player must maintain control of his actions. We will not get sucked up into habitually playing the sucker cards that draw weaker players into pots - you know, like the ones we beat all the time. We do know we don't prefer to gamble. When the cards change for the better, we make sure we are still power players.

Sometimes we go for a considerable length of time without power cards. When that happens, we will quit for the day and play power poker tomorrow. In the long run, it's all one poker game.

Discussion 213

Garbage Aces

It is recommended that the reader begin this series with Part 101.

Poker is not a card game played by people.

Poker is a people game played with cards.

The following are the fifty best pocket cards for starting a hand in hold 'em. The chart is not calculated on the probability of becoming a winning hand; it is based on the probability of being the most playable hand and making the most money. In the following chart, "T" stands for ten and "s" means suited.

rank		rank		rank		rank		rank	
1	AA	11	JTs	21	J9s	31	76s	41	QT
2	KK	12	QJs	22	AJ	32	97s	42	54s
3	QQ	13	KJs	23	KTs	33	A2s	43	K9s
4	JJ	14	ATs	24	87s	34	65s	44	J8s
5	AKs	15	AQ	25	Q9s	35	77	45	75s
6	TT	16	T9s	26	T8s	36	66	46	J9
7	AQs	17	KQ	27	88	37	AT	47	44
8	AJs	18	QTs	28	KJ	38	55	48	T9
9	KQs	19	98s	29	QJ	39	86s	49	33
10	AK	20	99	30	JT	40	KT	50	98

Aces have the supreme rank. No other single card is higher than an ace. We like aces and, after large pairs, the combination ace and a big card is our favorite starting place. But many players get carried away with aces.

One of the most important things to know about aces is there are players who will play any ace. Included in our useful list about each of our opponents should be information about what kind of aces each plays.

Playing any ace is prevalent in the lower limit games, say, up to $20 - $40. After that, players tend to be more knowledgeable. But there are misguided opponents who will play any ace any time in no limit games, mostly at the lower blinds levels. Soon we find we must look for the garbage ace habit everywhere.

Our chart, on the previous page, places ace combinations in the high rankings down to ace / jack, off suit, ranked number 22 in the third column. After that, no ace combination off suit appears on our chart and there is only one instance of a suited ace, number 33, because of the remote possibility of a straight flush or nut flush. In other words, after ace / jack, often ace / queen, we commonly throw away our aces.

Suppose we entered the pot in late position with an ace / four because the pot was already four handed and we wanted to see the flop with this kind of multi-way action. The flop comes ace, ten, nine, in different suits. One of our four opponents comes out betting and gets a call from one of the other four.

Any chance we have the best hand? Not much. We throw it away and should have done so to begin with.

Garbage ace players limp in to see if they can pair their ace. They sometimes do, and have to throw them away, a waste of good players' checks. This is the situation many, many players continually get into in small games. We want to know who those players are so we can play them accordingly.

Do we ever play ace / rag? Only when we're ready to bluff or are desperate to be active. It's often good to semi-bluff, as opposed to an outright bluff, and holding ace / rag in late position is a good situation for such action against a player who will likely fold in the face of a raise.

A few evenings ago, Murphy raised on the button with ace / deuce, suited, to try to steal the blinds. The big blind called. The flop came deuce, king, deuce. Even better, the blind, with kings up, bet into Murphy. But this is a piece of luck and it sounds like a TV WSOP story.

We can flirt with ace / rag sometimes, in the right places, maybe when we need to be active. But ace / ugly is a sucker hand and is usually destined to be no more than second best because of the lack of a strong kicker. Most often, it is an expensive second best.

We throw the ace / zero trap away with regularity. The garbage ace is not *playable*.

We're going to strictly no limit hold 'em discussions next but, before we go, there should be a few observations about limit games, especially low limit games.

The house makes money from the rake. Lots of money. The rake pays for the section of the casino the card room occupies. The usual competitor for the space is a group of slot machines. To keep the poker room space and make a profit for the casino, then, requires a lot of rake.

In some houses, the rake is 5% and stops at four dollars per hand. In most houses, the rake is 10% to 15% and stops at four dollars. Some houses don't stop until five dollars.

Many houses now have a bad beat jackpot. For the jackpot, they extract yet another dollar from the pot. We know of some houses that rake 10% and stop at five dollars without the bad beat feature. For a game like $2 - $4 limit hold 'em, this is pretty heavy stuff. Then add in the tokes and you have a tidy sum.

One day last week, friends at a local poker room asked Murphy to sit in on a $2 - $4 limit hold 'em game that was showing signs of collapse. He played awhile and quit after showing a $2 profit. Murphy won a few short chop pots but, mostly, he remembers winning four large pots and losing some large pots in this loose game. We know the person who wins the pot, pays the fees of the four dollar rake and the one dollar jackpot. Now, if the four pots Murphy won contributed $12 to the house and $4 dollars to the jackpot and that $16 were placed with the $2 Murphy took home, he actually won $18. So he received only 11.1% of his actual winnings.

But, of course, Murphy didn't have to stop when he was a $2 winner. Let's say he won the next pot, heads up. He might have won in the neighborhood of $14 with, say, $4 going to those ominous slots in the top of the table, for a net win of $10. At this point Murphy would have $12 dollars to take home, but would have won a total $30 for the house and himself. In that case, he would have netted 40% of his real winnings. He'd have to win several pots in a row, or a high percentage of pots in which he played heads up, in order to take home even 60% of his real winnings. Pots won in three or four way action bring bigger wins, but a good player wins a smaller percentage of those four way pots, especially in the typical loose $2 - $4 game.

In any case, winning the day in the small limit games requires a rush of good cards and, over the long haul, the rake can't be beaten.

A card room table will rake at least $100 per hour. In a $2 - $4 game with a $40 buy-in, that's brutal; two and a half players have been eliminated automatically by the rake. We all have seen, many times after two hours, all the same players at a table where none of them is a winner, all of them losers because of the rake. All the $2 - $4 players will eventually go down the rake slot.

Here's the message: Any time you feel ready to play in a higher limit game, go to that game. There are more winners in the higher games where the rake is the same as in the lower games but calculate to a lower percentage of the pots. And the pots are much bigger, so there is more to win.

Better yet, we'll go to no limit hold 'em next.

No Limit Hold 'Em and the Hustler

It's How You Say It

by Sam O'Connor

Can poker players go to heaven?

There must be a special casino for poker players, where the waitresses are prompt and everyone is a winner. So, it's poker player heaven. But what will the dealers be like?

The poker players that will be admitted to poker heaven, after their last hand is dealt on this small planet, are those that never harbored a bad feeling toward a fellow player. So surely, no dealers will be needed in that heavenly casino, because no one knows of a single player who never had a bad feeling.

Holding a bad beat hand is exasperating for anyone. But the loser often confuses things when he utters the overly familiar and officious phrase, "Nice hand".

"Nice hand" is directed toward the winner of the bad beat pot with all its underlying sarcasm, thinly disguised as a compliment. The frigidity of "nice hand" can be compared to the bracing chill of a shift boss' smile.

Actually, "Nice hand" ranks second in frequency among two word phrases at the table. The most frequent, unfortunately, is "blinds, please". But, if we reflect for a moment on other possible two word phrases, we realize the choice of available two word wonders could be a lot worse.

Texas Hold 'Em type games, with their many hand possibilities and their frequent draw outs, are chiefly responsible for breeding the brief and familiar "Nice hand". Gone with the riverboats are the occasions when gentlemen occasionally heard, "Congratulations, Sir. A very nice hand, very well played." Alas, the days of expansive civility are gone forever.

But "nice hand" and its variations can have more than one derisive meaning. And the meanings depend entirely on how you say it.

The more formal acknowledgements expressed in the river days of yore are comprised of far too many words for today's rapid fire draw out crowd.

Over time, the original phrase has been slowly reduced from "A very nice hand, very well played" to "A very nice hand" and then further diminished to the familiar two worder, "Nice hand".

The two word wonder with its efficiency and vaguely disguised varieties of disgust add mystery to the epithet. In its brevity, it is easily issued by the loser of the hand and the phrase reveals only sparse evidence of its true intent.

There are many benefits for the loser in the two word wonder. For one, "Nice hand" brings an element of immediate relief. It douses the inner flames of disappointment and gives the loser an opportunity for a snide remark of easy availability, if he so chooses that meaning.

"Nice hand" is most often the choice and is often cleverly delivered. The look on the loser's face, of course, won't tell us much about the true meaning of his two word epithet, even if he's smiling. After all, we're talking about a poker player here.

There are also benefits for the winner. After "Nice hand" from the loser, a return of "Thanks" from the winner is often the opportunity for the winner to have the last word.

Or it could mean that he doesn't care what the loser thinks.

Or it could be an acknowledgement, as he stacks his chips, that he was lucky. In that unlikely event, "Thank you. I was just lucky" would be refreshing but is seldom heard. Maybe it's because the winner feels he deserves the win. For instance, if the winner has tried to make a nut river flush three times before and has fallen short, he may somehow feel that it was his time for a lucky draw and that he deserved it.

The "Thanks" may be entirely sincere, but probably not, because on that occasion we surely would hope for the full two word return of "Thank you".

There are even benefits for the entire table. "Nice hand" and the return of "Thanks" signify the removal, in most part at least, of the silent cloud of vitriol rising over the table from the beaten players (there could be more than one). The two word wonder and its one word acknowledgement will help burst that purple cloud. Then we're off to the next hand.

But often overlooked are all the improvements that can be made on the usual remark by adding just a touch of class.

Admittedly, the two word wonder, "Nice hand", in its directness, has a certain instantaneous effect, akin to a sharp needle. In any case, it has all the desired properties needed to bring prompt satisfaction.

However, let's consider a phrase like "A very nice hand, sir". Such a phrase possesses a surprising musical essence that can never be attained in the brevity of "Nice hand", and it has certain other advantages over the two word wonder. The longer phrase has a better chance of leaving the recipient wondering what might really have been intended. Those taking the time to utter such original and lilting phrases can achieve a distinct advantage.

The next time we lose the big one to an unlikely draw out, we'll once again be inclined to deliver the "Nice hand" zinger. But let's give some thought to the longer, more musical variety. It can bring infinite satisfaction.

Discussion 300

Migration to No Limit

It is recommended that the reader begin this series with Part 101.

Poker is not a card game played by people.

Poker is a people game played with cards.

Making the Change to No Limit Hold 'Em.

It seems the natural evolution for new players is to first play internet hold 'em. It's an easy entry contest. There is a game at any time, which suits the player's itinerary. The player can quit whenever he wants. There are plenty of other new players, so the competition is at peer. Money can be won.

Encouraged by his winnings, the player decides to play in an internet tournament. If he does well there, he may go on to bigger tournaments or he may decide he needs to come face to face with people, instead of just facing a screen. The screen is unique in that it shields him from intimidation by his opponents. But, on the downside, he can't see if they have kibitzers or other unknown help such as trackers and calculators. It also hurts him in his efforts to bluff or call a bluff.

One of the problems of some players transferring from tournaments to cash play is in what the chips represent. The tournament player ordinarily views the chips as tools. The cash player, on the other hand, may view the checks as money. The money view can inhibit the new cash player's play.

If the beginner has confidence in his ability, it may be time for him to play among a gathering of humans. And the gathering of face to face humans is necessary to the real game of poker.

The next step is probably to play in a $2 and $4 limit hold 'em game at a real live table of players. These games are readily available in most states, either at the organized city casino, or at the organized reservation casino. Or maybe the game will be on a boat.

Whatever the venue, our player will face people and hear chatter for the first time. He'll experience the human influence pervasive in every game. Nothing new, exactly; he played at home or in the military service, or someplace. But now he has embarked on a higher echelon of live play hold 'em.

Soon, in the two and four blinds limit game, he will tire of the multi-way pots and the opponents calling his turn and river bets because of pot size. He'll tire of the draw outs, the high chance of pocket aces not winning, and the rake of four or more dollars per hand, which was all he won with his last bet. He would like to protect his hand better. He's playing good poker but he wants to walk away with a better win, more often, with fewer bad beats.

The next step could be a gradual acceleration of limits maybe to a $10 and $20 limit game or, perhaps, a $20 and $40 game.

In the larger limit games, he likes the bigger bets that will help protect his hand. But he still sees many multi-way pots, depending on the nature of the individual game. The increase in size of the bets does slow the gambling a bit, and the rake is not as disproportionate. He encounters better players and he likes that; he can count on their play more. He'll probably play at this level for awhile.

You know, there is another game out there that can sometimes be found, that makes pretty good sense. It is the $3, $6, $9 limit hold 'em game. The nine dollars at the end offers a little more leverage than just another six dollar bet, and some good small limit players much prefer this game when they can find it. I have often wanted the other limit games to be, say, $10, $20, $30 or $20, $40, $60. Perhaps even $80 after the river would be good in the last example. But the house doesn't want this kind of structure; somebody might run off with some serious money that would otherwise disappear into the rake slot. The game would break up sooner and the house would be bereft of its constant, pervasive, continuing rake. It's disappointing that, even in the limits of $500 and $1,000 and higher, most structures allow only two levels of limit betting.

The next step for the player looking for a more predictable win is no limit. To get a taste of no limit hold 'em, our player now goes to the small no-limit tournament. (Perhaps he has been playing small tournaments along with his increased limit playing. Or he may have encountered no limit on the internet, which is not the same game as live no limit play.)

In the live tournaments, he will experience the concept of an infinite choice of bets and he'll be introduced to the frequent all-in play. Disproportionate blinds will demand the need to play more hands. He'll get pushed around some but, if he's a good player, he'll learn how to push the others around as well. This is necessary experience for bigger tournament play. And it is a good way to learn some of the essential methods of no-limit cash play.

Finally, he will migrate to no-limit face to face cash play. THIS is the Cadillac of the game of hold 'em.

No limit cash games differ from no limit tournaments in many ways, but one difference is very important. In tournaments, the player can lose only his entry fee. But he can lose far more than that in a cash game. In that sense, all tournaments are limit events.

In cash games, the players' checks are real money. The player can take them to the cashier window and exchange their face value for government currency, any time he wants to. Likewise, in cash games, the player never has to be short stacked. In most cases, he can buy more checks at any time.

Also, the blinds never accelerate, so he doesn't have to play marginal hands. In these examples, cash games are easier to manage. But they can be more expensive, too.

No limit cash games require and deserve good management. The good player is wary of the no limit cash possibilities, both in winning and in losing. Here are some marks of a good player's self management:

- He plays only when he has the bankroll to support it, a bankroll especially ear marked for poker.

- He must be able to buy checks in an amount approximately, but no more than, one tenth of his bankroll.

- He must be confident in his play and comfortable with the amount at risk.

- He must be satisfied with a good win and not be upset about a loss.

Discussion 301

Entering the No Limit Arena

It is recommended that the reader begin this series with Part 101.

Poker is not a card game played by people.

Poker is a people game played with cards.

Are you ready to enter the no limit fray? Are you sure?

Those who embark on the no limit hold 'em voyage must know these things:

- Playing no limit with the smallest of blinds, $1 and $2, will require a much larger bankroll than its limit counterpart.

- The size of players' stacks, ours and the opponents', will become a large part of our no limit strategy.

- Unlike the limit game which centers on hand odds, pot odds, and the right pocket cards, no limit will center more on people. It has been speculated that limit hold 'em is 80% <u>obj</u>ective and no limit is 80% <u>subj</u>ective, perhaps even more than 80% in the larger games. Anyone who hasn't enjoyed making a study of people by this point in his life probably should not attempt the no limit game.

- While profit for the day's play in limit games comes from a series of winning hands, profit from no limit will come from two or three very memorable hands, hands we will play over and over again on our way home. The other small pots, win or lose, will serve as strategy tools for those two or three big hands.

- Profit in limit games depends on reading the hand and computing existing odds, while profit in no limit will depend on reading people, using position, observing stacks and having an awareness of the implied odds.

- No limit winning will depend on setting traps and avoiding traps. It will also depend on making bluffs and catching bluffs. All of these will require knowledge of the opponents and an understanding of various insidious hold 'em maneuvers at the no limit table. These maneuvers will be used by some of our various opponents and they will be used by us against all of our opponents.

Each of the above items will be discussed in detail in the following pages.

When we have a thorough understanding of how these things work, and we have the ability to recognize and execute them under fire, we will have joined the vast membership of the Hustler's Club and we will be able to make money as knights in the holy game. When we can do that effectively, we will be eligible to join the exclusive Dominator's Club.

Having the ability to win will depend not only on knowledge but also on experience. The reader cannot expect, because he has perused these written pages, that he is now an effective poker power player and poker hustler. Experience is necessary, without question. Therefore, the more we play using the tenets contained in these pages, the more experience we will have, the more consistent we will become, and the more we will win.

The Bankroll and the Amount to Buy-In.

The beginning no limit hold 'em player may want to buy the minimum amount at first to limit his losses. And it may be a good way to tiptoe into the shallow end of the no limit pool. Then, as the beginner feels more comfortable in the game, he soon finds that being short stacked is not a good way to play and he will soon want to have the same stack advantage of other players. Then, he may want to buy the maximum amount (usually $200) in the capped buy-in games, thereby limiting his losses and placing himself on stack par with most of the other players. When he has mastered the capped buy-in, is winning, and is full of confidence, he will attack the no cap buy in table – the real no limit hold 'em poker.

So, how much should we buy in this real no limit poker game? Well, at least as much as is needed to be effective through one hand with full raises. Later, we will want to buy as much as the top stacked player at the table, but that takes confidence and experience and can be postponed awhile.

Let's say we're playing $1 and $2 blinds. We have purchased $300 in checks. Now, let's say our first raise (pre-flop) is $10. That means we'll place $12 into the pot. Let's say we're re-raised $20 ($30 dollars total) and that we, in turn, raise $60. (It happens when we have good pocket cards.) This means we have a total of $102 in the pot, pre-flop. If we want to bet after the flop, we will want to make a bet with teeth in it and we'll bet $198, all we have left. Oops. We're all-in after the flop.

If our last bet is called, such a scenario may win us the pot and double our stack. Good for us. But less than $300 in players' checks would have fallen way short of what was needed and only marginally served us in the above case. If we had more players' checks, we might have won much more money with bets after the turn and the river. Additionally, our higher stack might have discouraged an opponent's call because he wouldn't have been able to look forward to a free turn and river.

Now let's say we were drawn out on and we have to buy more ammunition. Fine. But we should be able to do that at least twice. So we'll assume we need the round number of $1,000 in order to approach the table at all. And, in this case, more is better.

We should be able to repeat our day's poker adventure without threat at least ten times. That means we should have a bankroll of $10,000. Not only that, it should be a bankroll that is not needed for living expenses or the kids' college tuition. The pressure of winning is enough; we don't need the additional pressure of having to win. That is the true definition of a bankroll. Want to try it with less than $10,000? Fine. But, again, more than $10,000 would be better.

A review: After the no limit beginner has played a few weeks in the capped buy-in game and is successful, he will see the disadvantage of being short stacked. (Many novices never get to this point.) When he reaches this plateau, he will want to buy as many players' checks as the other players at the table, or at least as much as most players at the table.

He will seek games that are truly no limit, including the amount that can be bought when he sits down.

We're now underway. Hold on tight. Experience costs money. And there is no way to escape the need for experience. At first, it will be a bumpy ride. But soon the good player will be in the winner's circle and find it is well worth it.

Discussion 302

Introduction to No Limit

It is recommended that the reader begin this series with Part 101.

Poker is not a card game played by people.

Poker is a people game played with cards.

Welcome to No Limit hold 'em, the game often called the Cadillac of Poker and the game most often preferred by the power player.

In no limit hold 'em, the action is fast and, when we play with power, the rewards are plenty.

We have learned and we fully understand the power player's method of play in limit games. Now, in no limit, we will have increased power in protecting a good hand which will bring fewer bad beats. We will have much more power in the art of bluffing and we will win much larger pots.

With no limit, much of the power player's frustration with limit games will be eclipsed. We'll have more power to get rid of the limper that draws out on us and we'll be rid of the limited betting that encourages those draw outs. We'll play more heads up and three handed pots, so our chances to win the hand will be better.

The "scientific" player, who lives by calculating the odds for making a draw out hand, will be reduced to bowing to big cards and big bets. If he is wise, his objective style game will be placed on automatic while he concentrates more on the players in a more subjective, people oriented game. Watch it happen: The players without people skills will be left behind.

There can be no doubt about it. No limit is the power player's game. It's what makes him a successful Hustler.

First, a fleeting word about Pot Limit. Pot limit hold 'em is not just a stepping stone between limit hold 'em and no limit hold 'em. Much of it is similar to no limit, mostly because the power player bets the size of the pot a lot in both games, but there isn't much "all in" spoken in pot limit. And

71

the blinds are usually different; they are usually higher in pot limit in order to promote action. In that context, pot limit is more of a gambling game than no limit. So the power player prefers no limit because he is looking for less gamble and surer wins. In no limit, he finds more protection, stronger bets and raises, larger pots and bigger and more frequent wins.

Back to no limit.

Players new to no limit must immediately learn they cannot afford mistakes. This doesn't mean they can never lose a pot. It does mean that they cannot often be wrong about their measure of a large calculated risk. It means they can't afford to be wrong when all their players' checks are in the center of the table.

At the end of a playing session the no limit player can look back at his play and attribute his win or loss to two or three of the day's hands. Those are the hands in which he could not make a mistake and, if he didn't make a mistake, he won the pots that made his day.

In limit games, the player is used to making some mistakes and still booking a win because he has made fewer mistakes than his opponents. In no limit this same player, making key mistakes, will fall early in the day.

Another characteristic of new players in no limit is failing to get value for a good hand. Because of the ominous large bets coming on the turn and the river, many are afraid to play the hand through.

While ending the hand after the flop is often a good idea, hands that are good enough to be seldom drawn out on deserve more money than can be obtained from an early after-flop win. We'll discuss this at different intervals in the following pages. Some days we get good hands infrequently and we need all the money those infrequent hands deserve.

On the other hand, going all-in after the flop is done much too frequently by the novice player when he could be making a reasonable bet and getting more for his winning hand. The early all-in brings him a short win in most occasions where a bigger win may have been probable.

And then there is the inevitable occasion when the all-in move needlessly results in a busted bankroll. Habitual all-in bets work every time but once.

More important than ever, the no limit player must know his opponents and play them well. He must place those opponents on a hand and seldom waiver. He must be right most of the time and right almost every time he is involved in a large pot. We're going to cover a lot of ground in this area.

Almost every card room has a $1 - $2 blinds no limit hold 'em game. The power player prefers this game to, say, $4 - $8 limit hold 'em because he can exercise power tactics better and more often. $1 and $2 is a good place for players new to no limit to gain experience. And, because the $1 - $2 no limit game has so many novice players, it is the game the power player can Dominate. And it is the ultimate subject of this book.

These smaller $1 - $2 games are played just like their big brother larger games, although the house's rake in the smaller games will be a little more grinding because it will consist of a larger percentage of the pot than in bigger games, but that fact is minor compared to the advantage gained in playing against inexperienced players.

The biggest difference between small and large no limit games lies in the ability of the players, something the power player can take advantage of in small blinds hold 'em because those small games are full of acknowledged beginners and players who think they are not beginners. (We like the last category a lot.) In all other respects, the only difference between big and little no limit hold 'em lies in the color of the players' checks.

We use the same chart that we did for limit hold 'em. Only this time, we'll concentrate more on the importance of strong bets from good positions. Position in no limit is much more important than in limit games.

Reading the opponents will be tantamount to winning. This Cadillac game is all about people.

We'll be handling more money, more power now and playing our players even more. Those are the keys to Domination.

Discussion 303

Getting Started, Setting the Pace

It is recommended that the reader begin this series with Part 101.

Poker is not a card game played by people.

Poker is a people game played with cards.

Getting Started.

We begin gathering information about the game and the opponents from the moment we sit down, or while we're taking our chair. We'll learn from the hand being played while we settle in, before we see a new hand dealt. We notice how many players are in the pot and the size of the pot. Let's say there are three contestants.

Right away we know the game probably is not a limper game, which could mean all the players are experienced. With this single, simple observation, we've begun to size up the opponents and the game.

The next thing we notice is how much is being bet. If the bets are roughly the size of the pot, it could mean the players are experienced and aggressive.

If there is a showdown, we get to see at least one of the hands, maybe all of them, and we know what kinds of hands those three contestants are willing to start with.

The next thing we'll check out is the size of the stacks at the table. We'll want to know our place in the high stack pecking order. We'll make sure we're near the top.

If the reader is new to the game, he may want to play a short stack strategy. That way he can't get hurt badly by the experienced player's traps and other maneuvers. He can always buy more and try again. However, if we are confidant in our play, we make sure we have enough money in front of us to move most anyone to the middle of the table. We'll be after the big bucks.

We'll also look at who has the most small checks at the table, usually $1 checks. This person will have been very active recently, and we'll usually find he will continue to be active most of the time. He could be an LA, i.e., loose aggressive player.

Wow. We haven't even gotten our cards yet and already we have a pretty good, albeit broad, idea of three or four of the players at the table and the general complexion of the game.

Now, let's say we arrived in time to see one or more of the players make a bet.

Did he bet less than the size of the pot? If he's like many small blinds players, he bet about half the size of the pot or less. That tells us the game may not be too sophisticated. It also tells us the player making the bet is afraid of his money or lacks confidence in his play, or he's not too good at placing an opponent on a hand. Or it could mean the size of his bet reflects his opinion of the value of his hand. Further observation will place him more solidly in a category on our list. One thing we know for sure, he's not aggressive. We are leaning toward placing him in the TP category, i.e., tight passive player.

And which of the players did the calling? They could be calling stations.

When the smoke cleared, who won the pot? Was it the bettor or the caller? Depending on the hand, we could learn about who bluffs and who is likely to call. And, of course, we try to see all the showdown hands, the most definitive indication of how the players play.

How do these players stack their players' checks? How do they handle their checks when they make their play? Do they hesitate, or do they move with confidence? These are the tells that let us know what kinds of players we're up against.

The ones you know the least about after, say, ten minutes are the tight players and, although they could be either aggressive or passive, we can temporarily conclude, at this early interval, they are tight.

In other words, when we haven't played yet, or even received a hand, already we should know something about the game in general and more than that about at least one third of the players at the table.

Continuing with a sharp eye, we'll have the whole table lined up to some degree in less than five minutes. Refinements to our opponent data base will continue to be mentally logged as we play and as long as we play. Eventually, the broad categories will be pared down to the individual play of each and every player.

A good habit, after some time at the table, is to go around the table mentally, player by player, and review what we know about each of them.

We'll want tells on the most active. We'll want to study their habits in the blinds. And so on.

We'll determine who the tight players are very early. Yet they are the ones we'll know the least about in the beginning few minutes. Sometimes it's enough to know they are just plain tight and we won't be in their pots unless we have a very good hand. Later, they may be the ones most easily bluffed.

We start the learning before we're situated in our seats. And we never stop learning while we're seated.

Setting the Pace.

No limit hold 'em is played slower than limit games. There is a lot to consider and so we like it slow. We want the others to know we think very carefully about each action in the game, each new card, each bet, check, or raise.

In no limit hold 'em, we are playing in a game where the bets are bigger and we can double our stacks in one hand, or lose it all. So we have to be good. Our decisions have to be well informed and they have to be right.

What if a premium starting hand doesn't come to see us in, say, the first fifteen minutes?

Then we wait. This is one time we have to wait. There are many players who make it a habit of testing the new player in his first hand. The first hand must be a good one. So, we wait and we finally get a hand to play.

Maybe the curious will search our first hand, but maybe we won't get much action because we're seen as a tight player. That's all right. We'll build our power image with later hands in later action.

We should establish our power in ten minutes or less. Sometimes, it takes awhile. Either way, we remain patient and we stay focused.

Let's say we've waited for some time and we still haven't played a strong hand.

We certainly have been in the blind a few times and maybe we've seen a flop or two, but, we haven't been in any serious action and we're first to act in the next hand. We look down and we have pocket aces. With a tight image (indeed, a player who has never played a pot), our power raise in early position might drive the others out. In this case, we could consider limping in. It will bewilder the others some. They'll place us on being a tight passive player. But, chances are, one of them will test us with a raise, in which case we'll raise back the size of the pot. Our tight passive image is now erased. We have, with that action, become a tight aggressive player who protects his hand. The action has increased our power image.

What if we have already established a good image and we have pocket aces under the gun?

In that situation, the following rule is recommended, but not mandatory: If we have been active lately, we raise straight from the shoulder. If we haven't been very active, we'll play those bullets in the manner discussed in the paragraph directly above. Both are power plays. Raising from the shoulder is preferred because of the danger of everybody limping in and leaving us with no information about what they may be holding. And, ultimately in no limit, - think about this - the immediate raise will make a bigger pot even though there are fewer players. And we'll have a better chance of winning the hand.

The dollar size of the game should not affect the way a power player plays. If it does affect his play, he's in a game too large and shouldn't be in it. Players should be comfortable with the game they're in, the type of game, the size of the stakes, and the opponents at the table. Calm, confident and aggressive play depends on it.

The player must think of the casino checks he has in front of him as units, not money. If a player thinks he's betting a piece of the farm or the kids' college, he shouldn't be in the game. The only amounts the power player should notice are the number of units involved in the action.

No limit is king, and we're underway.

Discussion 304

Pockets to Play

It is recommended that the reader begin this series with Part 101.

Poker is not a card game played by people.

Poker is a people game played with cards.

The following are the fifty best pocket cards for starting a hand in hold 'em. The chart is not calculated on the probability of becoming a winning hand; it is based on the probability of being the most playable hand and making the most money. In the following chart, "T" stands for ten and "s" means suited.

rank		rank		rank		rank		rank	
1	AA	11	JTs	21	J9s	31	76s	41	QT
2	KK	12	QJs	22	AJ	32	97s	42	54s
3	QQ	13	KJs	23	KTs	33	A2s	43	K9s
4	JJ	14	ATs	24	87s	34	65s	44	J8s
5	AKs	15	AQ	25	Q9s	35	77	45	75s
6	TT	16	T9s	26	T8s	36	66	46	J9
7	AQs	17	KQ	27	88	37	AT	47	44
8	AJs	18	QTs	28	KJ	38	55	48	T9
9	KQs	19	98s	29	QJ	39	86s	49	33
10	AK	20	99	30	JT	40	KT	50	98

Many hold 'em players will play big cards of any kind at any time in any position. Of course, we know that's very bad play and we wonder why those players do it. I think it is, in many instances, because they haven't had a hand in a while which might be a good excuse. But more often, I think it's because they simply want to be in the action and don't know any better. The biggest problem the novice has in playing too many hands is that the novice plays past the flop much too often. It becomes much too expensive.

Consider power players. Sometimes we play large cards from any position to stay active. But we'll come in raising and we'll get away from the hand easily.

78

We all know the hands to start with by looking at the above chart and from former discussions in limit hold 'em. Now, in no limit, we must be more discriminating in our play than ever before.

The big pairs can still be played from any position, and they can be played strongly from any position. After all, what is the best we can hope for in pocket cards? Big pairs are the answer and we play them with gusto.

Remember, we are playing more of a people game than we were in limit action and we often are playing a mix of sophisticated players and beginners. So it's even more important that we learn all our adversaries' playing habits and tells.

If, after our raise, our pocket kings are raised and then re-raised, there can be pocket aces out there and our kings could be worth just so much spider spit. More often those aces that top our kings are made on the flop.

Many a no limit player has gone broke by refusing to let go of his kings against possible aces, queens against possible kings, and so forth. No limit is a game where one more call can be very expensive, maybe all the money we have in front of us.

Big Slick falls into the same category in no limit as it does in limit hold 'em, with the same warnings. We won't fall in love with the big guy. If we don't flop some help, ace / king should probably be thrown away. If we do hang around, what will we be hoping for when we pay that big bet price? Are we paying to pair our ace or king? Anybody could be paired after the flop, or maybe two pair or a set. Anybody. Be ready to give Big Slick the heave ho.

The ace / rag pocket is ranked the same as in the limit game. We'll be even more careful with this ace / nothing. Still, it is possible we might make a power play on the button with the small ace, especially if our cards are suited and we draw to a nut flush. And it's a good enough start when we haven't been active for awhile. But we'll get away from these ace / rag traps easily. It usually takes two pair to win with this starting hand.

We rank suited connectors higher than small pairs, but we're not fond of either of them in no limit; compared to limit, they are much too expensive to draw to. If played at all, they will be played from the late seats because we can see a cheap flop (not usually our style) or because we need to be active (more our style).

Whether connectors are suited or not is relatively immaterial. In fact, we may be in better shape if they are off-suited because flopping two or three cards of our suit may result in bringing us the smaller of two made flushes, a second best hand and a lot of expense. Being connected is more important. And throwing them away is usually the most important part of all.

Small pairs are expensive. We're supposed to flop some help, but a player can draw to them twenty to thirty times or more without flopping a set. Compare that cost with the wins from past sets over a period of time and we'll see we often are not ahead in no limit. How about getting in cheaply with a small pair? For the new no limit player, baby pairs are a self induced trap. In no limit, we throw the little ones back into the muck, hoping they'll grow up to be aces. We'll discuss it later.

Back to two big cards in the hole. We'll look at these pocket busters and then consider position later. The first seven rankings on our chart can be played, or at least tested with a raise, from most any position, except when there is a big raise from a player in front of us. When we get the big cards, it would be a mistake not to play them; we waited long enough. In the case of a big raise in front of us, whether or not we play depends on the cards we hold and who did the raising. We'll be careful.

Let's consider our chart. The pocket starter rated number 14 is ace / ten suited. This starter is played, by many players, through to the river and beaten often by ace / jack, ace / queen, or ace / king. Often players who are playing in the pot flop a pair of aces and the big kicker wins. With ace / ten, we may have been as weak as fourth best in that contest. Those kinds of losses at the river will drown the no limit bankroll.

Can ace / ten or ace / jack be played? They can and should be played in the last positions, when the action has been passed to us or dinked to us. At that point, we are not holding a limping hand, we come in raising. The power player wants the blinds and the limps now. Even if we get a call from one of the blinds, we probably have the best hand before the flop. But let's watch out for the flop. If the board cards appear to connect to the adversary's hand, we'll let go of our little ace with dispatch.

Position playing is discussed later. The subject of ace / ten suited from various positions is addressed in detail in Discussions 334 through 339.

The key to no limit: Know your players. Be able to throw hands away.

Discussion 305

Pockets and Position

It is recommended that the reader begin this series with Part 101.

Poker is not a card game played by people.

Poker is a people game played with cards.

The following are the fifty best pocket cards for starting a hand in hold 'em. The chart is not calculated on the probability of becoming a winning hand; it is based on the probability of being the most playable hand and making the most money. In the following chart, "T" stands for ten and "s" means suited.

rank		rank		rank		rank		rank	
1	AA	11	JTs	21	J9s	31	76s	41	QT
2	KKK	12	QJs	22	AJ	32	97s	42	54s
3	QQ	13	KJs	23	KTs	33	A2s	43	K9s
4	JJ	14	ATs	24	87s	34	65s	44	J8s
5	AKs	15	AQ	25	Q9s	35	77	45	75s
6	TT	16	T9s	26	T8s	36	66	46	J9
7	AQs	17	KQ	27	88	37	AT	47	44
8	AJs	18	QTs	28	KJ	38	55	48	T9
9	KQs	19	98s	29	QJ	39	86s	49	33
10	A	20	99	30	JT	40	KT	50	98

Position means much more in no limit than it does in limit games. The reasons are simple.

We can't make as many mistakes and get away with them in no limit. We are probably playing with better players. A third reason is that in the proper position a marginal hand becomes much more powerful because of the no limit bet.

When the no limit game is played in good company, there is often three way action and sometimes four way action. But, just as often, we have heads up betting after the pre-flop raises have chased the others away.

81

The following illustration is significant. Consider, for a moment, playing in a no limit game where most pots are bringing four way action. We'll assume, for the sake of illustration, all four players go to the river. These facts become obvious: When we lose one of those four way pots, we lose only our own money. When we win a four way pot, we win three times the money we would have lost.

Therefore, we can lose two pots, win one pot, and be ahead in a limit game. However, in no limit heads up action, or close to it, lose two, win one, and we are way behind.

On the bright side, win one good pot, heads up in no limit, and we could be the day's champion.

Murphy is fond of saying, "When you first sit in a game, watch awhile and let the game play a tune on you." That's a musical way of underlining the past couple of Discussions. Wait for the big cards for a first hand and, meanwhile, learn how this particular group of players has set the rhythm of the game. In getting to know the players and the game, we can determine what starting hands are worth a bet in various positions.

We've established that we should have chart number seven, ace / queen suited, or better, to enter the pot from an early position. In this case, application of the word "better" is actually much better. Now, how about the lesser type pockets?

Some general rules for the lesser pockets. We can play the chart ranks down from number 7, ace / queen suited, to number 15 ace / queen off suit, when we're in the middle positions. We can play the remainder of the ranks through number 30 at random and with discretion in the late positions, depending on our intentions, the players, and the tempo of the game. All other rankings seldom can be played and then only as a semi-bluff. Again, all these rules are general. But they should be thoroughly understood.

Please note that king / nine off suit isn't anywhere on our chart. Nor are any cards in need of stature. Those kinds of starters are not acceptable at any time with a full table of players.

Like my girl friend said, "Don't ever call". We don't like to enter the pot without raising and, therefore, the hands in the above paragraphs are ranked for raising.

If the pot has already been raised and, because of the nature of the opponent or other reason, we can't re-raise, we throw our pocket cards away; we don't ever call. We open the pot, or raise, or throw it away.

If we're not sure we have the best two cards going in, then we don't want to see the flop; it's too expensive, both in terms of money and in terms of the cost to our power image.

As established in previous pages, when we raise we always raise at least the size of the pot. Our adversaries must think seriously about whether they want to play this hand with the power player. If all the players at the table are playing up, in other words, they are not making cheap bets at big pots, the rule of thumb is to raise at least three times the amount of the last bet. (That means we put in four times his bet.)

The purpose for raising in no limit games is the same as the reason for raising in limit games except, in limit games, it isn't nearly as effective. The main reason for a power player to raise before the flop is to find what the others might have in the pocket. The second reason is to try to take the pot before the flop. The third, and distant, reason is to build the pot for a good bet after the flop.

For the power player, the third reason (to build a pot) is distant because, before the flop, he has only two cards, less than half the five cards needed for a hand. Anything can happen with the flop and he'd rather not risk his money on the come; he wants to assure his win from power. Two cards are not yet full power; five cards in the very next move by the dealer will determine who has the power cards. It's only one move away.

Two good cards are only the start of power. So we raise pre-flop mostly to gain information. We bet after the flop for bluff or value and, if we have a good hand, we are now interested in that bigger pot.

Discussion 306

Pocket Aces and Flops

It is recommended that the reader begin this series with Part 101.

Poker is not a card game played by people.

Poker is a people game played with cards.

Once again, the flop is where the hold 'em hand is usually won and lost. Sure, there are draw outs on the turn and river, but not as many in no limit as in limit hold 'em and, in any case, our decision to continue the hand to the end usually is made after the flop. Likewise, the opponent's decision to draw to the turn and the river is made after the flop.

So, we can conclude, the flop is the largest factor in the game. It is the only time we get three cards for making one bet. We'll have a five card hand after only one amount of betting pre-flop. Then the flop tells us the direction our action will take.

While we gain some information about our opponents' hands before the flop, immediately after the flop is usually where we confirm our decision. It is where we determine if we are going to continue the hand. We made an educated guess about the opponents' hands before the flop when they called our raise from their various positions, but now on the flop, a check or a bet will tell us more accurately what our opponent has in his pocket.

When we believe we have the best five cards, we bet vigorously. If we believe we don't have the best five cards, we throw our hand away. Flop time is the biggest and most important bet or muck time. And, with rare exception, we don't ever call.

Let's consider our big pair starters. We'll start with the best, a pair of bullets.

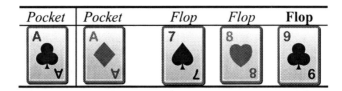

Whoa! We could be in trouble. We like aces and they usually hold up in no limit because, with our pre-flop raise, there aren't many players in the pot. But this is a good example of how aces can go bad. We don't yet know they are bad, but it's time for caution.

If the blind is in the action and he is known for calling from the blind at the one raise level, he could have two middle pair, a set, or a straight. If he bets, we won't wait to find out which it is. When he bets, we'll throw our two aces away; he has shown strength in the face of weakness. Is he a known bluffer? We still throw our aces away; anyone can have a hand and it's too expensive just to find out if we guessed right. Believe it or not, we will get more pocket aces.

Exception. Does our opponent have a dependable tell? Well, if we've found that tell, then it's a different story with a different ending.

If the blind is not in the pot and we are first to act, we usually check. Good players know another good player doesn't open early with a raise when he has a ten / nine or, most certainly, five / six. The opponents have put us on a large hand. So, it's time for us to see who wants to bet. If there is no bet, we might find we are free to bet after the turn, but it is still wise in most company to check along.

If someone behind us bets after the flop, we have some pondering to do. Does this bettor call raises with middle cards? Does he bet on the come? Does he often bet merely as simple procedural habit when he is last to act? Does he bluff? We'll react according to our answers to those questions and other things we know about this aggressor. Remember, he called our pre-flop raise and, if he's a good player, he should have big cards. This is no limit and our answers are important because the next two bets can be very expensive.

If we think we should still be in the hand, we don't ever call; we raise. If the opponent shouldn't be in the hand, he may throw it away. If he calls, he doesn't have his hand yet. If he re-raises, he may be there with a big hand. (Now it's really time to know our player.) In any case, as long as we're still firmly in the hand, the opponent won't get a free card to that four card straight unless he checks along with us. If he checks along with us, he likely doesn't have his hand yet and when there is no help for him on the turn, it will bring us out swinging a betting club that's at least twice the size of the pot! No way is he going to make his hand on the river without paying.

85

Let's try a different flop. Same numerical value on the cards, only this time they are all diamonds.

Pocket	Pocket	Flop	Flop	**Flop**
A♣	A♦	7♦	8♦	9♦

Charge! We could win it right here with one pair. If we don't win the pot on the spot, we have a lot to draw to. The difference between this hand and the first hand is this one is *playable* because we have the same high pair but it is we who are on the big draw.

If the blind is in the hand and has hit his hand with a flush, straight or two pair, he will likely check. If he bets, we'll raise him (that is, we'll know our opponents and raise most of them). If he has a flush, it's a small one. However, he is more likely to have a straight than a flush and, if so, he will be afraid of a flush. If he has two middle pair, they will almost definitely be checked in fear of the possible flush.

If there is no blind in the hand, we come out swinging. And if there is no raise behind us, it's our hand to win. If there is a raise, we'll play our player and we'll play pot odds in drawing to our hand. (There will be much more on pot odds in the following pages.)

Checking the hand is not in our arsenal at this time. We'd like to give our opponent a free card if he would draw a diamond and make his flush because ours will be bigger. But what if he hits a second pair to our one pair of aces and we don't get a diamond? Or, what if he hits a straight and we miss our diamond? No, we can't allow these things to happen. We must make a sizable bet – now!

We don't use the term "outs" in these discussions because they often are misleading. A player saying he had nine outs and missed making his hand sounds like he got a bad beat when, with forty five unknown cards, he had one chance in five of making his hand. We therefore prefer the chance ratio or percentage, twenty percent in this case, to the misleading "nine outs", which makes a little sound like a lot

86

Discussion 307

The *Playable* Hand

It is recommended that the reader begin this series with Part 101.

Poker is not a card game played by people.

Poker is a people game played with cards.

In our previous Discussions, we found:

- Always put the opponents on some kind of hand before the flop.

- Place the opponents on a hand after the flop, usually reassuring, but sometimes correcting, what we placed the opponents on before the flop.

- After the flop, if we think we have the best hand, come out firing.

- After the flop, if we think we may not have the best hand, check it to see who wants to do the betting.

- After the flop, if there is a bet and we think the opponent could have a better hand, throw the hand away before we're more involved at a big cost.

- After the flop it is usually win or lose time. This is when we often make our biggest decision. Will it be a small loss or a try for a big win?

This Discussion will be about the *playable* hand. Just because we have a good hand does not make it *playable*. The best hand often loses.

A *playable* hand must be in the right position with the right players with the right stacks at the right time and it must offer the opportunity to win with aggression. When all those elements are present, the hand is *playable*. Please notice we did not include the best hand as a necessity. We are interested only in the *playable* hand.

Let's start with pocket aces again and a different flop.

87

Pocket	Pocket	Flop	Flop	**Flop**
A♣	A♦	J♣	A♥	10♠

We're pleased with our set of aces. But let's consider something. In good company, if we have the aces, what do our opponents have? They must be holding something. Kings? Queens? Oh my, a king and a queen?

While we're always pleased to have a set of any kind, one of our opponents may easily have flopped a straight. So, our hand must be checked. (By the way, the novice who tells us "I made a small bet to see where he was at" is someone who will never reap the rewards of the power player. What's wrong is obvious and we won't even talk about it.)

If the player in front of us bets into us, we'll think about what we know about him for a moment and then probably throw our three aces away.

The same thing applies to a bet from a player behind us. Throwing away three aces is hard to do while we're learning, gets easier as we lose with those aces, and quite easy to throw away when we have considerable no limit experience. But, in the above illustration, when there is a raise from a good player, the big set of aces is not *playable*.

The exception to throwing away, of course, lies in evaluating the bettor who makes a habit of charging the pot and on whom we have a huge and dependable tell. He's ours in this situation and we love it.

Answers to questions about the opponent are important. Poker is a game of people. If he has a set of jacks or tens, or any other combination besides king / queen, we're in the best possible shape; we have a likely winner and he may stay with us in this hand for a while. If we're not sure what he may have, we throw our hand away.

We'll again underscore the value of the last position at the table. Weaker hands are *playable* more often from the late positions. For instance, jack / ten suited is more *playable* from the button than king / queen is from under the gun. (Another reason why the bettor in our example may have had a king and a queen.)

A working straight or flush flop is *playable* from the last position, but awkward to play from an earlier position. If we were in the last position with only a hand to draw to and the action was checked to us, we might be the ones betting to take the pot. It's the kind of thing good players take turns doing. Maybe it'll be our turn for bet-and-take-it the next couple of times.

Not long ago, Murphy was playing in a no limit game at the Bellagio. He was on the button. He raised the pot with virtually no hand and the small blind called. The flop was a neutral flop helping neither the blind nor Murphy. The opponent checked and Murphy bet his junk hand, taking the pot. It was a *playable* hand of junk.

The loser began grousing loud enough for Murphy to hear it. "Nice bet." (Pause.) "Yeah, really good bet." (Pause.) "Wish I could make a bet like that." So Murphy smiled and assured the sarcastic little man he soon would.

Let's continue with another flop:

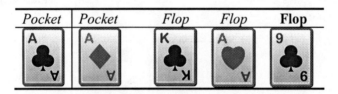

Many players will check this hand to try to build a pot. The power player, in this situation, usually will come out betting to prevent the opponents from drawing to a straight or flush. The power player will bet his usual formula of the size of the pot, or slightly more. The power player wants the opposition to guess, "Is he strong or is he bluffing?" If we have been active lately, we may get a call, better yet, a raise. We won't slow play the hand and, if we're raised, we will move in with an extra large re-raise. We want that pot before our opponent proves to be right or something scary happens to the board.

This time, in the above illustration, we have a *playable* hand from any position. We can lead from an early position and keep on coming. We'll make the opponent pay to draw to his hand. If he calls, we hope he doesn't have clubs, but we're not afraid; we'll win in most of these situations.

Discussion 308

Pocket Kings and the Flop

It is recommended that the reader begin this series with Part 101.

Poker is not a card game played by people.

Poker is a people game played with cards.

One of the big questions has always been: When should we fold pocket kings before the flop? That question calls for a short answer: Anytime we suspect possible aces.

Moreover, if an ace comes on the flop, we're gone. After all, our opponent called our big raise. Right?

Now that we've given the short answers, we'll explore a few more steps in varied situations.

We are holding the king of diamonds and the king of spades, our second favorite hand.

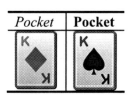

We're sitting in a middle seat and the pot has been opened with a raise. He's a good player. We re-raise. Everybody else folds. The opener re-re-raises.

In no limit, those are aces !! In fact, there are many times when the good player will have moved all-in.

We throw the kings away.

There may be games of a looser nature in which it would take one more round of raises to establish the opponent's aces, but that rule would normally apply to a limit game.

What's your favorite word for getting something sticky on your hands? Something you might accidentally get on your hands that pocket kings might stick to? Eeeeuwww. A soon as you are re-re-raised in no limit hold 'em for what is, by this time some, very big money, you can offer those two sticky cowboys a hasty ride into a mucky sunset before you lose the ranch. And then wash your hands.

Consider another situation about pocket kings experienced by one of my students. The kings stuck to his hands and he lost to aces with a possible flush.

We hold pocket kings and the player immediately to our right holds pocket queens. He raises the pot and we re-raise. All other players fold and the original raiser to our right calls. At this point we know we have him beat. (We know this if he is not in the habit of slow playing big hands.)

Had this particular player re-re-raised, we would have folded. So, the situation begs the question, "Should a player re-re-raise with queens, representing aces, thereby taking the pot?"

The answer is, "A very conservative player can do that once or twice in a bold move and get away with it. But, if a very active player tries to bluff with that maneuver, he'll get called." And therein lies some of the advantage of the power player in knowing his opponents. But, of course, even the active player can have pocket aces. And so most of us will play it safe because we're talking big money here.

When the active player with the queens is taking the chance of representing aces against our kings, he also is taking the chance that we have aces. Again, we must know our opponent.

Let's play a hand.

We are in an early seat with pocket kings. We open the pot with a raise and we get a caller.

The flop shows us the ace of diamonds, the four of clubs, and the queen of hearts.

Pocket	Pocket	Flop	Flop	**Flop**
K ♦	K ♠	A ♦	4 ♣	Q ♥

What do we do? We have to check to the caller. He flat called with something, not enough to re-raise, but he has something. We have to put him on an ace combination or a pocket pair. After the flop, he can easily have a set of queens or aces up with queens or just aces. If he bets, we'll let go of those kings! If he didn't have anything, so what? It was his turn to win a small one.

Let's change the story.

This time we're in second position. The opener has raised the blind and we have re-raised with our pocket kings. He calls our raise and we get the same flop as above.

If he bets we must fold. That's the trouble with kings – there can always be aces. If he checks to us, we play our player. Will he raise over the top of our bet? Or will he slow play his aces, if he has them? We must know our player really well if we are going to bet or call.

A rule of thumb is we make our big pre-flop pocket kings raise with the gamble that there won't be an ace in the flop. If there is, we don't play the hand unless we know his playing habits really well.

We'll change the story again.

This time there are no aces in the flop. The flop shows the jack of diamonds, the four of clubs and the queen of hearts.

Pocket	Pocket	Flop	Flop	**Flop**
K ♦	K ♠	J ♦	4 ♣	Q ♥

With this flop, no matter what position we're in, it's full speed ahead. Full speed does not mean we bet a small bet to get a call or a big bet to build a pot. We, as power players, are calm, rhythmical, and we bet the size of the pot, or more, to win the pot. No give away tells or patterns here. We'll bet and take it before that ace falls.

If we are raised, we play for the opponent to have queens with an ace and we re-raise the size of the pot or more including our call money. We'll get this settled right now.

If we are only called, we know the caller has either a pair, probably jacks (!) and didn't want to bet them, or he has a drawing hand to a straight.

It helps to know our player. But we have two of the four kings and so we doubt the drawing hand. If he had queens, he'd have bet if he was in first position, but he might have cautiously called if he was in second position.

If there is no scare card on the turn, we move all-in or similar such big bet. If there is a scare card (ten or nine?), we check the hand through the river unless we get more help in the form of our own straight.

If we get a bet from our opponent, we don't ever call. We raise or throw the hand away. (Have we made our necessary player observations?) We play the player.

In summary, kings are good to play if there is no ace showing.

We also need to observe that if the player shows strength in betting or improbably calls, he likely has a set.

In power play methods, it's easy to establish there are no pocket aces at the table against our kings. But, like all pairs, kings need help in a lot of cases. Besides a board ace, we'll watch for possible straights and flushes.

Don't be afraid to check any large pair that isn't helped. But, if you feel you have the advantage and might lose it, don't be afraid to make a big bet. We're still playing our players.

Pocket kings are not just one notch below pocket aces; kings are way below aces because aces are the best and can't be topped by another pair.

Discussion 309

Blinds and Big Slick

It is recommended that the reader begin this series with Part 101.

Poker is not a card game played by people.

Poker is a people game played with cards.

A Word about Blinds. One of the most important things to watch for in any player is how he plays his blinds. Action from the blind varies more widely than any other position. The trouble with studying opponents' blind play is that blind play for each player is infrequent; each blind comes around only every nine or ten hands. (Even though it seems more often.)

How does the power player play his blinds? Emphatically, he needs an unusual hand in order to raise from his blind. The exception to play two rags with a call occurs when everybody in the pot has only called our big blind. We'll take the free flop. We can also call in the small blind if we're sure the big blind won't raise; we get a 50% discount.

When we have a big hand in either blind, we raise when the betting comes around to us. And if we can't re-raise a raise, we can't call the raise that was made. Remember, we will have to act first after the flop thereby erasing most of our *playability*.

When we have a hand, we charge. Are we bluffing? The opponent will have to call to find out. There are occasional exceptions which will be discussed later, but raising from the blinds is generally the power player's method. It suits his image.

Some players call all raises and play most of their blinds. Their theory is they have their money already in the pot and they have to protect it. Actually, the blind money they've donated is no longer theirs. If they are entering the fray behind a raise because they have a discounted call, they may have a point. But, to call a raise, they still should have a hand. Our problem is these frequent blind players can be holding most anything.

Some players will play the big blind differently than the small blind. The decision to be more active in the big blind is usually due to the amount of money they have invested and so they've decided to be foolish about that small amount.

Other players never raise from the blind before the flop. These players could have two aces or two deuces, but never a raise. They are hard to read and we need to pick up on their no-raise-from-the-blind habit. They, too, could be holding most anything. On the good side, without a raise they know nothing about us.

Some players in the blinds, no matter what they are holding, never lead the betting after the flop. Their theory is that they aren't expected to have a hand and, therefore, someone will bet their hand for them. Often, their plan is to check and raise.

Other players, after they've checked and raised from the blind a couple of times after the flop and have shown a good hand, will use the check and raise to bluff. Know who they are because they are rare in small games. We'll place them in a very high category.

Again, we only get to study these blinds players now and then. Not just because each player has a blind every ten or so hands, but because they don't play their blind cards every time around and we have to wait even longer to study them. Information will come slowly but it will become not only useful, but necessary.

Borderline Hands and Big Slick.

Maybe Big Slick should be called Big Nasty. He probably presents more problems than all the other pocket cards because he should be played in various ways, depending on position, stacks, and opponents. Because of complications, he's hard to play. After all, when we get ace / king, we hold the two biggest cards in the deck.

So many players always play him, unsuited, like he's rated much higher than the number ten pocket hand we've given him. Listen to them; they are the ones who complain about Big Slick.

Here's the rub: Sometimes he should be played strongly and sometimes he should be promptly thrown away. The complainers don't know the difference.

Other borderline hands are easier than ace / king to throw away. We can quickly get rid of ace / rag, connectors that don't connect, doubtful pairs, etc. But Big Slick doesn't like to slip away; he likes to stick around.

A lot of how we play ace / king depends on our position. Under the gun, we usually get rid of ace / king before he makes trouble. He becomes more attractive in the middle positions and he gets kind of gorgeous at and near the button.

This time, we'll play big slick from the third seat from the big blind. That places us in the fifth position after the flop, usually at the middle of the table.

The Hand.

We have the ace of diamonds and the king of hearts. We open the pot with three times the amount of the big blind.

A player behind us calls and the big blind calls.

The flop:

Pocket	*Pocket*	*Flop*	*Flop*	**Flop**
A ♦	K ♥	K ♦	10 ♣	J ♥

We have top pair and best kicker. We appear to have a good hand, but we have to be careful with this flop. We have a big blind who could have anything and we have a late seated player. Both smooth called our raise. The blind is now under the gun.

The Big Blind Bets. He bets the size of the pot. What we do now depends almost entirely on what we know about the blind. He's betting into a power player who made the initial raise. Does he have two aces? He might, if he sandbags his blinds before the flop. Does he have a straight? If he plays ace / queen with a cold call, he could. How about three of a kind? Does he lead with three of a kind from the blind? Or, in this case, does he just have a draw to a straight?

We have three times the blind invested in this fiasco and, if we don't know the answers to these questions and don't have the feel for a dependable tell, we must give our Big Slick the burial he deserves.

The Big Blind Checks for a Trap. In this scenario, we studied our blind player and we know he likes to set those check and raise traps. So, when he checks, we check along with him. If the third player bets and the blind raises, we're out of the hand with no further cost. If the third player doesn't bet and the blind has a hand, he'll come out betting after the turn and we'll make a decision based on what we know about him. If the third party bets and the blind doesn't raise, we have all the best of it and the choice of raising a large amount.

The Big Blind Makes an Honest Check. In this case, we feel we're in fair control and we come out charging. We bet the size of the pot. The player behind us calls but doesn't raise, which probably means he needs another card. It could also mean he has top pair with a lesser kicker or, more likely, a pair with a straight draw. We'll put him on the pair and draw. Actually, we all have a straight draw and, if anyone has a queen, he has the best of it in the draw.

The Turn. How would we like to have aces up on the turn? Be careful with your answer.

Absolutely not! At the moment we have the best hand and an ace could make somebody a straight. At least, it will give somebody a chance to represent a straight and put us to a guess. No. No ace, please. We'd rather have a piece of garbage.

How about a queen for a straight? That would make things more manageable than an ace. But no queen, please; it could result in the bane of no limit poker – the split pot.

We'd like to maintain the status quo, or better. The turn: The ten of spades.

Pocket	*Pocket*	*Flop*	*Flop*	*Flop*	**Turn**
A♦	K♥	K♦	10♣	J♥	10♠

Yes! The third player, and possibly the blind, made two pair along with us. Neither player has three tens because bottom pair would have been too expensive to play. Neither player made his straight. Both likely have two pair. It's time for us to devour those little pairs. We have an ace kicker riding shotgun.

After the blind checks, we make a super sized bet (no more drawing) or we could go all in, depending on the stacks in front of the opponents.

Lessons illustrated:

- Big Slick is dangerous. We have to know his strengths and his shortcomings.

- The second order of business after we've lined up players is to pay more attention to how they play the blinds.

- We'll be aware of the blind check and raise. It can be dealt with.

- When we don't know about the players, or if we're in a bad position, we throw ace / king suited, or unsuited, into the muck.

- When we have the edge in any dangerous hand, we don't allow more drawing. We move in.

Postscript: In a pre-flop all-in situation, either our all-in or theirs, Big Slick gives us more benefit than his usual tenth place spot on the chart because he doesn't have to be *played* after the board cards fall. With Big Slick, we are sitting with the two highest cards in the deck with five cards to come that we don't have to pay for. In fact, a study of winning hands would probably place him third, with only pocket aces or kings being superior in the coming draw. We have to observe, however, that he is fairly even with other pocket pairs. Altogether, he's a good all-in bet before the flop.

Discussion 310

Big Slick and Sets

It is recommended that the reader begin this series with Part 101.

Poker is not a card game played by people.

Poker is a people game played with cards.

The Turn.

Let's take the hand we had in the previous discussion.

This hand, our hand, opened the betting from a middle seat and had two callers. After the above flop, we bet, hoping to take the pot but, that failing, we have a good hand to draw to.

Now we'll change positions.

We're on the button. Someone ahead of us opened before the flop, got one caller, we raised and the opener called us. We're now heads up.

On the flop, our opponent checked to us and we bet the size of the pot. Again, we wanted the pot at that time, but he called.

Here's the turn.

If the opponent bets, we'll be surprised; he opened and is a good player. He just called us last time. How could the turn have helped him?

If he checks to us, do we bet? Be careful.

To bet would be foolish.

We don't have a turn card to bluff with. We raised and our opponent, an experienced player put us on large cards, so it's not likely we can buy the pot at this point. Besides, we already tried twice. And we're not going to bet on the draw with a 20.4% chance of catching a river diamond.

We'll take a free card. Maybe an ace, king or jack will win for us. Altogether, we have only a 40.9% chance of catching an ace, face card pair or a flush. No bets. We'll take the free card.

If the river brings an offsuit seven, nine or ten, and our opponent bets, does he take the pot? We have no pair to call him with. But consider this: He opened the pot, is a good player who opens under the gun with big cards, so he likely does not have the straight. He hasn't re-raised us and hasn't led with the betting since he opened the pot, so he probably doesn't have a pair and, if he bets at this point, he is probably bluffing.

With ace / king, we could have the best hand. What else do we know about him? Does he bluff? Does he bluff foolishly? (This would be a really foolish bluff.) Do we have a tell on him? Maybe he deserves a call.

But here's the *play*: If we're pretty sure he's bluffing we could raise and take the pot!

Okay, let's try the same hand with a different turn card.

Pocket	Pocket	Flop	Flop	Flop	**Turn**
A♦	K♦	J♣	3♦	8♦	Q♣

Our player comes out betting. Again, what do we know about him? Does he open under the gun with a queen? Ace / queen? If so, we throw our hand away.

We have many possibilities but, in total, only a 43.1% chance on the river of improving our hand to something better than a pair of queens. In the meantime, he also can improve on the river, threatening our already slim chances. So, if we've placed him on a queen in the hole, we throw our hand away.

Now, what if he checks? In that case, we have a bluff card. Unlike our opponent, we are in a position where a queen in the pocket is much more likely. Because of position, our hand can be *played*. It'll be a semi-bluff.

First, we may be bluffing with the best hand. Second, we probably don't have queens to beat and we have many ways of improving our hand on the river.

If the river brings a nine or seven, we probably don't have to worry about the straight, because the opener is a good player and probably wouldn't be playing that kind of trash in the face of this kind of action.

With an ace, king, jack or ten on the turn we might split the pot, but maybe not. A high card on the river deserves a good bet. A rag on the river means it's showdown time.

Now, here's a different position for our opponent. Instead of an early position, he has a middle position. We're on the button.

If our middle seated opponent comes out betting, representing a pair of jacks, we throw our hand away while the price is right and we have little invested.

If he checks to us, we bet because we don't think he's paired and we think he won't be able to call us. We want the pot now. If he calls, we put him on a hand. Second pair maybe. Second pair and drawing to a straight or flush? Maybe.

The turn brings the queen and the middle player comes out firing.

Here are some things to think about: He didn't bet after the flop and we didn't put him on top pair. He's betting now on the queen. Is he the type of player who would play ten / nine suited from a middle position? He could have the ace and king of clubs in the pocket but, on the other hand, he didn't re-raise us before the flop. And, if he had ace / king in the pocket, would he have called with only a jack and two rags on the board?

After all, we're on the button, we raised, and for all he knows, we could have a strong pair. So why is he betting when the queen of clubs hits the board? It's time to know our player really well. In many cases we could make the call.

Look out! This betting pattern for a good player says he may have three of a kind! Will he play a pair of pocket eights from middle position? Many players will. And, if he's really good, he waits for what we know is an unlikely queen before he makes his move.

A hidden set is the meanest hand in hold 'em. This could be the time. The hidden set of three of a kind lies like a crocodile in the murky flop with only its eyes showing. It lies waiting patiently to suddenly rush out of the murk and snap us off.

If the hidden set checks to us, we take a free card, an advantage of being in the late seat.

If the river is good to us, we bet. Otherwise, we play showdown, unless we know something special about our opponent.

Lessons learned:

- It's a people game! Knowing the players is first in importance in no limit hold 'em and it is tantamount to winning.

- It's a game of big cards.

- Position changes the play of numerically equivalent hands. Suited Big Slick is marginal to play from any position but better played from a middle or late position.

- Playing the players is even more important than usual when none of the contestants has a strong hand. (Many big pots are won here.)

- We make straights and flushes accidentally. Many broke and whining players tell stories about how they got beat when they had "19 outs".

- Look out for the hidden set! Knowing our opponents helps tremendously with this.

Discussion 311

Large Suited Connectors

It is recommended that the reader begin this series with Part 101.

Poker is not a card game played by people.

Poker is a people game played with cards.

A Bill Boyd Story.

When the razz game at the Golden Nugget, 1960, grew late into each afternoon, the winners and losers had pretty well been decided. The winners were ready to call it a day and the losers were staying a bit longer than they should.

The later the hour, the more the phone rang. Bill Boyd would answer it.

"Card room."

Immediately, at least three voices from the table would sound off in unison, "If that's my wife, tell her I just left."

"No, ma'am. He's not here. He just left."

Bill would put the phone back on its hook and say to one of the players, "Your wife says when you do leave, stop and pick up the cleaning on your way home."

The instruction would always bring a round of laughter. Bill Boyd enjoyed delivering the message and waiting for the reaction. It was his kind of humor.

When the hapless husband finally left, the others at the table would be sure to whoop, "Don't forget the bread and milk," and other such encouragement.

If you wanted to maintain an image at the Nugget poker table, it didn't pay to be loser, stay too long and have a wife who needed something to be brought home.

Image at the no limit hold 'em level is many times more important than it was in the Nugget razz game. It is more important than in any other poker game we can name or think of. If we want to win more pots than just the pots planned by our share of good cards, we have to have the power image. Better yet, we must be the Dominator.

Connectors.

We play high card connectors with regularity. We like Big Slick and his cousins, ace / queen, king / queen, and sometimes queen / jack or even jack / ten in the right game and in the right position. And it's slightly better when our cards are suited. But when we play these suited and connected cards, we are playing the cards principally for their high value, not for the connectors or the suits. We won't get ordinary in our play; our decisions to bet or raise with these connectors are based on value, not on the draw.

Then why is this discussion about suited connectors? Because it adds a bit of spice to the hand. It is natural for us to contemplate them; they always will be considered by us and, therefore, must be discussed.

In no limit hold 'em, we sometimes bet a little more eagerly when we have suited connectors to draw to, just as we do in a semi-bluff. If we haven't gotten our straight or flush after the flop, and the turn hasn't placed us in the high card winning category, we can let go of the drawing hand because the price to see the river will not be cheap. In good company, it will cost us at least the size of the pot just to see one card.

When we draw to our somewhat good high cards and make the straight or flush, we will make it accidentally. During this action, our table company sees us drawing to strength instead of hope and we maintain our image. As a result, we will be winners most days. We can leave the game on time and bring home the cleaning without having our spouse's summary command bellowed across the card room.

Middle connectors, like seven and eight or eight and nine, are rarely played and only in the last positions. Again, we might play them as semi-bluffs or we might play them to stay active in a long dry spell. We throw them away when they aren't helped by the flop and, that way, we won't let the players see what kind of hand we raised on.

If we win with the middle connectors, and have to show them after a call on the river, we have a pot to add to our stack, but we also have a change in image to deal with. We may get a little more action on our next few plays, so we'll play some solid power hands. If we still can't get the solid hands, maybe we should quit for the day. More on this later.

Large Flush Draw.

Suppose we open the action with a raise on ace / king suited. We were not re-raised. On the flop we get two of our suits but no help for the value of the ace and king.

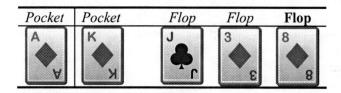

Pocket	*Pocket*	*Flop*	*Flop*	**Flop**
A♦	K♦	J♣	3♦	8♦

We opened pre-flop with this hand and now we have all the best of it. This is an exception to the cautiously played Big Slick of a previous discussion.

Ordinarily, with Big Slick, we're afraid of one, maybe two, pairs among our opponents. But this time we have callers and, for them, a neutral flop. We have the combination of our ace and king, each a candidate for an overpair and, additionally, the possibility of the nut flush. This all means we don't want to retreat.

We can make a pot sized bet, depending on the game. Our opponents know we opened with something strong and they don't know what we have. Our bet will represent a large pocket pair for the kind of company who will believe it.

We could win it right there, which is preferable. On the other hand, instead of betting in some games with some opponents who might not believe we raised with a pocket pair, we'll take the free card if we can.

What do our opponents have? They called our power playing opening bet. The player two seats from us called and the button called, each without re-raising. Again, who are these two players? What do we know about them? When we have decided who and what they are, we'll place them on a hand.

Key to this scenario is the fact the opponents did not re-raise. After the flop, we're not afraid of the jack; if one of them had pocket jacks, especially the button, he probably would have re-raised. We'll suppose we're playing in good company and there are no pocket threes. Pocket eights? Maybe. What do we know about our opponents? In any case, if there are pocket eights we'll soon know.

What we must realize is that our hand, although not paired, is *playable* even though we are in first position in the betting. We have something to draw to and the opponents don't have anything to draw to. They don't know what we have and, because we raised from a middle position, they can easily place us on a large pocket pair.

Sound the charge! We'll bet and see what the opponents want to do about it.

It's a semi-bluff. If one of them is paired (in the pocket?), he may call. But, even if he does, he has called only and he's not proud of his hand. He just wants to see the turn. We hope he makes a flush.

Chances are we'll take the pot with the after flop bet.

However, if we get a raise, be careful with this player's strength-from-apparent-weakness big bet, one of the danger signs of a hidden set. The set could be those eights we were considering and decided we would soon know about. What do we know about this opponent?

Playing Big Slick in the gray area is all about playing the players. So is spotting those hidden sets. Is the opponent who raised our bet out of his usual pattern? If so, he could have those three eights.

Discussion 312

Small Pocket Pairs and Small Aces

It is recommended that the reader begin this series with Part 101.

Poker is not a card game played by people.

Poker is a people game played with cards.

We've explored the wonder of pocket aces in no limit. Kings are next. They're played like aces, but, when we play kings, we are wary of aces on the flop. Queens are next after kings. They're played also like aces, but we are wary of both aces and kings on the flop. And so on.

Now we see why pocket jacks are not as attractive as they might have been in limit hold' em. We have to be even more wary because now there are three card ranks to avoid and there are many chances that one of them is going to fall on the flop. And, after the flop, there is the turn and the river. There are two 26% chances that an ace, king or queen will fall after the flop. Two because one can fall either on the turn or on the river, or both. Tens in the pocket? Two 35% chances. The odds are not in the jacks' or tens' favor.

Jacks can cost a lot of money. We'll play them under select conditions. We'll play them in later positions and in those situations when we think we can take the pot before the flop. We'll fervently hope for a helpful flop or a neutral flop. Pocket jacks with no flop help, or a neutral flop, are not usually *playable*. But, when there is a neutral flop and the action is checked to us, usually we can bet. And when the board cards are all less than our jacks, in most situations we'll bet a ton.

Pocket pairs smaller than jacks or tens can cause even more consternation. We don't play them often and when we do, it's usually the result of a semi-bluff, such as being called trying to steal the blinds and the limpers' bets and bringing a little action. In those situations, we've already sized up our opponents or we wouldn't have raised them with nine / nine or worse in the first place.

But let's say an opponent has called our raise. Now, on the flop, we know how to deal with him. There is a lot of playing our players in small pocket situations. We'll try not to spend too much money.

The situation is awkward because we're always hoping for help from the deck. Power players hate that.

Let's move on to ace combinations.

Ace / king and ace / queen, especially when suited, are nice because they are usually *playable*, although best played from the middle and late positions.

Any ace on the flop will probably give us the best pair of aces because of our kicker. They are strong hands and we know how to play them.

Again, with ace / jack we're a little nervous. An ace on the flop might not give us the best ace if the opponent is in the early position and has quickly called our raise. Good players regard ace / jack in an early position as a trash pocket. So, with ace on the flop, our good player who is first after the blinds probably has our ace / jack beat.

But let's look at an ace / jack hand.

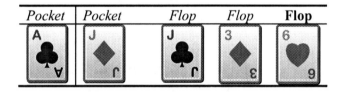

Starting with ace / jack in the pocket is something we do in some situations. When we do, managing to flop a jack which is high on the board is even better than starting with pocket jacks and is far better than flopping an ace which could be beaten because of our small jack kicker.

When we get our jack on the flop, it's better because the ace kicker is ours alone and is not shared on the board. The ace, the supreme kicker, helps to ensure our win. On the other hand, starting with pocket jacks and flopping an ace gives us no help at all and probably hurts us.

When a king or queen is flopped, we've lost our *play*. But the same would be true if we had started with pocket jacks.

In the above hand, if the flopped jack had brought connectors with it, such as a ten and a nine, we could also be in trouble. The same holds for three of a suit.

Just look at all the trouble our pocket jack can cause. To sum it up, ace / jack is a trash pocket hand in no limit hold 'em. In many cases, maybe most cases, it is not *playable* after the flop.

In the above hand, we've raised the pot before the flop and we were called. If it was the blind, the jack may have helped him, or the six might have paired or connected him, or maybe both the three and the six gave him an open straight to draw to.

If our caller is behind us, he likely has a king or a queen to draw to, maybe with an ace. Knowing our player, we have probably put him on some kind of high card hand.

On those rare occasions when we get a flop such as the one above, we can come out with a strong bet. With top pair, we probably have the best hand, at least for the moment. But the advantage could be fleeting. With that lonesome jack on the board, we want the pot now before the opponents improve their hands.

If we're called, we might catch an ace in the next two board cards. Maybe the ace will pair the opponent and leave us with the superior two pair. Big pots are won that way. Nevertheless, the opponent may have the best draw to both a king and a queen or to a straight, so an oversized bet after the flop on the above hand is definitely in order. We'll play our players and if we bet, we'll bet big.

A single ace in the pocket with a second card less than a jack complicates things exponentially. The lower our second card, the harder it is for the coming board cards to stay under that second card and the harder it is for us to keep our advantage. Additionally, middle cards hitting the board that help us, often help the opponent even more.

So we'll play small aces seldom and play them cautiously. How we play ace/garbage will depend a lot on playing our players and, mostly, on our position. (More on that later.) Meanwhile, the reader can review Discussion 213 for a review on garbage aces. Is ace / jack an ace garbage hand? Yes, it is. Didn't we just demonstrate that?

Discussion 313

Borderline Starters

It is recommended that the reader begin this series with Part 101.

Poker is not a card game played by people.

Poker is a people game played with cards.

Do celebrities tell the truth when they are asked personal questions?

The heavyweight boxing champion, Joe Louis, had financial problems that were well known. He was much too generous with friends and he was a pushover for a sad story or a good story about a bad investment. He liked everybody too much and the government said he didn't like the IRS enough.

When Joe's boxing career was over, he was in dire financial straits, a time when he should have had retirement income. But he had a friend in Bucky Blane, one of three owners of the Golden Nugget and the Nugget's general manager. Buck engaged Joe as a greeter in the casino.

Joe Louis would stand in the main aisle of the Nugget, nicely dressed, and smile at the people who walked by. He was a quiet sort of man and was reluctant to approach anyone. Many hundreds of people passed by without knowing who had smiled at them. Maybe if management had placed a Champion Everlast big buckle on Joe, he would have been recognized and gotten a little more attention, maybe not.

I was a poker dealer at that time at the Golden Nugget and I finally shook his big hand after a player at my table convinced me it was Joe Louis. Sometimes employees are the last to know.

The main aisle of the casino was shared between Joe, the casino greeter, and Howard, the poker greeter. Howard was among those of us who didn't recognize Joe, so naturally Howard approached him to play poker.

Howard asked Joe if he'd like to play at one of the tables. Joe simply smiled and said he didn't have any money.

Sadly, I think it was the truth.

110

The Truth about Borderline Hands.

They should be played only when the situation calls for it.

Today we are sitting on the button and we haven't played a hand in a while, partly because the player on our right has the habit of stealing the blinds when it's our turn. Such impertinence.

Actually, in this particular instance, the player on our right has saved us money because he is very active and, in stealing our thunder, has kept us from some very bad flops. But we know he often starts loose. We have also observed that, if he pursues a hand past the flop, he has some good cards.

In the following hand, everybody after the blind mucks their hands except the player to our right who, once again, opens the betting.

We look down and find we are holding the ace of diamonds and the jack of diamonds. We raise the opener three times the amount of his opening bet.

The big blind calls and, our main opponent, the opener on our right, calls.

We place the blind on some kind of high drawing hand. Any time a blind calls and we don't know much about him, except that he cold called our raise, we have to give him credit for some high cards and, because he's the blind, we automatically include the possibility of a drawing hand. In other words, the possibilities depend on what we know of him as a player.

Our pot usurper to the right of us also could have anything, but whatever it is, he has something of value because he called our raise. Probably high cards, or at least one high card. It's important to note that he didn't re-raise.

We don't much about either of our opponents' hands pre-flop but, without our raise, we wouldn't have as much as a single clue what the opponents are holding. If we hadn't raised, both players could have two rags and a free draw. Being able to place both opponents on some kind of hand demonstrates what the raise before the flop is for.

The flop comes ace of clubs, three of diamonds, and the four of clubs.

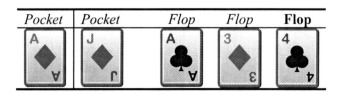

Pocket	Pocket	Flop	Flop	Flop
A♦	J♦	A♣	3♦	4♣

The blind checks his hand.

The next player also checks.

With our pair of aces, we bet the size of the pot.

The blind missed his draw and mucks his hand.

The remaining opponent thinks a while and calls. We now are fairly sure he has an ace. But he isn't proud of it.

The turn brings us the king of diamonds.

Pocket	Pocket	Flop	Flop	Flop	Turn
A♦	J♦	A♣	3♦	4♣	K♦

The opponent says "Okay" and, for the first time, takes the lead. He bets more than the size of the pot.

Here's what we know. He is in the habit of stealing blinds, even when it isn't his turn. He'll start with a loose hand, but continues only when the flop is fairly strong. We haven't heard him say much before this hand and he never says anything during a hand. He called our initial raise. He hesitatingly called our bet after the flop. We believe his hesitation to be a true hesitation. After the opener, he didn't take the lead until the king hit on the turn.

Now, let's make our decision. Since he never took the lead or re-raised us, he doesn't have big slick. This is confirmed by his "Okay" when the king hit the board; it's foolish table talk and he's too anxious to impress us. He over-bet his hand. If he had a solid hand, such as aces and kings, this type of player would have made a bet the size of the pot in order to get a call.

Looking at us through his eyes, we believe he sees we are on the button and perhaps have ace / rag, maybe two pair. If he is right, he thinks, we will throw away our two pair in the face of his aces and fake kings.

The trouble with his thinking is that we don't think he has kings because he didn't play his hand like an ace and king. We just might have the highest pair of aces with our jack. We could be wrong, of course. And, in our favor, is our 20% chance of catching another diamond, 7% chance of catching a jack, etc.

On the other hand, he'll be drawing too. We can't call. We don't want to give up the pot. The opponent is tentative and defensive. So we'll semi-bluff. And there is the good chance we'll be bluffing with the best hand. Additionally, we definitely have the best draw to the nut flush.

We raise twice the size of the pot.

The opponent was hoping we would fold our hand. Therefore, he is not in a position or frame of mind to call. We take the pot.

Post script: Our opponent is anxious to tell us what a good decision he made and shows us his ace of spades and queen of spades. We compliment him on his decision. He didn't tell the truth and neither did we, but then none of us is the ingenuous Mr. Joe Louis.

Lessons illustrated:

- Ace / jack is a dangerous pocket combination.

- Know the players. Know the positions. We were on the button.

- Know the general tells. "Okay" and too big a bet gave our adversary away. Try to sense when an opposing player is off balance.

- When making the last big decision, take time to mentally replay the hand and access what you know about the players.

- The best answer to a bluff is often a counter bluff.

113

Discussion 314

Borderlines, Rivers and Short Stacks

It is recommended that the reader begin this series with Part 101.

Poker is not a card game played by people.

Poker is a people game played with cards.

The hands we're discussing are borderline or hard to play hands. It is necessary that power player readers have absorbed our previous discussions and know how to play the large card hands from every position. Power readers should also know how to maximize the margins of the hands won and the amount of money those hands can win for them. Prior Discussions are important.

The big pocket hands are the hands that win most often in hold 'em. Those hands win our arithmetical share, or probability share, of the table winnings. Our profits will come from astutely playing the borderline hands.

The most difficult and the most rewarding hands we play at the table are marginal hands. When played with diligence, they are not only rewarding financially, but rewarding in extreme personal satisfaction as we wallow in our self-applause for a hand well played. Many will say that is what the game is all about.

If we play these borderline anomalies correctly on a regular basis and we count our winnings at the end of the day, we'll often find much, sometimes all, of our winnings are the winnings we gained from the borderline hands.

The River.

By the time we get past the turn and plunge into the river in strong play, we should have made some kind of hand and it should be destined to be the winning hand. In other words, we should not be in a position of having to pray to the poker gods to grant us a surprise hand, a hand which is a surprise to our opponent and is also a surprise to us. If we talk to the poker gods at all, we should only be asking not to be drawn out on.

If we were drawn out on at the turn, then we should no longer be in the hand and we shouldn't pay for the river card - unless we have pot odds for a small call. We should never be consciously in a desperate situation, although we may sometimes be there without knowing it. (Again, the opponent's slow played small set is the usual culprit.)

After a few draw outs on the river, the power player sometimes wishes there were no river. But, if we play our power game, and the pot sized bet we make is called on the turn, the river bet will in the long run add to the money we take home.

When the weak player makes a couple of river draw out wins, he is encouraged to play more of them. In the long run, his attachment to the river will contribute even more to our winnings.

Occasionally, when we draw to our winning hand of, say, two large pairs, we'll make a five card hand on the river, a full house perhaps, or maybe a straight or flush by accident. We'll accept that bit of luck because we're entitled to our share of it, but we won't consciously need it nor depend on it. That is to say, we usually won't know we need it. (Maybe we'll beat the opponent's slow played set that we didn't know he had.)

Here's something that has happened to all of us. Occasionally, making the five card hand on the river harms our win. The additional river "help" to our hand is sometimes overwhelming evidence to the opponent that we have a hand and the help robs us of a call when the cards are out. And then there is the "counterfeit" in the form of an additional board pair that replaces our winning second pair and ties the opponent's hand with our hand. Those things happen now and then so the poker demon can have his little joke. But, if we do it right, we win in the long run.

The Money on the Table.

We've established the top three elements of poker play: The Players, The Big Cards, and Position. The fourth element, if named, would be The Stack. The player with the short stack will be picked on by those with the big stacks. The weak stack will be moved toward the center of the table by the others as often as possible until he's knocked out of the game or has to make another buy.

The power cash player is never short stacked. When he isn't winning, he still has confidence in his play and he buys more players' checks so he can get value for that big hand when it comes. Tournament play, of course, is another subject with a different strategy. But, in cash games, we will always have a stack that is big to bring a fierce growl and sharp teeth.

The opponents' short stacks are vulnerable. But we should watch the attitude of the short stack player. Often he will play "scared money" for awhile. In other words, he will play defensively; he will play tight so he can double his short stack. But after what is often a short time, he will suddenly take the attitude of, "I'm not getting any cards, if this is as good as it gets, I'm all in." We hope this happens in a pot with us and we, therefore, should try to sense the moment when he adapts the new attitude. At that moment he has made the leap from tight to loose. That moment will feed the table and we hope will include the observant power player.

Again, in a money game as opposed to a tournament, the power player makes sure he has a strong stack. That way, we maintain all our ammunition for winning. And, if we can't get the good cards, we go home.

The short stacked player will be called, not only because the others want to move him in, but because he will seem desperate.

Borderline Hands. We play a borderline hand when:

- We haven't been active for awhile, don't want to leave the game, and need to avoid the tight player stigma.

- We try to take a pot when we're on the button, but we are called by one of the blinds.

- We're already in the pot because we're the big blind and no one has raised.

- We have sensed a weakness in a late position opener and we have raised to take the pot, but he has called our raise.

We have already discussed ace / large hands and ace / rag hands. We will dissect a few more of those kinds of hands in the coming discussions. We'll also discuss playing middle connectors and suited connectors and other trash hands that have been foisted upon us, or ill chosen by us.

Discussion 315

Borderline Middle Connectors for Profit

It is recommended that the reader begin this series with Part 101.

Poker is not a card game played by people.

Poker is a people game played with cards.

Borderline Hands.

We play a borderline hand when:

- We haven't been active for awhile and need to avoid the tight player stigma.

- We try to take a pot when we're on the button, but we are called by one of the blinds or a limper.

- We're already in the pot because we're the big blind and no one has raised.

- We have sensed a weakness in a late position opener, we have raised to take the pot, but our raise has been called.

Let's look at middle connected cards from the blinds.

We're in the big blind with the seven and eight of hearts. The pot has been opened but not raised and three players have called. The small blind folded and it's up to us. We tap the table signifying we will not exercise our option to raise; we'll take the free flop even though we're in the dark about the opponents' hands.

This, of course, is another exception to the "don't ever call" rule. We don't have raising pocket cards and we can't usually steal the pot, pre-flop, in the position of the blind. (More on this later.)

If we should raise to drive out some of those other three players, we might get a re-raise and have to throw our hand away. We might as well take a free draw.

The flop:

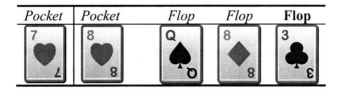

This is not a good flop for us. With three other players, we have to be wary of a queen among them. We're first to act and we check our hand. If there is a bet, even if it's from the button, we throw our hand away. That ends the boredom and we can get on with the next hand. (This boredom stuff can get old; we have to stay alert and watch our players. Focus! If we stay bored, we go home.)

If the flop is checked around the table, it could signify no one has a match for the queen. No raise before the flop and no bet after the flop.

This is important: At this point, we are invested only to the extent of the price of the blind.

The turn:

We're under the gun and we might have the winning hand.

Many players will bet this hand. We'll check it because we have little money invested and would rather get on with the next hand. There could be an inside straight draw or a club flush draw among our three limping competitors. If we bet, we could take the pot right now, but it would be a measly profit of four times the blind. However, if we wait, we could take the pot without risk and with one more card it could develop into a money pot. We'll check.

If the turn had paired our seven, we'd take charge. We would make an oversized bet (more than the pot) and stake our claim immediately. No draws for anybody, especially if the turn seven had been in diamonds. An oversized bet would do it; no one else has much invested either. We wouldn't mind a foolish draw call from an opponent; that's one reason we would bet: to build a pot if someone wants to play and take poor pot odds.

The river:

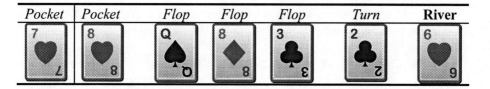

Pocket	Pocket	Flop	Flop	Flop	Turn	**River**
7♥	8♥	Q♠	8♦	3♣	2♣	6♥

The six is probably a neutral card. We'll possibly showdown and win those called blinds.

If the six were a club and someone bets, they can have our two dollars. If the river is a high card and someone bets, we give it to them as well. And the reason is still because we don't have anything invested. On with the next hand.

A queen would be one of the best river cards. We would bet the size of the pot because we certainly have the best second pair. And, as on the turn hypothetical, if the river is a seven, we have a betting hand. We just might get a call. Although, in no limit, we would check if it's the seven of clubs because, once more, there could be a flush and we have so little invested.

In this story, someone could have a four and a five because there have been no information bets or raises. Any bet from such a player will get rid of us. Nothing gained, very little lost.

Now, we'll change positions. We're on the button and we're in the pot because we tried to take the blinds by raising. Both blinds call our raise. (Well, that raise didn't work.) But, we haven't played a hand in a short while; we need to show some action and we have the seven and eight of hearts.

After the queen, eight, three, flop as shown above, the hand is checked to us.

There was no re-raise before the flop, but the blinds did call our raise. What do we know about these players? Are they in the habit of "protecting" their blinds? Do they re-raise in the blind when they have big cards? Do they cold call a raise to draw to a hand? Will they slow play when the button raises? As usual, in these kinds of hands, we must be sure of our players.

If the action is checked to us and we believe neither player is likely to have a queen, we can bet the size of the pot or three times the amount of our raise. If we are called by one of the blinds, we are probably still in good shape. Of course, we'll be anxious about the turn.

On the other hand, if we are re-raised (check/raised), we have found the queen – or maybe a set. The queen may even be accompanied by an ace. We throw our hand away.

If we get a call and no raise from a fairly good player, he is probably on a draw, likely a middle draw. Or he could be slow playing a set, but we should have decided that before now.

The turn, deuce of clubs, is no help to anybody. We now act according to what we know about our opponent. The biggest danger: A set of threes. We know our opponent didn't get help on the turn, nor did the turn help us. If we bet, he can't call – unless he has that set. So, since the pot is ours at this time and, if we believe a set isn't likely, we bet the size of the pot. He shouldn't be able to call. If he does, we'll look out for that slow played set. If he raises, we'll muck the hand.

What do we know about our opponent? Does he slow play a set? Does he make bad bluffs? Good bluffs? Remember, we raised before the flop and bet after the flop and, in this case, with no raises or re-raises from our adversary. He has little idea of what we hold and we've put him on middle connectors. At this point, we need to know our opponent.

Assuming the turn is the above deuce and we have not put our adversary on a set of threes, we bet so that he won't want to draw to those connectors.

If the six is a club and he bets, we have a serious decision to make. We believe, at this point, it's not a set. But what about a flush? About those connectors we put him on, could he be lucky enough for them to be clubs?

The middle connectors could have been the seven and eight of clubs and he's been calling us through the betting with a pair of eights. Depending on the player, we might have to find out.

Now we really, really have to know our player. A tell would be a big help. All things being equal, we'd probably search him with a call. After all, his calling with a pair of eights and making a back-in flush on the turn and the river is unlikely.

If the river is a high card and he bets, we give it to him.

Again, if we help our hand anywhere along the way, turn or river, we come out swinging. No draws by opponents to straights and flushes are allowed without paying the power player's toll.

We have the position. From the beginning, if no queen was being held by the opponents, this second pair pot probably has been ours all along. All we had to do was find out.

This could turn out to be a relatively large pot. Knowing our players and how to get information from them will make the difference between a good win or a stinging loss.

Confused at this point? Playing border hands is complicated. Read it all again. This is where the profit is. Lessons learned:

- We study the players so that we are prepared when the tight situation arrives.

- When we are in the button position, or near it, we can take command. A soft hand has to check to us. In the right company, we could take the pot at any time.

- In the button position, we can charge the pot, taking it or building it.

- Although we have suited connectors, our best prospect of winning is nearly always with a pair or two.

Discussion 316

Defending Against Connectors

It is recommended that the reader begin this series with Part 101.

Poker is not a card game played by people.

Poker is a people game played with cards.

Borderline Hands.

This discussion will revolve around slightly higher connectors. Although these cards are higher than those discussed earlier, they can sometimes be more troublesome than the middle connectors because they are harder to throw away.

We are in middle position with the queen of diamonds and the jack of diamonds. We enter this pot for one or more of the usual reasons:

- We haven't been active enough.

- The pre-flop action has been passed to us and we can make a power move by opening with a raise.

- There are players behind us we can intimidate because of their short stacks or for other reasons such as just being players weak in judgment. (Again, it is best to have the strong players on our right and the weak players on our left.)

We open the pot from the middle with three times the amount of the big blind. A player behind us calls and the big blind calls. The others will watch.

This time the blind is a good player. He doesn't slow play and he has been throwing his blinds away. We'll put him on some kind of good hand. He could have a drawing hand, but this player has been playing mostly big cards. He didn't re-raise, however; he merely increased his blind to the amount of our opening raise (he called). So he could, at this point, have anything but a large pair.

Our hapless caller behind us is a loose passive type and his pocket cards will be a mystery until after the flop. We won't disregard him, because anybody, even a weak passive player, can hold good cards and his calling station style of play could be hiding a good hand.

The flop brings the queen of clubs, the ten of diamonds, and the eight of diamonds.

Pocket	*Pocket*	*Flop*	*Flop*	**Flop**
Q♦	J♦	Q♣	10♦	8♦

We are lucky on the flop. We like having top pair and a somewhat high diamond flush to draw to. We won't get excited about the possible straight flush because that kind of excitement makes good players play bad. "Forget about it." When those straight flush things are made, they should always come as a surprise. And, much of the time, such a premium hand won't win premium money anyway because of its obvious dangers to the opponents.

The blind checks his hand. Remember, we have a good player in the blind. He likes to play big cards and the larger type connectors. So, we're wondering, how could this flop not have improved his hand? Are his cards larger than a queen?

Nevertheless, we must take charge because our advantage could be fleeting. There could be board overcards in our future and we'd rather not have to draw to win. Also, we have a good player who checked to us and is dangerous. So, we take the bull by the horns.

We bet twice the size of the pot.

The player behind us folds.

The blind calls. (!) He's not likely to pay the high price of our bet for just a draw.

The turn shows us the jack of spades.

Pocket	Pocket	Flop	Flop	Flop	Turn
Q♦	J♦	Q♣	10♦	8♦	J♠

The blind checks his hand.

We bet the size of the pot.

The blind moves all in.

Whatever the blind is holding, he has played the hand well and the play has fallen almost exactly how he had hoped it would. He has a good hand, a hand that we were willing to bet for him. There was a calling station behind us that he thought might be willing to add to the pot, but our flop bet was too large even for the calling station.

The blind didn't re-raise our flop bet because he wanted another bet after the turn. He was able to get a bet after the turn and then move all-in after the money was in the pot.

When the jack was not a diamond, he knew we did not have a flush and now he is not willing to let us draw to it. With the jack he can now represent a middle straight or an ace high straight. He's all-in. (Actually, this sounds a lot like Doyle Brunson.)

Let's review our player. He's a good player and he knows the value of a hand. He likes to start with high cards. He sometimes plays the higher connectors. He likes to build pots and set traps. He's a very good bluffer. (Yep, Doyle Brunson.)

Let's make our decision.

- We know this good player would not play a nine with anything except an ace, if then. Even if he held an ace with a nine, he couldn't have continued the hand through the after-flop betting.

- Our opponent playing king / nine is out of the question. And jack / nine is quite unlikely for this good player.

124

- If he held a pair of nines, he'd have been compelled to raise before the flop, good player that he is, in order to protect his hand or, more likely, he'd have thrown the pair of nines away.

- If he had held an ace and a king, he would have had to take the lead and hope to take the pot. If that didn't work, he'd have thrown Big Slick away. He would never have called our big bet just to draw to an inside straight.

- He has no idea the jack helped us and his only chance to win the pot is to bluff.

We call.

Our player is a gentleman and, as soon as he is called, he turns his hole cards over, a king and queen of hearts. We show our two pair. The river is a deuce of clubs and we take the pot.

Lessons illustrated:

- Know the players.

- Play the opponent's hand through his eyes.

- Take time to analyze throughout the hand. This is no limit; take some time.

- From the opponent's position: Don't get cute. Be a power player. A power player probably would have won in the blind's spot. Instead of playing coy after the flop, the power player would have bet into the opener while the power player thought the position of the blind had the edge.

- Don't call and draw from the blind, take charge. Because we had shown strength before the flop and made a bet after the flop, a bet from the blind would have gotten rid of us. The opening good player with the queen / jack in our position would probably have decided his queens were too weak to face higher queens and higher bets. The blind could also have a higher pair. The power player in the blind doesn't allow the draw and takes an early win, instead of a very expensive loss.

Position

Little Bud and Big Bucks

By Sam O'Connor

He was too small to be in so many fist fights. But Bud Nelson occasionally would appear in the dealer's chair at The Boulder Club with scraped knuckles and a purple eye or a fat lip. All the sawdust employees and regulars were accustomed to the symptoms, so no one was ever surprised by his appearance and very few commented.

Bud's real name was Larry but few people knew that. He was the youngest of three brothers and the two much older brothers called him "Buddy". But the people of Las Vegas' Glitter Gulch knew him as "Little Bud".

He may have been small, but he was wiry, and he was a scrapper. He walked with a swagger that was aimed to make up for his lack of size and to warn people to stay out of his way. Little Bud seemed quite sure of himself and he was almost always on the side of good.

Bud fit in perfectly in a sawdust joint like the Boulder Club, and the Boulder was right down his arroyo. He looked like the Colorado countryside he came from, raw boned, tough skinned and sun burnt. He had worked on his brother's horse ranch, but he gave up the cold wind and the hard work of Colorado ranching in 1959 for the less demanding desert town of Las Vegas.

The Boulder Club managers were taken with Bud's rancher look and they gave him a dealing job in the no limit dime ante draw poker game at the back of the sawdust joint.

Bud's frequent drinking partner was Freddie Ivans, the swing shift poker boss at the Golden Nugget. They worked shifts that had the same hours, across the street from one another. Bud would join Freddie after work at the Nugget's famous Nymph and Satyr Bar. They'd start with the call liquor of their choice at the Nymph and Satyr and then make their way down Fremont Street tasting the healing waters that were available here and there. After the third drink, the label on the whiskey bottle didn't make much difference.

Freddie was a good friend to Bud and Little Bud confided in him often. Freddie took the avuncular role and played it well. Tonight, Freddie had some news. He waited until after the second drink.

"Shoeshine Nick is playing in the big game at the Dunes. He's losing pretty bad and says they need a new dealer. He wants to make a deal with you."

"I don't have any money to loan", Bud said facetiously.

"You wanna make more money, or not?"

"You know Shoeshine?"

"Sure, I've known him since Adam got kicked out of Eden."

"I suppose you knew Adam, too."

"Might have."

"Did Adam make any money?"

"Not without Shoeshine."

"Wasn't Adam a fruit picker? What's he doing now?"

"Contemplating his navel."

"He didn't have one."

Freddie gave it a minute's thought. "Let's have another round."

"Bud, you wanna make more money, or not? How much you making now?"

"Fifty a day. Sixty some days. Good money."

"At the Dunes you'd make a hundred to three hundred a day. The smallest check on the table is a hundred. The winner tosses the dealer two or three at the end of the shift."

"It's a carpet joint. I wouldn't be able to wear my boots."

"Shoeshine wants you to see him at the Dunes tomorrow. And I'm sure you can wear your boots, if they're clean."

Las Vegas in those days was a cameraman's nirvana. One of the favorite movie camera effects was to film an arriving limousine in front of the Dunes Hotel, then pan slowly up to the great Sultan atop the entrance. The Sultan, impressive in his turban with sparkling jewel, fists insouciantly thrust on hips, gazed down with triumph over the eager minions entering his den of pleasure. Who knew what exotic adventures awaited within?

In the old days, the Dunes was probably the most mob-run place in Las Vegas. Sure, all the hotels were mob-run or mob-influenced. There was the Sands with the mob-connected entertainers and then there was that other hotel where Jimmy the Weasel and Sam Giancana lounged poolside. But, still, none was so blatantly centered in the mob as the Dunes. And it was there that the mob's stewards liked to play poker.

The poker "room" at the Dunes was no room at all. It was a roped off area situated at the back of the casino next to the entrance to the main show room. Poker was run by Gene Stone and his sidekick, a scratchy voiced little guy known only as "Shrimpy". They were from "back east". You know, from the old school, before Senator Kefauver shut down the nation's back alley gambling in 1952.

Little Bud came slowly through the front entrance of the Dunes with all the swagger he could muster. He was acutely uncomfortable in the carpet joint and he hid his nervousness the best he could, which made him all the more conspicuous. He headed straight for the poker room and, just short of entering, stood to the side, atop the two descending steps where Shoeshine Nick could spot him from the poker table.

Nick approached and gave Bud a quick nod and hello. Without further words, Nick took him to meet Gene Stone.

Little Bud got his audition at the main table. He dealt to Charley Rich, Major Riddle, Chicago Nate, Shoeshine Nick, Johnny Moss and Ray Ryan who was killed shortly later in a car bombing. They all liked Bud and approved his dealing. Gene offered Bud the dealer's job. But Gene was surprised when Little Bud said he would have to think about it.

Just before he said goodbye to Little Bud, Shoeshine Nick stuck a matchbook in Bud's shirt pocket. It was a common way to pass information when you didn't want to risk being overheard. The note in the matchbook read, "Meet me at Bungalow 12 at the Stardust tonight - 5:00 o'clock"

What did Nick want? Bud's mind was racing. Nick wants to talk? Sure. But about what? Something about the dealer's job, surely. No, wait. Nick was a player, not a manager. Wait. What exactly was he? This seemed a little dangerous.

There were rows of bungalows behind the Stardust, but a bungalow with a number as low as twelve couldn't be very far. Right?

Where IS that bungalow? Bud's mind was racing. Maybe the walk to the bungalow wasn't really that complicated, maybe it just seemed that way. Ah, there it is. Bud wasn't sure he was glad he'd found it.

Nick wasted little time with salutations. "Bud, Gene tells me you have to think about taking the job."

Bud nodded.

"There is so much money to be made. I'm not talking about the salary and the tokes; that's small stuff. I'm talking about big bucks."

Bud's eyes narrowed.

"Look. Take the job. After a few days, I want you to put out a double."

"A double? Two run-up hands? I'd have to be crazy. Besides I don't know how."

"My people have played in your game at the sawdust joint and they say you're capable. Look, just don't make the hands too big. I don't have to tell you, four aces over four kings is very suspicious. Make sure my hand barely beats the other guy."

"I'm not capable. And even if I was, I'd be nuts to try it in that company. I could get killed."

"Okay, forget the pot split. I'll give you a flat $20,000, just so you know how much you got coming. Make it a good double. And don't take too long making up your mind about it. Take the deal while you can."

The next day Bud eagerly called Gene Stone at the Dunes. The conversation was brief and very worthwhile.

That night Bud met Freddie at the Nymph and Satyr Bar. Bud told Freddie he was offered the job, but it wasn't an ordinary dealer's job. There were certain conditions imposed by one of the players.

"You mean you didn't take Nick's proposition?"

"How the hell do you know about that?"

"It was a test to see if you were going to deal an honest game. Well, at least that's what Nick told me today."

"Really? Or did he tell you that story when he figured I wasn't going to take the proposition?"

"I don't know. Poker players that make deals with Adam can be hard to figure. Anyway, the job is still yours – without any complications from Nick. It looks like you've won."

The next morning Little Bud was early getting to work. With a little sawdust on his boots, it was good to be home.

Discussion 330

Playing From Early Positions

It is recommended that the reader begin this series with Part 101.

Poker is not a card game played by people.

Poker is a people game played with cards.

We have advised folding some hands that even tight players play with a call...like A/J, 8/8, 10/9 suited and so forth. At this point, it seems that power players play fewer hands than tight players, which makes us the tightest players of all. Is that right?

No.

Power players play more hands than tight players and fewer hands than loose players. Let's take a look.

Early Position. We play fewer hands. It seems sure that power players play fewer hands in early position, especially-under the-gun (UTG), than any other type player, including both types of tight players, passive and aggressive. There are two main reasons:

- Information. Power players want to discourage limping, reduce the number of contenders, have fewer draw outs, and maintain a power image. We raise pre-flop; we want mainly to find out more about the opponents' hands before the flop. We, therefore, must raise from early position before the flop and we need an extra good hand with which to raise because we will be first to act after the flop.

- Position. Power players are more conscious of position than most players. In simplification, the tight player wants to make a hand; the loose player wants to play. While both these types consider other things to some extent, the power player is thoroughly disciplined in players, odds, position, stacks, tells, bluffing and many other things. Notice that the third item in the foregoing list is position. We want an extra good hand if we're going to act first after the flop.

There are other, although small, reasons for playing fewer hands in first position. When the power player is jockeying for his choice of seats at the table, he tries to place the stronger players to his right. If he has been successful in doing this, he has the strong players playing near the button when he is in the blinds. Additionally, the strong players are in the blinds when he, the power player, is under the gun and must open the betting.

Those are more reasons to wait for the extra strong hand in first position, or just to wait for the button which is only two hands away, before making an aggressive play.

In addressing this question, we're suddenly conscious of how many hands we play in first position, under the gun (UTG). The answer is, almost none. Certainly less than five percent. In fact, we usually can look at one card and know we're not going to play. There are only two reasons to look at the second card. One is if the first card is an ace or a face card. But we do look at the second card each time, because we want to repeat the same motions at the same speed each time we act, in order to pre-empt sending any tells. But around ninety five percent of the time, looking at the second card is mere play acting.

In prior pages, we have discussed in detail which card combinations are suitable to play from an early position. Basically, it is any of the first three in the first column of the chart.

rank		rank		rank		rank		rank	
1	AA	11	JTs	21	J9s	31	76s	41	QT
2	KK	12	QJs	22	AJ	32	97s	42	54s
3	QQ	13	KJs	23	KTs	33	A2s	43	K9s
4	JJ	14	ATs	24	87s	34	65s	44	J8s
5	AKs	15	AQ	25	Q9s	35	77	45	75s
6	TT	16	T9s	26	T8s	36	66	46	J9
7	AQs	17	KQ	27	88	37	AT	47	44
8	AJs	18	QTs	28	KJ	38	55	48	T9
9	KQs	19	98s	29	QJ	39	86s	49	33
10	AK	20	99	30	JT	40	KT	50	98

Remember, we're discussing raising UTG or raising from the blind. The first three pockets ranked, with an option for Q/Q depending on the game, are must raise pockets from any position, including under the gun.

133

The next seven rankings can be played (raised) if the players and the rhythm are right. We have thrown members of those seven rankings away many times when in first position when there are troublesome players to our left. We are free to raise the pot with one of the rankings of four to ten when we have figured out how to handle the troublesome players and we are comfortably in control at the table.

To underscore, we observe the following: All of the above was written with only no limit games in mind. The rules can be relaxed in limit games because, after all, we can be re-raised only the amount of the structured limit. If we are fairly sure of our hand (one of the top three rankings, or a routine raise from a habitual raiser) we can re-raise. If we are not sure of our hand, we don't ever call; we throw our hand away. In limit games, the amount we save is often the amount we win.

Contrasted to limit games, in no limit we must measure our chances in terms of making some large bets with each flop and turn of the card. So we'll want a good hand to start with.

In summary, the power player plays fewer hands from early position than most other players. He knows he is risking big bucks when he violates the practice. He knows he'll get his chances later.

The power player plays far more hands from the late positions than other players. When we add just a few additional hands from middle position, we find that, in total, we play many more hands than either of the tight categories of players. This keeps us active and gives a chance to mix our play and win some dollars.

Discussion 331

Playing From Middle Positions

It is recommended that the reader begin this series with Part 101.

Poker is not a card game played by people.

Poker is a people game played with cards.

Our last Discussion showed Power Players play more hands than tight players and fewer hands than loose players. And we play them much better.

We've established that power players play fewer hands from first position than any other type player, including very tight players, because we are more aware of the weakness of the position and we have the need for as much information as we can get before the flop. If we act first after calling, we have no information. We do gain limited information when we are called or re-raised. However, if we are re-raised, we will need a very powerful hand to re-re-raise; we won't ever call.

First position hands, therefore, lacking the strength of favorable position, are usually hands to be thrown away.

If you haven't reviewed the previous Discussion 330 concerning early position play, please do so before reading this discussion further.

Middle Position.

Generally speaking, the second column in the chart below shows pocket cards suitable for raising from a middle position before the flop. But there are many warnings and exceptions to the chart. We are getting into a very discretionary area and one of the most difficult areas to play. Readers should be very experienced in play in order to use the second column from middle position. Even experienced players should allow far more weight to the first column when playing from the middle.

rank		rank		rank		rank		rank	
1	AA	11	JTs	21	J9s	31	76s	41	QT
2	KK	12	QJs	22	AJ	32	97s	42	54s
3	QQ	13	KJs	23	KTs	33	A2s	43	K9s
4	JJ	14	ATs	24	87s	34	65s	44	J8s
5	AKs	15	AQ	25	Q9s	35	77	45	75s
6	TT	16	T9s	26	T8s	36	66	46	J9
7	AQs	17	KQ	27	88	37	AT	47	44
8	AJs	18	QTs	28	KJ	38	55	48	T9
9	KQs	19	98s	29	QJ	39	86s	49	33
10	AK	20	99	30	JT	40	KT	50	98

In prior Discussions, we have set out at length the importance of position, the importance of knowing the players, and the importance of knowing our current image at the table, before choosing to play one of the hands in the second column of rankings. Moreover, we're not at all proud of rankings after eighteen for this kind of middle position play.

Here's a story about middle position. Is this familiar?

Yesterday, the cards were not kind. Murphy was able to catch a couple of hands after while and he got some action, which made him winner. Next, he played a bluff which lost him the pot, reduced his stack and removed his tight aggressive image. And then the good cards stopped coming.

He had to play some hands he wouldn't have ordinarily played in order to stay away from a tight image and to get some action on a future hand, if ever one were to come his way. It didn't.

So Murphy had to stop playing the looser hands because it was becoming ridiculous. And still the cards never came. After he sensed that he had regained a tight image, he bluffed three hands in a row and quit winner.

It's worth repeating. The good cards never did come, but Murphy quit winner.

The three ending bluffs in the above example were one bluff from the button which was the easy one, and two bluffs from middle position which were harder. Middle position is far and away different from early position, even though it is only two or three players away from early position. But it is much, much different because Murphy was dealing with perhaps only half the table; so the position was much stronger than its early position neighbor.

To play properly from middle position, we must have intricate knowledge of the players in front of us and behind us. When the pot is opened before it gets to us, we must know a lot about who opened it and whether or not we can play (raise). If we raise, what will any action from a player behind us mean?

If we must play marginal hands because we have been somewhat inactive, middle position is best. It is much better than the early positions, for reasons already stated. It is also a little better than late positions because we are expected to steal from those positions. However, we must note that middle position may not be as *playable* after the flop because we are almost always playing opponents behind us. But a raise from middle position makes a stronger statement before the flop than from late position and a friendly flop, even a neutral flop, will give us the pot.

The chart sets out the benchmark for hands played from middle position.

The hands include the first and second columns in the rankings, although we should stop at number eighteen. We'll be careful because middle position play often decides a player's winnings for the day. Exceptions to the starting chart are executed carefully and with considerable calculation.

Conclusion: Power players play more hands from middle position than tight players do. We power players can do it because we don't ever call from middle position. We can do it because we take the lead at the right time against the right players when our image calls for it. We do it because we know our players and we are aware of the opponents' opinions of us and because we know how to shift gears as our luck changes – without being on tilt. We can do it, because we have the knowledge and we are power players.

Discussion 332

Playing from Late Positions

It is recommended that the reader begin this series with Part 101.

Poker is not a card game played by people.

Poker is a people game played with cards.

Power players play more hands than tight players and fewer hands than loose players.

The last two Discussions have addressed power player action from the early positions (we play far fewer hands from early positions than other players, even tight players) and power player action from the middle positions (we play more hands from the middle positions than most other players). If you have not participated in these last two Discussions, please review them now before reading this Discussion.

Some lower limit tables have ten chairs for the players, some even have eleven. The big number of seats is designed by the house to control the money and the rake. In the lower limit games, there are few winners because a steady rake from small pots sends a constant flow of money from meager sources down the slot and into the rake box. As the chips go back and forth across the table, they seem to gradually wear out. The house, therefore, needs as many players at the table as it can get to disguise the somewhat obvious volumes of escaping money.

The more players there are at the table, the better our hands have to be. This makes the eleven handed game more troublesome than the nine handed.

It follows that, with fewer players, the weaker hands become stronger. In a five handed game, we bend the chart considerably. A five handed game is the aggressive player's delight and the power player's good fortune.

Another school of thought allows nine chairs for the players in no limit. More than nine players, they reason, would not increase the rake because the full rake is usually taken after the flop at any active table and the rake isn't as obvious because there is a lot of money on the table. We prefer this view from the house management.

We designate the first four seats at the table as the early seats, including the blinds. This is because the under-the-gun seat is the first to act before the flop and the blinds are the first to act after the flop. We, therefore, have two sets of seats acting first, two in the blind and two under-the-gun seats. The next three chairs are the middle seats. And the last two are the late seats in a nine handed game, the button and next to the button.

rank		rank		rank		rank		rank	
1	AA	11	JTs	21	J9s	31	76s	41	QT
2	KK	12	QJs	22	AJ	32	97s	42	54s
3	QQ	13	KJs	23	KTs	33	A2s	43	K9s
4	JJ	14	ATs	24	87s	34	65s	44	J8s
5	AKs	15	AQ	25	Q9s	35	77	45	75s
6	TT	16	T9s	26	T8s	36	66	46	J9
7	AQs	17	KQ	27	88	37	AT	47	44
8	AJs	18	QTs	28	KJ	38	55	48	T9
9	KQs	19	98s	29	QJ	39	86s	49	33
10	AK	20	99	30	JT	40	KT	50	98

The first, second and third columns show the acceptable pocket cards for entering the pot with a raise from the two late seats. But this rule of thumb is probably the least observed rule of the power player. The columns will be mangled and twisted, intentionally, more than any other chart rule we've presented. And, of course, the reason is because of the variety of complexions of a game, affected by the types of players, our image in the game, and the betting rhythms of the game.

Just as we are very strict about the first position, a lot of judgment is needed to play the late seats because a lot of hands will be played. If the pot has been raised and we cannot re-raise, we can throw most of those hands away. In those cases, the hands with which we might have ventured a raise, go to the muck.

However, if the pot has only been called, we can raise with many hands. Now, we'll be careful in deciding to make that raise. How is the rhythm of the game? What is our image? Are the players who limped in tight or loose? What are the blinds likely to do? (We should know what the blinds are like, because they are the same blinds for us to observe every time the button goes around the table.)

Here's a good question. If we are next to the button, what will the button do when we decide to steal when it's his turn to steal? (We should know him pretty well by now, too.)

Let's say we've raised in a position just before the button.

If the button didn't call us, we will be the last to act after the flop. This gives us a decided advantage. If the flop is favorable, we are in a position to bet or raise. We don't ever call unless we have pot odds and only then if our image of not calling isn't more valuable.

If the flop is marginal to our hand and has been checked to us, we have the choice of betting, or checking and getting the free turn. Remember, we're the pre-flop raiser. Sometimes our choice will be repeated on the turn and we'll get a free card on the river.

This last "free card" move from last position is one thing that gives our drawing hand and last position additional advantage. Being in a good bluffing position is what moves so many of the chart hands into a *playable* place in last position.

The last two columns of the chart hold very little merit and those columns are there mostly to demonstrate how weak they are. However, they can be used as maneuver columns. Maneuvers include stealing pots, before or after the flop, opportunity to draw to hands, and action to maintain image. Some other uses will be covered in later Discussions.

We don't ever call before or after the flop. We've already noted the rare exceptions.

We're real good at throwing away those maneuver hands in the face of a bet, or when they just don't work out. We get rid of them early. We're also good at capitalizing on them when they do work out. Capitalization on marginal hands, in no limit, is usually a surprise to the power player's opponents as well as to the power player. And that, in turn, usually means we've just won a big pot. Much more on this later.

We're going to play some hands in the next few Discussions.

Discussion 333

Blinds and Big Slick

It is recommended that the reader begin this series with Part 101.

Poker is not a card game played by people.

Poker is a people game played with cards.

A Word about Blinds. One of the most important things to watch in any player is how he plays his blinds. Action from opponents in the blind varies more widely than any other position. The trouble with studying opponents' blind play is that blind play for each player is generally infrequent; each blind comes around only every nine or ten hands. (Even though it seems more often.)

How does the power player play his blinds? Emphatically, he needs an unusually good hand to raise from his blind. The exception in playing two rags occurs when everybody in the pot has only called our big blind. We'll take the free flop. We can also call in the small blind if we believe the big blind won't raise. We get a 50% discount in the small blind.

When we have a big hand in either blind, we raise when the betting comes around to us. And if we can't re-raise a substantial raise that was made by the opponent, we can't call; he's telling us he has a big hand and we'll have to go first after the flop. However, if the raise is a small raise made by the button, who is the habit of raising on the button, maybe we can make an exception. But, remember, we still have to act first after the flop. Blind hands usually are not *playable* and, therefore, usually thrown away.

When we do have a good hand in the blind, we charge. Are we bluffing? The opponent will have to call to find out. There are occasional exceptions discussed elsewhere in this book, but raising is generally the power player's method. It suits his image.

Some blinds players call all raises and play most of their blinds. Their theory is they have their money already in the pot and they have to protect it. Actually, the blind money they've donated is no longer theirs. If they are entering the fray by calling a raise because they have a discounted call, they may have a small point but, because of the raise, they still should have a hand.

Our problem is these frequent and habitual blind players can be holding most anything. Another good reason for raising before the flop.

Some players will play the big blind differently than the small blind. The decision to be more active in the big blind is usually due to the amount of money they have invested and they have decided to be foolish about that small amount.

Other players never raise from the blind before the flop. These players could have two aces or two deuces, but never make a raise; they want someone else to bet their hand for them. They are hard to read and we need to pick up on their no-raise-from-the-blind habit. They, too, could be holding most anything. But, on the plus side, they know nothing about our hand either.

In the same vein, some players in the blinds never lead the betting after the flop no matter what they are holding. Their theory is that they aren't expected to have a hand and, therefore, someone will bet their hand for them. They often plan to check and raise.

There are other players who, after they've checked and raised from the blind a couple of times after the flop and have shown a good hand, will use the check and raise to bluff. We'll soon know who they are and remember them, because they are rare in small games. When we find them, we'll place them in a very high players' category for small games.

After we've lined up all the players at the table, our next assignment is to pay apt attention to how they play their blinds. The information will come slowly but, especially in no limit, it will become not only useful, but necessary in order to book a win.

Borderline Hands and Big Slick.

Maybe Big Slick should be called Big Nasty. He probably presents more problems than all the other pocket cards because he should be played in various ways, depending on position, stacks, and opponents. Because of these complications, he's hard to play. After all, when we get ace / king, we hold the two biggest cards in the deck and we can get kind of excited about it.

There are many players who will always play him, unsuited, like he's rated much higher than the number ten pocket hand. Listen to those players; they are the ones who complain about Big Slick and how he let them down. These players handle Big Slick like the owners of an untrained pit bull; they don't know what to do with him.

Here's the rub: Sometimes ace / king should be played strongly and sometimes he should be promptly thrown away. Position is almost everything in those decisions.

Other borderline hands are easier than ace / king to throw away. We can quickly get rid of ace / rag, connectors that don't connect, doubtful pairs, etc. But Big Slick doesn't like to slip away; he likes to stick around and embarrass us.

On the other hand, Big Slick can win a lot of money. But we have to be careful and we have to know how to play him.

This time, we'll play Big Slick from the third seat after the big blind. That places us in fifth position after the flop.

We have the ace of diamonds and the king of hearts. We open the pot with three times the amount of the big blind.

A player behind us calls and the big blind calls.

The flop:

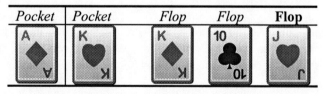

We have top pair and best kicker. We appear to have a good hand, but we have to be careful with this flop. We have a big blind who could have anything and we have a late position player. Both cold called our raise. The blind is now under the gun and we'll look at the following situations:

The Big Blind Bets. He bets the size of the pot. What we do now depends almost entirely on what we know about the blind. He's betting into a power player who made the initial raise. Does he have two aces? He might, if he sandbags his blinds before the flop. Does he have a straight?

If he plays ace / queen with a cold call, he could. How about three of a kind? Does he lead with three of a kind from the blind? Or does he just have a draw to a straight? We have three times the blind invested in this fiasco and, if we don't know the answers to these questions and don't have a dependable tell, we must give Big Slick the burial he deserves. Knowing the answers to the questions may give us enough knowledge to raise, but in this situation, we never call.

The Big Blind Checks for a Trap. In this scenario, we studied our blind player and we know he likes to set those check and raise traps. So, when he checks, we check along with him. If the third player bets and the blind raises, we're out of the hand with no further cost. Nice play, good discipline. If the third player doesn't bet and the blind has a hand, he'll come out betting after the turn and we'll make a decision based on what we know about him. If the third party bets and the blind doesn't raise, we have all the best of it and the choice of raising a very large amount.

The Big Blind Makes an Honest Check. We know he made an honest check because we are familiar with his play. In this case, we feel we're in fair control and we come out charging. The player behind us calls but doesn't raise, which probably means he needs another card. It could also mean he has top pair with a lesser kicker or, more likely, a pair with a straight draw. Actually, we all have a straight draw and, if anyone has a queen, he has the best of it in the draw because his draw is open ended.

The Turn. An ace? How would we like to have aces and kings on the turn? Be careful with your answer.

Absolutely not! At the moment we have the best hand and an ace could make somebody a straight. At least, it will give somebody a chance to represent a straight and put us to a guess. No. No ace, please.

How about a queen for a straight? That would make things manageable. But no queen, please; it could result in the bane of no limit poker – the split pot. We'd like to maintain the status quo, or better. The turn: The ten of spades.

Pocket	*Pocket*	*Flop*	*Flop*	*Flop*	**Turn**
A♦	K♥	K♦	10♣	J♥	10♠

Yes! Good turn card. The third player, and possibly the blind, made two pair along with us. Neither player has three tens because bottom pair would have been too expensive to play. Neither player made his straight. Both likely have two pair. It's time for us to devour those opponents with our best two pair and supreme kicker.

This is the kind of hand that wins big pots, the kind that is close to an opponent's hand but is a clear winner.

After the blind checks, we make a super sized bet (no more drawing) or we could go all- in, depending on the stacks in front of the players.

Lessons illustrated:

- Big Slick is dangerous. We have to know his strengths and his short comings.

- The second order of business after we've lined up players is to pay more attention to how they play the blinds.

- We'll be aware of the blind check and raise. It can be dealt with.

- When we don't know about the players, or if we're in bad position, we throw ace / king suited, or unsuited, into the muck.

- When we have the edge in any dangerous hand, there is no more drawing. We move in.

- We're not interested in the big hand; we need only the hand with the edge which often wins much bigger pots.

Postscript: In a pre-flop all-in situation, either our bet of all-in or theirs, Big Slick gives us more benefit than his usual tenth place spot on the chart because he doesn't have to be *played* after the all-in and the board cards will fall no matter what else happens. With Big Slick, we are sitting with the two highest cards in the deck with five cards to come that we don't have to pay for. In fact, a study of winning hands would probably place him third in pre-flop all-in, with only pocket aces or kings being superior. We have to observe, however, that Big Slick is fairly even with the other pocket pairs in this situation. But, all things considered and on balance, he's a good all-in bet before the flop.

Discussion 334

Position Drawing

It is recommended that the reader begin this series with Part 101.

Poker is not a card game played by people.

Poker is a people game played with cards.

What do we do with a four card flush? Or a draw to an open ended straight? Of the two, we prefer the flush because it's bigger. It's also easier to make than the straight after we have four of the suited cards.

We'll explore the pocket starters below in the next few Discussions. They'll be discussed with several positions in mind and with several types of opponents. We'll use the ace and ten as pocket cards because we like the flush better, but the strategy will apply to all drawing hands. We simply use the ace and the ten to try to keep the comparisons between apples and apples.

In our illustration, the reader knows that an ace and a jack would be more favorable, ace and queen better yet, and so on, but we'll take the more difficult hand for our purposes. It's still a nut flush.

In the first situation, we're under the gun. We'll assume all stacks are about equal and all players are good players. No bets from our opponents will be small and therefore, for illustrative purposes, pot odds calls will not be part of the discussion.

We are holding the ace and ten of clubs.

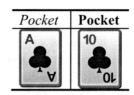

We're under the gun and we shouldn't be in this hand. We throw the hand away.

Okay, no more tricks, let's go to a middle position. No one has opened the betting. (If someone has opened the betting, we throw the hand away.) As we all know, we don't ever call before the flop. In this case, we want to play the hand and open the betting, so we raise three times the amount of the blinds. We get a call from the small blind.

The flop brings the king of clubs, the three of clubs, and the queen of hearts.

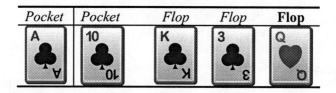

Pocket	Pocket	Flop	Flop	**Flop**
A♣	10♣	K♣	3♣	Q♥

The small blind bets the size of the pot. We don't know what the small blind called our raise with, but he jumped a raise fence and must have something strong. In the past, his small blind has never been important enough to "protect" and this time he's in a raised pot voluntarily that he could have gotten out of gracefully. He probably has big cards and all he needs in order to gain the advantage is a pocket king or queen. Actually, he could have both. We'd have to know more about the player to know if he'd check two pair, kings and queens. But just a single pair gives him a distinct advantage.

We have, roughly, a one in five chance of making the club flush on the turn and approximately the same odds again on the river, enhanced only slightly by the inside straight possibility. But that isn't our biggest problem. The big problem is the hand can't be *played*. In the face of his bet, we throw the hand away.

Again we run across the italicized word, *played*. It simply means we have a good hand that we can do little with because of position. A limit poker player might call along with the limit bet, but our no limit bettor, if he's a good bettor, will make it too expensive for us to draw. In fact, if we were in his place, it would be VERY expensive. In the face of the opponent's bet, the hand must be thrown away.

Changing stories, let's assume the small blind checks to us. Now, this hand in this betting position can be *played*. It's a bet-and-take-it position in most situations, regardless of what's on the board. After all, we did the pre-flop raising.

Even better, we have a king and queen showing and a blind checking to us. A semi-bluff could be in order, depending on our recent activity and that of our opponent. If we bet, we bet our uniform bet of the size of the pot, so we don't send any tells. We have lots of nice overcards, including our ace down in the hole. (We could write a song about that.) The opponent should also be afraid of clubs working. All conditions are "go". Considering the opponent and recent activity are favorable, we bet the size of the pot.

If we get a raise after our bet, it means the small blind got lucky and we throw our hand away.

If he calls, we're fairly confident. We have a lot of chances to make the hand, but we'll be careful. He'll likely check to us after the turn and we'll likely check along if we haven't improved our hand. That way, we'll get two cards, turn and river, for the price of our after-flop bet. With two draws after the flop, our odds are about 2.1 to 1 for making that flush.

Changing stories once again, we'll take a new position. We're on the button. There are still only two players, the middle opener who called the amount of the big blind, and our raise. The blinds have folded. The opener has called our raise.

After the flop, the opener checks to us. We're faced with the same decision as immediately above. We'll likely bet the size of the pot.

Now let's say the opener bets into us. He bets the size of the pot. In that case, we're faced with the decision of either raising or throwing our hand away, depending on what we know about the opponent and recent activity. We don't ever call a sizable bet. It's likely we'll throw our hand away.

In the next Discussion, we'll continue with the same hand. Things will be different when we get more players in the pot.

Discussion 335

Position Drawing

It is recommended that the reader begin this series with Part 101.

Poker is not a card game played by people.

Poker is a people game played with cards.

We continue the matter of pocket clubs from the previous Discussion. This time we'll add a player.

As long we're under the gun with this marginal hand, we'll muck the ace / ten.

So let's move to the middle position.

We are holding the ace and ten of clubs. The hand is dangerous from the middle position, but let's say we think we'll get the players behind us to fold if we raise.

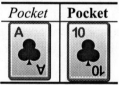

As you know, we don't ever call, especially before the flop. We want to play the hand, so we raise three times the amount of the blinds. We get calls from the button and from the small blind.

The flop brings the king of clubs, the three of clubs, and the queen of hearts.

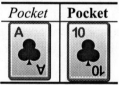

This is not a small pot. There is the big blind and there are three players with three times the blinds for a total pot of ten times the big blind.

149

If the blind comes out betting, we seriously consider throwing our drawing hand away. Blinds don't usually bet after the flop, though, especially in the face of a strong pre-flop raise and a strong two paint flop. Also, good hand or bad, blinds tend to check.

So, if the blind bets after the flop, we have to judge our betting player. What do we know about him? Will he bluff in this situation? Or does he have the goods? What does he think of us? And, this is important, what does he think of the button player? Would he bet into all that, if he didn't have a strong hand? If we don't have much of a clue, we'll credit him with strong cards and we'll muck the hand.

Now, we'll suppose the blind checks to us. We have a button caller behind us who jumped the raise fence and, assuming he is a strong player, is holding something good. Since he called our raise, we'll put him on an ace. We have the choice of a semi-bluff or checking the hand. And what we do depends on what we know about the button player. If both opponents are ready to be bluffed, we might take the pot with a strong bet together with the strong board.

If we bet and we get only calls from the button and the blind, it confirms our placing the button with an ace and the blind with a drawing hand. On the other hand, we likely could get to see the turn and the river without more betting - but wait; this may not be the time for a freebie.

If we check to the button, we are giving up the role of aggressor and we are placing the button in the position to steal the pot! So, maybe we should bet, keep the aggressor role and see what the button wants to do. After all, we've placed him on an ace which he hasn't paired. Betting and getting called is a whole lot better than checking and calling.

Let's talk about it some more. If we decide to check, the button bets a large amount and the blind folds, so our calling the button is out of the question. We don't call, especially in this situation. (There are exceptions, but this is not one of them.) We'll be transferring the initiative to a player behind us. If we call, we must be ready to call the next bet, a big one, after the turn. If we don't get help on the turn, are we ready to call that big bet? It will have cost us a lot of money to see the turn, too much. Next, will we be ready to pay three times the turn bet to see the river?

It's easy to see that, if we want to see more cards, we must keep the initiative and bet our hand after the flop. If we don't feel right about that, we check and throw our hand away after the button bets.

Checking and raising likely will let us see two more cards without any more betting. But if we check and raise, we must be prepared to be moved all-in if the button has a good hand. That's too big a risk. Also, when we muck after a re-raise, or there is an all-in move by the button, we've lost much more money than if we had made the first bet after the flop.

In general, most decisions whether or not to play are made after the flop. Most pots are won or lost after the flop. Drawing hand decisions are nearly always made after the flop.

What's the biggest lesson learned here? Ace / ten suited is a very dangerous hand in middle position. We shouldn't raise with it pre-flop unless we're fairly sure no one behind us will call. In most cases, we'll be throwing the hand away after the flop.

Discussion 336

Position Drawing

It is recommended that the reader begin this series with Part 101.

Poker is not a card game played by people.

Poker is a people game played with cards.

We continue the discussion of pocket clubs from the previous pages. We'll change positions once more.

We're on the button. It's a nice place to be.

We again are holding the ace and ten of clubs. The hand is now a good hand because we're on the button, but not if the pot has already been raised. If the pot has been raised, we throw the ace / ten away.

Pocket	**Pocket**
A ♣	10 ♣

Once more, we don't ever call, especially before the flop. We want to play the hand, so we raise three times the amount of the blinds. If the pot has already been opened by a limper, we still come in raising. In this example, we get a call from one of the blinds and a call from the opening limper.

The flop again brings the king of clubs, the three of clubs, and the queen of hearts.

Pocket	*Pocket*	*Flop*	*Flop*	**Flop**
A ♣	10 ♣	K ♣	3 ♣	Q ♥

It's up to the blind to act. He checks. The limper checks. Well, isn't this nice? We'll bet and probably take the pot.

152

If the blind raises an amount that is more than favorable pot odds, he got lucky and we throw our hand away. If the limper raises (not likely), we throw our hand away.

When we initiate the after flop bet and we are called, we have all the best of it. A call from either the blind or the limper isn't wanted, but we're still on the button with a good drawing hand. The limper, as indicated by his action, is playing a scared hand. So is the blind if he continues his hand.

Let's say the deuce of diamonds appears on the turn. Both players check to us. It's decision time. We don't have anything but a draw. But one of the opponents, or more, could have a large scared pair.

It's time to take stock of the players. If one or both can be bluffed at this point in the hand, it's time for a big move. But if, in reading the players, we decide a bluff is dangerous, we can check along and take another card. However, in doing so, we have exposed our hand.

Let's say we take another card and the four of hearts appears on the river. It's showdown time because we have lost our aggressor advantage and we will not make the easy-to-read Desperation Bluff. (There will be much more on the Desperation Bluff in Discussion 441 later.)

The decision whether to bluff after the turn is crucial to our winning the pot. If we don't bet after the turn, we possibly can still out draw the opponents on the river, but we will be counting on completing the best draw and we've lost our advantage in *play*. After the river could be showdown time and we haven't helped our hand. We could wind up third best.

Phil Helmuth once made the boast he could win in a typical small no limit game without ever looking at his pocket cards. Oh, that Phil. He was undoubtedly thinking he would have the best of it by watching the players for tells, watching the patterns of the players' action, having the most chips at the table, playing position and placing others on hands because of their positions. We also know he would dominate the table with his unusual brand of chatter. Phil probably would have won the above hand even if it was third best.

But I don't know about your boast in other situations, Phil. Once the open pair or a big bet hits the board, you'd better look at your pocket cards. But Phil is a Dominator and that is what this book is about.

153

Discussion 337

Position Drawing

It is recommended that the reader begin this series with Part 101.

Poker is not a card game played by people.

Poker is a people game played with cards.

We continue the discussion of pocket clubs from the previous pages. This time we'll change the number of players and take the big blind.

We are holding the ace and ten of clubs in the big blind.

If the pot is raised, we throw our hand away. We have a weak hand and virtually nothing invested.

But, our pocket cards make a suitable hand for an un-raised blind. The amount of the blind is called by three players. It's up to us to act pre-flop. We have little information, our hand is not worth a raise and we'll have to act first after the flop. So we check to see the free flop.

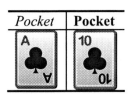

We have limped into the pot, one of the few times we, as power players, allow ourselves to do that. If there had been a raise, we'd have mucked the hand. If there had been only one player limping into the pot, we would have raised, maybe even if there had been two, depending on who they were. But, with three players already in the action, we limp in with the rest by checking our option to act.

The flop brings the king of clubs, the three of clubs, and the queen of hearts.

Pocket	Pocket	Flop	Flop	**Flop**
A♣	10♣	K♣	3♣	Q♥

Now we're first to act and, of course, we have to check.

Okay, let's get some terms clear. Someone says, "I had three way action." What does this mean? It's supposed to mean the speaker had three players in the pot with him for a four handed pot, and that's the way we'll use it. It means we get three players to one for our money.

We have about a 5 to 1 chance of making the flush with one card or abut 2.5 to 1 with two cards to come. We'd like to get the first one free. Plus, we have a small percentage opportunity to make a straight with the jack. Plus, we have lots of big cards. There are better drawing hands, but we have one of the best drawing hands available in hold 'em.

With three way action, we have the best of it in the odds department, when there is a bet the size of the pot. We want to play the hand. But that's not all there is to it. There is the matter of cash flow management.

We are getting three way action and we have better than a 40% chance of making some kind of winning hand. If we were short stacked and we check and then go all-in after someone bets, it could be lucrative. We would see the rest of the board cards without having to risk more money. We'd be getting good money and pot odds and there wouldn't be much at risk. But the power player is never short stacked in a cash game. There are more reasons not to be short stacked than there are reasons to be short stacked in this unique situation. We've been over all that in previous pages.

So, if we are not short stacked, we have to think about calling any pot sized bet from one or more of the other players in order to draw just one card, the turn. If we miss, we then have to call another bet, usually a much bigger one, in order to see the river.

If we could do this kind of hand three times in a row and commit all the money necessary to do it at the beginning of the first hand, we would gladly do it in groups of three all day long because the odds of winning just one of them would make it worthwhile.

155

But right now we're looking at one hand, this hand, which we must finance one card at a time. In the long run, playing this kind of hand will pay off, but the question is, what is our cash situation in this hand, right now? Do we want to spend the money for a one hand 40% long shot?

Another good question is whether or not the hand is *playable* from our position. It's very awkward to be the first to act each time. If we play, we must check and call. Check and call is not our style.

What do we know about our opponents? Maybe they can be bluffed. On the other hand, we don't want just some of them bluffed and still be playing the hand with one player because, if we make the nut flush, we want everybody in the pot with us. We either have to bluff them all, or none of them. And just about the best way to bluff is with a check and raise. Are the opponents set up for this big power play? All three of them?

So we check our hand. Someone bets and gets a call. It's up to us. What do we do?

Assuming the bet is the size of the pot or maybe larger because the bettor doesn't want anybody drawing to the board, we fold. We don't have much invested. It was nice to see a "free" flop. A good flop, too. But, in our position of having to act first, we needed another club or a jack.

Some players will call this hand all the way through. They are usually the ones you hear telling their bad beat story, the one where they had "nineteen outs".

Discussion 338

Position Drawing

It is recommended that the reader begin this series with Part 101.

Poker is not a card game played by people.

Poker is a people game played with cards.

We continue the discussion of pocket clubs from the previous pages. This time we'll change positions.

We'll skip the middle position which, with four players in the pot, would be played much the same as the play from the blind, covered on a previous page. Instead, we'll place ourselves on the button. We like it there.

We are holding the ace and ten of clubs. Our pocket hand is an okay hand for the button. Maybe we can steal the pot, either before or after the flop.

The pot has been opened, there has been one caller and it's up to us. We raise with our hand and we are surprised with a call from the big blind and the other two players. Perhaps we should be raising more to keep the limpers out when we have a big hand, but this time it suits us.

Pocket	**Pocket**
A ♣	10 ♣

It's sometimes common, depending on the players, for someone to call our raise when made on the button because buttons try to steal the pot a lot. But we're a little surprised to be in a hand with three other players. We like the fact the two players before us didn't raise the pot. If they had, we'd have thrown our hand away. At this point we don't know why the blind called our raise.

Once more, the flop brings the king of clubs, the three of clubs, and the queen of hearts.

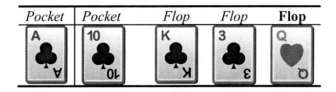

Pocket	Pocket	Flop	Flop	**Flop**
A♣	10♣	K♣	3♣	Q♥

If all three opponents check to us, we have to bet our hand. Not a small bet, not just the size of the pot, but more than that. The hand is *playable*. The oversize bet is occasionally a part of the power player's arsenal and this time we make good use of it.

It doesn't matter that the opponents know we want them out of the pot; the question for them is merely whether they want to pay to stay in with their garbage hands. Normally, we'll take the pot with the bet.

We assume, with our bet, the opponents have not paired a king or a queen, because they didn't bet. We'll place them on holding single aces and we'll come out swinging. A check and raise would be a gutsy move on their part after our big bet and, if it happened, we'd have to assume they have a set.

We like it, if they just call. A slow played set notwithstanding, they could have a pair, hidden or otherwise, but if they do, they're afraid of it. If a rag comes on the turn, another bet from us should take the pot.

But, if we suspect some slow play, we'll take a free draw. Of course, then we give up the initiative and it's more or less a showdown hand.

Again, knowing the players is essential. Ah yes, so many decisions still come down to knowing the players. Hold 'em is a game of people, accentuated by no limit.

Now let's change the queen of hearts to a king of hearts.

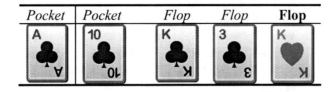

Pocket	Pocket	Flop	Flop	**Flop**
A♣	10♣	K♣	3♣	K♥

It's the same position. We're on the button and the action is checked to us.

In this case we have to check along. The open pair is deadly, especially kings, which could be part of trips. We have three other players and any one of them could have a king in the pocket or, more likely, a better ace. If any one of the other three bets this flop, the pot is theirs with our best wishes. In the face of any kind of bet the pot certainly is not ours.

Let's say no one bets and the turn brings us a club to make the flush. If the action is checked to us, we can bet a large amount, depending on the players. As in the description above, we have reviewed what we know about our opponents. So in this case, we have decided the chances of an opponent having a full house are small, but we don't want to risk an opponent catching a full house on the river. So, if we bet, we bet a large amount, so big that someone will not want to raise unless he has that full house. (If we get a raise, our knowledge of our opponent could make us call that raise. However, not many players in the small no limit arena will bluff with a check / raise.)

On the other hand, it's no disgrace to check along with our club flush and such action, or lack of it, is often recommended in the face of an open pair, especially with opponents on whom we don't have a good read.

If we should decide to make a bet after the turn and we have to go to the river because we are called, we try for a showdown. If we don't get the showdown and we get a bet by an opponent, it'll call for a big decision on our part. A defensive position, in this case, is not a good place to be. Again, this is a good reason to check along after the turn instead of making that big bet. Those big bets with an open pair are rough on players holding flushes and our decision will depend on what we know about the bettor.

We should point out that small open pairs, like threes, are not as dangerous as a pair of open kings. Many times we can place our opponents on hands that are not likely to contain a small card. Then again, sometimes we have to place them on ace / rag where the small open pairs can be very dangerous.

Conclusion. In a no limit game, open pairs are deadly. If this Discussion about open pairs of kings has not been very conclusive, it's simply because open pairs come with a black hood and scythe. The safe decision is generally to get out of there.

Discussion 339

Position Drawing

It is recommended that the reader begin this series with Part 101.

Poker is not a card game played by people.

Poker is a people game played with cards.

We continue the discussion of pocket clubs from the previous pages. This will be the last in this series of discussions about drawing from various positions with a varying number of players.

This time we'll change the flop. Instead of a strong club flop, we'll suppose a weak club flop.

Pocket	**Pocket**
A ♣	10 ♣

Once more, if we're under the gun, we throw the pocket cards away when an opponent bets.

We can make a raise from a middle position only because, with our knowledge of the players, we think we might be able to take the blinds. We raise three times the size of the blinds.

This time, we are called by the button and by the big blind. We'll still be in middle position in the after-flop action.

The flop shows us the seven of clubs, the two of clubs, and the nine of hearts.

Pocket	*Pocket*	*Flop*	*Flop*	**Flop**
A ♣	10 ♣	7 ♣	2 ♣	9 ♥

Parenthetically: It's always interesting when players can call an opening raise, but can't make a raise themselves, especially on the button. I suppose the reasoning is, "I was going to raise, but since the pot is already raised, I'll just call." This kind of fuzzy thinking is one area that subordinates the ordinary player to the power player.

Let's consider the button hand. What kind of hand can we put a player on who has decided to cold call a raised pot in which he has nothing invested? It's a hand he wants to play badly but the hand isn't good enough for him to re-raise. It makes us curious.

Because he jumped the raise fence, it's probably not a drawing hand. It could be a pocket pair, middle sized or better, depending on the player. Or it could be big slick or similar.

Now let's consider the big blind hand who called our raise. We ask the same question about the big blind. What kind of hand can we put a player on who has decided to cold call a raised pot in which he has nothing invested? Of course, this blind player may think he already has something invested. Actually, he has nothing invested because the blind money he donated is no longer his. However, he gets a discount in calling our raise. Is this how he thinks? Does he play most of his blinds to "protect" his blind? If so, he's called a raise to put his dubious practice into play. But because he called a raise, we're going to place him on more than just a drawing hand, maybe a big card drawing hand. Not knowing more about the player, we'll give him as much credit for a good hand as we gave the button.

If the blind comes out swinging after the flop, we'll call his hand three sevens and give him the pot. If the blind checks to us, we don't have good enough board cards to bluff because the opponents know we raised with stronger cards than are showing in the flop.

So we check to the button. It's time for him to bluff. He may likely represent a pair of some kind or a set. If he does, we may as well believe him. Middle position after a sizable bet is not the place to be with this flop and, because we can't be aggressive, our hand after the flop is not *playable*.

Our best hope: This weak flop could get checked all around and we'll get a free turn card.

161

In a previous discussion, we had big cards on the flop and we could, depending on players, make a bet into the button and maybe take the pot. If we were called, we had a flush, a straight, and high cards on the board to draw to. In this example, we have weak board cards which make representation of a good hand difficult, and we're in a weak position in the betting rotation. End of story.

So it's time to change the story.

We'll move our position to the button. The pot was opened with a call of the blind by a middle seat. We raise from the button. The big blind calls and the opening middle player calls.

Pocket	Pocket	Flop	Flop	**Flop**
A♣	10♣	7♣	2♣	9♥

Our pocket ace and ten are much more *playable* from the button. Even with a weak flop, we can bet the hand if the other two players have checked to us. We've raised and they have no idea what we are holding. They haven't helped with the weak flop and they've checked to us. It's time for us to make a bet the size of the pot, or slightly more.

There is always possible sandbagging in this situation, but sandbaggers with, say, a set, don't like to see players draw to working flushes. When the button (that's us) is the raiser, the good playing set holder knows the raiser on the button can often have suited cards and the good opponent, holding a set, wouldn't want to risk a check and free draw for the button. So, it's likely the good player that checks doesn't have a set.

It follows that a check and raise is not likely in this situation because the sandbagging player reasons he might not get a bet for him to raise.

Since the good player would likely bet his set in this situation and didn't, we're in a position to bet. Of course, if we get a check raise, we throw our hand away.

Any time one of the two opponents bets a sizable bet into us, we fold. Here's why:

We have represented power. The opponents didn't re-raise. The flop is weak. So a surprise bet from a weak hand and a weak flop made into our representation of power cards is a case of "sudden strength from apparent weakness." It's a red flag. It's a huge red flag.

The two weak elements, weak hand and weak flop, are representing a hand-in-glove fit. Someone could have gotten lucky (probable), or someone is running a clever bluff (seldom in small blinds games). Which one applies to our opponent? It's often best to be safe because it can get expensive from here.

Discussion 340

Position and the Power Image

It is recommended that the reader begin this series with Part 101.

Poker is not a card game played by people.

Poker is a people game played with cards.

We're going to once again look at hands from various positions with the intent of underscoring the last few Discussions.

This is a hand played a few days ago in a no limit hold 'em game. It was played by our hero, Murphy, from a position that was first seat before the button.

Murphy had won some pots without showing any weakness in his choice of hands. Most of them weren't shown at all, which is a good thing, and the others were strong hands which helped establish his power image.

Murphy also had the players sized up.

In the number one seat was a player that Murphy had encountered before. He played with a lot of attention to odds and little attention to position. (He even, in very bad form, had the dealer count the pot down at one interval, in order to calculate pot odds for his hand.)

The next player was relatively new to the game and was very cautious. (After playing for about an hour in only three pots, none of them past the flop, he announced, "I want you all to know I usually play a lot tighter than this.")

In the third seat was an older gentleman, very conservative and always with a hand when participating in the betting; he varied the size of his bets according the strength of his hand.

The fourth seat was a very experienced and good player who was dangerous but couldn't seem to catch a good hand. (He could be easily bluffed, but mostly Murphy and the man stayed out of each other's way.)

The next player was an experienced, but weak player, who was easy to read.

The sixth seat, to keep it general, was a fair repeat of the fifth seat. The seat next to Murphy on his right was filled by a man called "Vince" who liked to limp, then charge, then limp again. It was Vince's version of "mixing his play".

Murphy liked having the last three on his right because they were easy reads. The player to Murphy's left made the table complete in the ninth chair. He was a wannabe dealer in a dealing school somewhere in town, knew little about the game, and made some really naïve comments. He eventually got tired of Murphy stealing the button action from him and started calling the raises. Then he usually couldn't bet after the flop. And so, if he did bet, he had a hand.

The player Murphy knew the least about was in the number one seat, a player Murphy had played on another occasion; he was one that liked to consider a lot of odds. Murphy was lucky enough to beat him a couple of nice pots and Murphy sensed the odds maker was intent on getting his money back. Murphy thought of him as "Mr. Odds". We'll describe Murphy's hand against Mr. Odds, below.

Two players limped in and Murphy raised the pot, second from the button, with ace / three, trying to capitalize on his power image. The wannabe to Murphy's left folded and Mr. Odds, in the small blind, called. The two limpers folded.

The flop brought an ace, a seven, and an eight.

Murphy's hand:

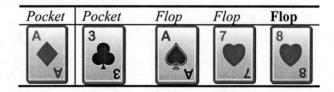

Mr. Odds' hand:

Pocket	*Pocket*	*Flop*	*Flop*	**Flop**
A♥	9♥	A♠	7♥	8♥

Mr. Odds checked. Murphy bet the size of the pot and got a call from Mr. Odds.

The turn was the king of spades.

Mr. Odds bet about 2/3 the size of the pot. Murphy raised four times the size of the opponent's bet.

Mr. Odds thought awhile, showed Murphy his hand, and slipped the best hand into the muck.

What happened here?

Consider the opponent. Murphy had beaten him a couple of pots and Mr. Odds was gunning for him. (He might play something relatively weak, although he didn't, considering he was the blind.) He liked to play the odds and he was weak on position play. After Murphy's raise before the flop, he only called. (Murphy put him on a drawing hand and Mr. Odds' ace was a small surprise.) After the flop Mr. Odds checked and called. (This action reinforced Murphy's placing him erroneously on that drawing hand.) Murphy knew the king didn't help the drawing hand, but Mr. Odds decided to bet on the king, hoping he would:

- Convince Murphy the king helped him.

- If called, make his flush on the river.

- Or, if that failed, make his aces on the river.

166

His weak bet of 2/3 the pot, told Murphy Mr. Odds didn't think he had a hand yet. Murphy didn't want Mr. Odds to draw to the hand, so he raised an amount that wouldn't compute to the odds Mr. Odds needed to make the call.

Mr. Odds' hesitation before he showed his hand, then mucked it, was mostly an act, although he did want to draw to the hand badly, who wouldn't? But the odds didn't compute to a call.

Murphy's bet had to be a big one to get the opponent to throw away a winning hand (nine kicker), although Murphy may have overdone it a little. The king on the turn was the biggest contributor; Murphy wanted the additional insurance of representing aces and kings.

By the bye, after losing the hand, Mr. Odds became the worst calling station seen in a long time. He kept calling, trying to play odds, hoping to make a hand. He was the poster boy for tight passive and he turned into easy prey.

This is an example of playing the player. This is an example of using the late position. This is an example of using the power image.

Now for a new question.

When Murphy made the bet four times the size of the pot, should he have put the opponent on an ace? That is a very good question.

Since Murphy hadn't placed him on an ace in our true story, the question is hypothetical and hard to answer. If Murphy had bet thinking the opponent had an ace, Murphy certainly would have been taking a bigger risk. We would be correct, if we suppose that Murphy thought he had the best hand when he bet. Still, in considering the characteristics of the opponent, the raise would have been the best decision and, as it turned out, it was. It's a good example of a bet to protect against a drawing hand.

Much more importantly, we do believe Mr. Odds would have called a smaller bet.

Let's try Mr. Odds' side of the hand.

As long as Mr. Odds was in the pot, he should have won it. And as long as we're being hypothetical, let's play the opponent's hand.

Actually, Mr. Odds shouldn't have been in the pot. If we were in Mr. Odds position and a strong opponent had made the raise where we would be first to act after the flop, we wouldn't have called Murphy's raise.

However, you'll recall this situation in the blind, although rare, is one of the exceptions to the "don't ever call" rule. The raise came from a player who is in position to steal at a time when we have a good hand. So, if we wanted to enter the fray, we would have re-raised, especially with careful consideration of Murphy who is prone to steal. The gamble would be to either re-raise and take the pot, or not be able to call a re-re-raise from a strong player. A re-raise would have won the pot.

Knowing that we might have won the pot with a re-raise, we'll follow Mr. Odds' play and merely call in this story. We'll see the flop to keep the scenario in progress.

The only thing to do after seeing the flop is to check and raise. It gives our blind position last action and we might take the pot because:

- We might well have the best hand.

- We have a great drawing hand to hearts and to a pair of aces.

- Even if we don't take the pot when we check and raise, it is one really great semi-bluff seldom seen in the lower blinds in hold 'em games and we have the drawing hand for back up.

That should win the money, which was a nice sized pot. That's what should have been done. Mr. Odds should never have let the hand reach the turn.

If we're called, we go all-in after the turn. Our early position has taken the initiative away from the late position because of our check and raise and we will take advantage of it. We're now in control and we'll make a bet that can't be called.

But, back to Mr. Odds' play. We have illustrated Mr. Odds likes to make bets the size of his hand value and for odds. He, therefore, could not have made the position power play that would have. He wanted to play the odds and call his way to the nut hand. Once more we see the value of the power play in no limit and the folly of playing strictly odds and ignoring position.

Three of a Kind

Eric the Red

By Sam O'Connor

"Know when to walk away and know when to run."

Kenny Rogers.

Eric was a big red headed young man who appeared one day in the poker area of the Boulder Club. He had a dominating manner not unlike Jackie Gleason in the Honeymooners. Eric was full of conversation, comments and guffaws and was generally loud, but likeable. Little Bud, the sawdust dealer, was glad to have this newcomer and his money in the game.

Alas, poor Eric. After he had settled in and the players were used to him, he started doing funny things with the cards. Funny things were not tolerated in Little Bud's game and Bud gave Eric the "tom" sign to cease the telltale motions and obvious intent. Eric showed Bud a big smile and was openly pleased that Bud didn't embarrass him in front of the rest of the players.

Bud needed a new player in the game and thought Eric had learned his lesson. Bud let him stay because, after all, Eric had never actually profited from his moves. And maybe Eric had learned his lesson.

Of course, at this point, Eric knew he was needed in the game. But he also knew he was in danger of not being invited back.

Little Bud wasn't the only one who noticed what Eric was doing that day. Also in the game was Rex Reynolds, a dapper young hustler who had once been a dealer. He was still proud that he once wore the dealer's apron, but he was even prouder that he no longer had to, because he was doing a good job of "playing the outside". Rex was a hustler of the type we called a "wise guy", a term we used back then not in the deeply sinister sense that John Gotti was a wise guy, or in the magisterial sense that the Magi were wise guys, but a poker wise guy that played all the angles.

And now a red-headed angle would soon be coming Rex's way.

A few days after that first day when Eric and Rex were in the game together, Eric paid the Boulder Club another surprise visit. He spotted Rex at the bar.

Grinning ear to ear, Eric approached Rex, leaned on the bar and, kicking a little sawdust, placed a foot on the brass rail. He offered to buy Rex a drink.

In the next half hour, Eric revealed that he played the saxophone and often made himself available as a sideman for local bands and those passing through town with a two week gig. But Eric claimed his real musical talent was organizing poker games for the headliners after the shows. That way, he said, he made far more money than a sideman is generally supposed to.

"There will be a country western show at the Cashman Arena in three days, and some of the music will be made by eager poker players."

Eric had Rex's attention.

"The performers are paid a percentage of the gate - in cash."

Rex's eyes widened. He nodded, inviting more information from Eric.

"And some of them are the up and coming stars of today."

Now Eric had Rex's full and eager attention.

The redhead said he'd introduce Rex to a big, post-concert poker party on the condition Rex loaned him money for the game. You see, Eric explained, he hadn't worked much as a sideman lately. The mortgage payments on his house were way behind, the kids were starting back to school and the cupboard was bare. If he could just make a nice score, his life would turn around.

Rex didn't usually stake players or loan money, but this was kind of intriguing. If he staked Eric, he could see the show, meet some interesting people and, most importantly, play in the poker game. He and Eric would stay out of each other's way at the table, of course, because Rex was well aware of Eric's past ethical lapses at the sawdust poker table.

The country western show was a good one. Eric didn't play with any of the bands that night, because, as he explained to Rex, there isn't much demand for a sax in a country band. But he got backstage because he knew the other sidemen, and he had no trouble organizing a big money poker game in a nearby hotel.

Rex slipped Eric some stake money.

Joining Eric and Rex at the table were Hank Williams, Jr., Roy Clark, Faron Young, and an obscure talent agent named Eli.

Also joining them were a lot of hundred dollar bills. With Eric and Rex it would be a nice and prosperous six handed game.

The talent agent wasn't making any headway in getting a new client from the players in this game so, when he had won a little money, he pleaded fatigue and left early. Rex was a big winner, up a couple of thousand, and Eric had won a little. All the entertainers were losers, and were deep into their newly acquired gate money.

It was late and Faron Young, full of damaged ego, delivered a few of the most colorful and direst obscenities, slammed the door, and stalked down the hallway.

Roy Clark, a super nice guy and a terrible poker player, was interested in trying to recoup his losses. Everybody kind of bowed out of what was left of the game, so Eric invited Roy to some heads up action – "to give him a chance to get even".

Rex watched in fascination.

The shoddy ways Eric manipulated the deck shouldn't be tried on a blind hellhound. Eric was good at picking up the cards but his false shuffles and cuts needed a lot of work.

And Roy Clark bought it all. Even though Eric the Red was a rough country cheater, he took about $3,000 of Roy's money, which was enough to buy a fine new car in those days.

The game was over and Eric and Rex started for home. In the car, Eric gleefully returned Rex's stake money, along with some interest, and Rex accepted Eric's invitation to go to his house in North Las Vegas to celebrate. Since the game and its scabrous undertakings had used up most of the night, the celebration would consist of a sumptuous breakfast with Eric's family.

Rex had no objections to some domestic time. He had a family of his own. Although he was single, his past had left him with the dubious distinction of being a thirty six year old grandfather. Like most hustlers, he didn't talk much about personal things, but when he did, it was usually about his daughter, her husband and Rex's granddaughter.

Eric and Rex stopped at an all night Mayfair grocery store, picked up steak and eggs and other things, and arrived at Eric's house to prepare. Inside the house were a red headed wife and two little red headed kids who looked like a TV commercial for "some cereal".

When Eric saw his wife, he reached into his pocket, threw the money into the air and, as the green stuff flipped and fluttered toward the floor, he shouted, "Here's the money, Honey!" Red headed wife screeched with delight as she gathered the fallen lucre.

Eric told his wife a wildly embellished tale of camaraderie and nocturnal poker as Rex listened in wonderment. Eric was suddenly a clever player and the slickest mechanic west of the Pecos. The poker story, as told by Eric, contained intrigue, danger and excitement; and the story culminated in Roy's share of the gate ending up in Eric's pocket.

The last part was true.

It was early morning and Rex could hear the two kids rattling in the bedroom and bathrooms. Then they entered the kitchen, asking about clothes to wear, breakfast and other morning things. But mother had something else in mind.

Red Headed Mother: "Have you kids said your prayers this morning?"
Red Headed Kids: "Well, no."

Mother: "Then repeat after me. Thank God for Mommy."
Kids: "Thank God for Mommy."

Mother: "Thank God for Daddy."
Kids: "Thank God for Daddy."

Mother: "And thank God for Roy Clark."
Kids: "AND THANK GOD FOR ROY CLARK."

Discussion 350

The Slow Played Hand

It is recommended that the reader begin this series with Part 101.

Poker is not a card game played by people.

Poker is a people game played with cards.

Maneuvers on the Flop.

The launch pad of winning in hold 'em is made of good pocket cards and good flops. It takes luck to get good pockets and then more luck to get a good flop. The luck part can't be controlled. But we have choices in management after we get that good or bad flop.

Our after flop choice is the most crucial decision time. It is the point at which we decide to charge forward or to quit the hand.

Finding the edge after the flop is important, whether it be the winning edge and a big bet or the losing edge and throwing the hand away. The biggest pots are generally won and lost with only a slight edge because of the hands' similarities – two pair over two pair, set over set, etc.

Poker is a people game played with cards.

This is not just a slogan, it is a fact and it is more important in no limit hold 'em than in any other poker game. The people game is a fact in which the reader should be deeply ensconced at this juncture. Those power players who know how to play people will find their required edge in the correctly chosen hands and they will win decisively.

When we find the edge in a hand, we protect our edge and bet with impunity.

We rarely slow play a hand. The reasons are not complicated:

- We're the power players and so we like the power image of either confidently charging or decisively mucking. It gives us a winning and dominating advantage.

174

- We don't like taking the chance of checking the goods and then no one betting our hand for us. When no one bets, we have lost a level of protection and we're not getting value for our hand. When no one bets, we give them a free card and we could lose our card advantage.

- We like to keep the opponents in the dark, which is best accomplished by playing all hands the same way; keeping our bets in a constant pattern while the strength of our hand varies. (Is that power player strong this time, or is he bluffing?)

- If we were to slow play hands, soon the thinking adversary would no longer bet behind us; he starts to slow play along with us. Then we have big trouble getting value for our hands.

- When we're not charging, we are losing our power; we are losing our image and our Dominating status.

The maneuver of checking and then raising is related to slow play. It's slow play with a kicker. We don't do it often for many of the same reasons we don't often slow play a hand. But occasionally we'll be in a hand with a known frivolous bettor, maybe someone who always bets when he's on the button, and we'll take advantage of his eagerness with a check and raise.

Now for the defensive side. When we are checked and raised by a good player and we could easily have the weaker hand, we throw it away. There is no shame in that. It's very important to get a few tells on this check/raiser, though. When he finds we muck our hands in that situation, he may start bluffing us with a check/raise. When we have a dependable tell on him, he'll be surprised when we raise him back.

Using the check/raise as a bluff is covered thoroughly in Discussion 447 in the Dominator section.

Playing for the unusual hand is also addressed later.

The following is an actual poker event and is presented here as an example of an opponent slow playing off balance. There is more emotion than reason in the opponent's play in the hand on the next page. He's out to get us and he has abandoned good judgment.

175

We'll let Murphy play the hand.

The first player after the blind, an aggressive player, opens the pot. He has pocket aces. Murphy is next to act.

Murphy looks into his pocket and finds the queen of hearts and the queen of spades. Murphy raises three times the opening bet. All players fold except the opener with aces. He calls.

The flop brings the king of diamonds, the ten of clubs, and the jack of spades.

Pocket	Pocket	Flop	Flop	**Flop**
Q♥	Q♠	K♦	10♣	J♠

The opener checks his aces. Murphy doesn't think the opponent would check a pair of kings and so he bets the size of the pot. The opener calls.

Red flag! Because the opponent is usually aggressive, Murphy now believes the adversary is slow playing his pair of kings for the river trap.

The turn slops the seven of hearts.

Pocket	Pocket	Flop	Flop	Flop	**Turn**
Q♥	Q♠	K♦	10♣	J♠	7♥

The opener checks his aces again. The usually aggressive opponent is fingering his players' checks. Murphy believes the opponent is planning to call any bet. The king is glaring at Murphy and the seven didn't help either player. Murphy reads the opponent's anxiety and checks along with him.

The river springs the ace of diamonds making three aces for the opponent.

Pocket	Pocket	Flop	Flop	Flop	Turn	River
Q♥	Q♠	K♦	10♣	J♠	7♥	A♦

The opener is disappointed Murphy didn't bet for him last time and he's determined he won't miss out on this last bet. He's thrilled with his set of aces. He overbets the pot.

His slowness followed by emotional eagerness has gotten him into trouble.

Murphy moves all in. The opponent takes a closer look at the board and can't call.

Lessons illustrated:

- We seldom slow play a hand.

- We watch for players who like to try for the unusual hand. They are tricky. Their trademark is being in and out of pots a lot. (We'll discuss the proper time and place for us to play in this manner in later Discussions in the Dominator section.) Most of the slow players fall into the loose passive category at the beginning of the hand and aggressive if they have made their surprise hand. We like these players because they feed us a lot of flop pots when the flops don't help their weak starting cards. We know who they are; we watch for aggression.

- The power player isn't usually intent on making the surprise hand, although the surprise play is covered more thoroughly in later Discussions. Usually, when the power player gets a surprise hand, he is as surprised as anyone.

- A bad beat, or being out maneuvered, will never get us down. We learn more about the opponents from those incidents. We don't chase those who have beaten us in a hand. If we're patient and we remain focused, their stacks naturally will belong to us at a later time.

177

Discussion 351

Playing a Set from the Blind

It is recommended that the reader begin this series with Part 101.

Poker is not a card game played by people.

Poker is a people game played with cards.

We've discussed the number one reason for making a raise before the flop. Altogether now: It is for information; it is to place the opponent on a hand.

Then, after the flop, we confirm what we've placed him on through his after flop action.

We don't waiver often from that conviction. Usually, when we change our minds later in the hand, we are simply talking ourselves into making a bad call or trying to justify why we can't make a raise.

When we place the opponent on a hand before the flop, decide to play after the flop because we've placed him solidly on a likely hand and we win the pot, we've done a good job. This is what the game is about.

Placing the Opponent on a Hand. More about three of a kind.

In review, "sets" are three of a kind with two of them in the pocket. "Trips" are three of a kind with two of them on the board.

Let's take an unusual situation, but one we all run into now and then. We have the big blind. We look down to find two threes in the hole. Someone opens the pot, gets two calls, then the small blind calls. It's up to us.

My girl friend says it's okay to call in this situation because we have already called and our money is committed.   ("Okay, Honey, I've answered the phone, what the hell do you want?").

Through some very weak play, we've been invited into the hand because we're the big blind. But my girl friend says we shouldn't get pushy just because we can call. With this weak hand, it is not okay to raise. We will likely throw the hand away after the free flop.

Let's consider our adversaries: We have a player under the gun who opened by calling our blind, two middle players, and the small blind. There are five of us in this dink pot.

We'll be second to act and the pre-flop opener is sitting to our left. We are hoping for a one chance in eight of getting another three.

The flop comes jack, three, five.

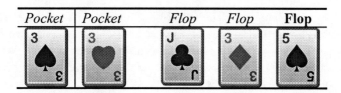

Well, heavens to Mergatroid. This flop has our attention.

But we have to be cautious in this five way pot. Since there was no raise before the flop, we don't have a very good idea what our opponents have, and there are a lot of opponents. (This is a good example of why every pot should be raised by somebody before the flop - but not by us this time.) Except for what we already know about our opponents, we're flying blind.

The jack is the least of our problems. The opener, just to our left, might have pocket jacks, but we're playing at a full table, in fairly good company, in no limit, so it's not likely that he has pocket jacks in an early position. And, if one of the other three players had held pocket jacks, they'd have raised.

The other players could be playing connectors but, in good company, the three and five probably didn't help them. And, even if the three and the five had helped the connectors, the players are still drawing to an unmade hand.

What's our biggest concern?

Three fives! But that is not the principle feature of this hand. The big awareness is we have almost no investment in the hand and there is very little in the pot.

Yes, we could get trapped by three fives, but the biggest trap could be set by our own foolishness. We could lose a lot of money chasing a small pot.

So, we're thrilled with our set of threes, but we're disappointed with the size of the pot and we will not get suckered into playing an out of position hand for very little money.

First After the Flop Action Example. The small blind checks. We check. Everybody checks. If there is no scare card on the turn, such as a five or a jack, we come out betting the size of the small pot. That was easy.

Second Action Example. The small blind checks. We check. The opener bets. Everybody folds. Yes, we mean everybody because we have little invested. We don't know anything about the opener's hand. We could be trapping ourselves. There is little to gain. We won't get involved. We throw our hand away. That was hard.

Third Action Example. The small blind checks. We check. The opener bets the size of the pot. The next player folds. The last player calls. The small blind calls. Now, what do we do?

This is suddenly interesting. Opportunity is knocking in the form of a much larger pot. Make no mistake, the pot is not suddenly large after the betting stops; it becomes larger as the betting progresses. The action has come around to us and there is a comparatively large pot we'd like to win. But, we still have very little invested.

Do we play this set of threes in the face of a bet? If we do decide to play, we must raise; there are too many hands at the table drawing against us. If we raise, we'll learn a lot about the hands that remain against us when the others fold.

We will stay in the contest, not because of money invested, but because of waiting opportunity. There is money to be won.

What do we know about the opener, the one that has now bet? He was under the gun when he opened the pot. Could he be just a little out of line and have opened with a pair of jacks? How about ace / jack? Surely not queen / jack or other connector. Has he been active recently? What is his attitude toward the game at this moment? Does he have reason to be pushing a marginal hand? Or could he be making a bluff after a weak flop, hoping the opponents have nothing?

180

What do we know about the late position and the small blind? Are they the types to call with a set of fives, instead of raising? Surely, they would raise. Or would they slow play a set of fives? Will they call a bet in order to draw to a small straight? Surely not.

The problem is we must learn after the flop what we ordinarily would learn before the flop by raising. Additionally, we must still learn what we normally learn after the flop. (That's why, in example one above, we couldn't bet until after the turn.)

If we are fairly sure there is not another set out there, jacks or fives, we can raise. But it won't be a customary raise. If we play, we will raise and we raise more than the size of the pot. But to do that we have made this decision: We have decided to take charge of a pot in which, to this point, we have invested only the size of the blind. And we have decided there is no other set being held at the table. Those are huge decisions and we had better be sure that a real opportunity has been presented to us. Because we have little invested, it is much easier to throw the hand away.

If the opener is playing his usual strong game, he has opened with a large pocket pair. If he bets, we can raise. But, we still don't have anything invested, and so we must be reasonably sure he has a large pair, or maybe two. If he gets a call from one of the other players (slow playing a set of fives?), the pot is bigger still, and we can raise, if we want to. We are at least betting from last position in this betting sequence.

If we raise, we're not much concerned with the opener, we want to see what the possible set of fives is going to do. If they call, the phantom set of fives probably doesn't exist and actually could be another large pair. If the possible fives re-raises, we're out of there with money wasted from chasing a pot in which we had nothing invested.

We are determined not to fall victim to set over set. Not many players, especially in the small blinds no limit games, can get away from losing to set over set. You're reading it here first. This hand could mean the difference between a win and a loss for the day. Recognizing set over set puts us among the few. It places us among the winners.

The key, once more and almost always, in a tight situation, is in knowing our players. If we can't put our players on reasonably assumed pocket cards, we throw this set of threes dirty trap hand away. There is no shame in it and we have lost only our blind, virtually nothing.

Whatever our decision, we have exercised caution. But, once decided, we have acted with strength. Both are the mark of the dominating power player.

Of course, we won't call, won't ever call, with a set of threes when an opponent has a straight working. Yes, my girl friend would approve.

Lessons learned:

- Small pairs are dangerous to play.

- Small anything, when we are first to act, places us in an awkward position.

- We won't chase a small pot when there is danger. Even when we've lost opportunity, it doesn't take anything off our stack.

- We will play our players!

- We'll bet a hand from any position, if we're reasonably sure it's the best hand. We'll be decisive about it and we'll bet it with gusto.

Discussion 352

Playing Sets and Watching Stacks

It is recommended that the reader begin this series with Part 101.

Poker is not a card game played by people.

Poker is a people game played with cards.

Betting a Set.

So much of no limit hold 'em revolves around a set of three, not in the number of hands played, but in the volume of dollars won and lost.

The game of hold 'em consists mainly of big cards and sets. (In review, "sets" are three of a kind with two of them in the pocket. "Trips" are three of a kind with two of them on the board.)

Sure, the straights and flushes happen, but they are usually accidental and can be seen. As such, they don't get as much action and value as a set because three of their cards can be seen on the board. Many of them are also accidental or river draw outs.

But the sets and big pairs are intentional and are often hidden.

It's great fun to raise with pocket kings and get called by big slick. The flop brings ace, king, rag. We check to big slick and he comes out with a nice bet. We take it from there, usually switch gears to a calling game and, depending on conditions, nearly always wind up with a big pot. This is the hand that no limit players wait for.

But playing the set isn't always that easy and is often tricky. We want value for our hand. But whether we end up winning much or not, the one thing we don't want to do is get drawn out on.

Steamboat's Pocket Eights.

Steamboat started this hand in the big blind with pocket eights.

183

There was a small raise from the button, small enough for Steamboat to think some of the other players will also call; it's been the pattern at the table. With this many players and only a small raise, Steamboat played the eights. There were four players in the pot.

The flop arrives with the queen of clubs, the eight of spades, and the ten of diamonds.

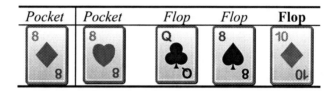

Pocket	*Pocket*	*Flop*	*Flop*	**Flop**
8♦	8♥	Q♣	8♠	10♦

Steamboat, of course, checks the hand. The next player bets. The player after that calls. The button raises. (How nice.) With two one gappers for the straight and no flush threat, Steamboat flat calls, disguising his hand.

The turn brings the five of clubs.

Pocket	*Pocket*	*Flop*	*Flop*	*Flop*	**Turn**
8♦	8♥	Q♣	8♠	10♦	5♣

Now there are two clubs on the board and Steamboat doesn't want to lose to a flush, so he moves all-in. The next two players fold. The button calls with what he has left, an amount equal to about one fifth of the pot.

The river brings the deuce of clubs.

Pocket	*Pocket*	*Flop*	*Flop*	*Flop*	*Turn*	**River**
8♦	8♥	Q♣	8♠	10♦	5♣	2♣

The opponent shows big slick suited in clubs.

Lucky draw? Sure. But this hand was <u>misplayed</u>!

The button, the final opponent, was the raiser before the flop. He was also the raiser after the flop. The flop raise was substantial and he was trying to steal the pot, but Steamboat placed him on a high pair, aces or kings, and wasn't far off.

There is nothing wrong with Steam's guess, as long as he leaves other possibilities open and remains observant.

The opponent could have a set. The biggest pitfall of the hidden set lies in the opponent holding a higher hidden set. When that happens, we are often just unlucky (see the previous Discussion). But, of course, set over set is not what happened here.

What was Steamboat's mistake?

Not keeping track of the raiser's stack!

The opponent played the hand very well.

The opponent tried to buy the pot after the flop knowing that, if he was called, he would be short stacked for a try at the gut straight and maybe more, since he had both the turn and the river to look at. But things turned out better than the opponent could have hoped when he got the fourth club on the turn. He was short stacked for a river draw to both a straight and a flush.

Steamboat's error was in concentrating on three opponents after the flop and not paying enough attention to the button/raiser.

If Steam had moved in after the flop, the button couldn't have called because the other players would not have added to the pot by calling, thereby denying the button pot odds.

The opponent was the raiser with the shortest stack. An early move-in after the flop was the only smart play and would have made Steamboat the winner. Watch the players' stacks.

When we make a bet into a short stack, our bet has almost no teeth in it.

Discussion 353

Big Sets and Value for the Hand

It is recommended that the reader begin this series with Part 101.

Poker is not a card game played by people.

Poker is a people game played with cards.

Let's look again at the hidden set trap. Sometimes the trap we're setting is a trap of opportunity for us. But how much opportunity?

Here's a recent hand played by Murphy.

The player in the number five seat did a lot of calling. Not only a lot of calling, but he was a take-the-lead player who was accustomed to betting less than half the size of the pot. In other words, he bet and he called as if he were playing limit hold 'em. Welcome to the game, Mr. Limit player.

Being a limit player, very large bets were hard for him to call. It's time for Murphy to take advantage and play his player.

Murphy is in the number one seat. He is in middle position in this hand with two red pocket kings, a nice place to be.

Murphy raises five times the pot to narrow the field and he is called by the number three seat (two to his left) and he is also called by Mr. Limit in the small blind.

The flop brings a deuce, a ten, and the king of clubs.

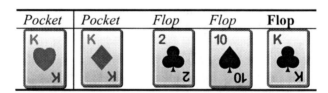

Pocket	Pocket	Flop	Flop	**Flop**
K♥	K♦	2♣	10♠	K♣

Mr. Limit, in the small blind bets half the pot. This is a nice continuation of events.

With a player behind him, Murphy calls. Ordinarily, with two open clubs he would raise the pot, but he'll take a little gamble for one more card because his call leaves the third player free to call a small bet and leaves the small blind free to once again lead the betting after the turn.

Murphy places the small blind on king / ten and the third player, an inexperienced young man, on a drawing hand. The default placement of a drawing hand for the young man is a slight reach, but a drawing hand is the young man's customary play and his calls are now giving every indication of the possibility of such a hand.

The turn shows the players the ten of hearts.

The small blind comes charging (!) out with a 50% increase over his last bet. This is a small bet in proportion to the pot, but a huge bet for Mr. Limit.

Oh, wow. Murphy calls with his kings full and the third man calls. Murphy's trap is set.

It should be pointed out that there could be four tens, but the chance is small, especially with the small blind leading with small bets; it should be expected for even Mr. Limit to pick up the pace a little with three tens after the flop.

The river is the five of hearts and so, unfortunately, the third player has missed his draw.

Mr. Limit comes out betting about 70% the size of the pot. This is a gigantic bet for Mr. Limit. On his face is an irrepressible expression of confidence.

How much does Murphy raise this smug little man? Murphy wants a call from him. Mr. Limit is smugly confident. He calls most bets when he has some kind of hand, as in limit games. But he's "afraid of his money" and he'll fold if his stack is threatened too much.

All-in is out of the question. Murphy can think of a couple of old adversaries he'd like to go all in with in this situation, but the gentleman with the proud tens full of kings is not one of them. If Murphy's raise sends Mr. Limit from confident to suspicious, Murphy could lose him.

Murphy decides that a raise twice the size of Mr. Limit's bet would be too little and a raise four times the bet size would be too much and, like Goldilocks, a raise three times the bet would be just right. (Actually, a raise three times the bet was, after Murphy's call, still slightly less than the size of the pot.)

The third man, of course, folds. Mr. Limit picks up his folding money and hurriedly peals off the amount of Murphy's raise.

Maybe Murphy should have bet a little more. That kind of thought sometimes comes to mind, but we should always stay away from it; Murphy made a good bet on the river and got a good call. The other kind of hindsight is for losers.

Lessons learned:

- Playing the players is not just for winning a little. Playing the players correctly can add value to a winning hand.

- House over house is another trap to watch out for. It is closely related to set over set and deserves the same kind of analysis.

- Slow playing a set with two of the same suit in the flop is dangerous and usually should be protected with a large bet. An exception (sometimes) is having the players fairly well placed on their pocket cards and having a calling player behind us who can add to the pot.

- We can slow play large sets somewhat freely, but small sets are more of a problem and require more caution.

Discussion 354

Playing Sets and Trips

It is recommended that the reader begin this series with Part 101.

Poker is not a card game played by people.

Poker is a people game played with cards.

First, Betting Sets.

Let's take the same pair of pocket eights Steamboat had in Discussion 352 and move them to the button.

The diligent Murphy will play this hand. Murphy tried to steal the blinds with this hand with a raise. But he got a caller.

Murphy was lucky. The flop arrived with the ace of spades, the deuce of hearts, and the eight of spades.

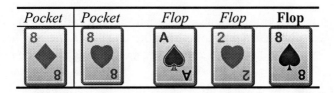

The ace probably hit somebody's pocket card and Murphy likes it that way.

The action is checked to the raiser, Murphy. What does he do?

He bets the size of the pot because, in this game, that's a strong bet but not an impossible bet to call. Murphy can't let the opponents draw to straights and flushes. But he wants to bet enough to encourage two pair of any size because they are hard to improve (one chance in five and a half per turn of the card). But they get no free draws to straights and flushes.

If the ace were the ace of hearts, Murphy's strategy is the same. No free flush draws.

If the ace were the ace of diamonds, maybe he could slow play a little and try a call, just to set a trap. In that case, he would hope the turn card is the king of clubs. That would place all four suits on the board and maybe the king would give the opponent some encouragement to do some betting.

It's important to distinguish between limit and no limit poker in this area. It is one reason why we have changed from limit to playing a dominating no limit game.

When we miss a round of betting in a limit game, we miss an opportunity to build the pot. We'll never get that round of betting back; it is gone forever and the pot is one round smaller than it would be if it had been a betting round.

However, in no limit, the important play is the trap; one wager in the right place can make up for several rounds of lost betting. It's a distinction the dominating power player is well aware of.

Most hands with a hidden set (is there any other kind?) will be won after the turn because it is unlikely we'll have four board cards, each with a different suit. So, barring no suits or dangerous connectors on the flop, our big bet is usually after the turn, but quite often after the flop.

Here's some wishful thinking. It's great to get a call after the flop and an unconnected turn card that completes the four suit rainbow. It's perfect to get another call and move in after the river. Dreams are made of this.

Now and then we'll get a call after the turn and we'll make a full house on the river at the same time the opponent makes his flush. That's still another, and bigger, dream.

Meanwhile, let's stop dreaming.

In review: We mustn't get greedy. Sets are not to be wasted, but we want to make sure we get the win and not the loss. The win will come usually after the turn, sometimes after the flop as we protect our hand and our win. We can only slow play as long as we aren't threatened by draws.

Betting Trips, Three of a Kind with Two of Them on the Board.

These are correctly called "trips". Nothing freezes a round of betting in no limit poker like a board pair.

With a pair showing, trap wary no limit players are ready to throw their hands away at the first rattle of a player's stack, no matter how many times the hand has been checked.

Many times the first player to bet is in the last position because everybody else has checked and he can make a representation. With a board pair showing, the bettor is representing at least two pair or maybe a set. Or it could be a bluff. We like all those things. (Funny how the open pair gives the novice player encouragement when, in reality, the pair belongs to everybody. Or maybe the novice wants us to believe he has trips.)

How do we play those trips?

We do the same thing that's done with the hidden set. We play along until it's dangerous. But we don't often get nearly as far with the open pair and trips. The part that's showing usually ends the hand much sooner.

If our bets with the open pair trips are being called, beware of the same trips.

Suddenly the kicker becomes important. An ace is the usual winner, although sometimes there is another pair.

Then there is the possibility of the hidden set with a pair on the board. That would make a full house for the opponent. Full house over full house can be expensive. In short, open pairs that make our trips can make someone trips with a bigger kicker it even can make a bigger full house. Nightmares are made of this.

Specialties

The Death of a Shuffle Machine

Written by Sam O'Connor

with apologies to Edgar Allan Poe

It's true! I'm very nervous, dreadfully nervous. I always have been and am today. But can anyone say that I am mad? The disease I had sharpened my senses, not destroyed, not dulled them. Above all was the heightened sense of hearing. I have heard all things in the heaven and in the earth. I have heard many things in hell. How then am I mad? Just listen and see how healthily, how calmly, I can tell you the whole story.

It is impossible to say how the idea first entered my mind but, once conceived, the notion haunted me day and night.

I was a poker dealer on the graveyard shift. I loved my job and the people I worked for. The bosses had never wronged me and the customers, for the most part, were congenial and often generous. What finally affected me was that damnable automatic card shuffling machine.

It wasn't the usual kind of shuffle machine, the kind you see in so many poker places these days. It was an experimental machine, one that cost less, gave less information about what it was doing, but still managed to shuffle the cards. What bothered me was this: the machine whined. It whined and whirred interminably.

While other machines were perfectly quiet, the new machine was not. It did its work well enough. But the distinct whirring, nay, whining, would sometimes reach extreme proportions and, while the card players never seemed to hear it, the whining was beginning to drive me insane. It reminded me of my ex-wife. Yes, that's it. It was much like my ex-wife was hiding under the poker table. The thought began to make my blood run cold and so, by degrees, quite gradually, I made up my mind to put the old girl out of her misery and rid myself of the shuffle machine forever.

And so now, I know you think I am mad. But madmen know nothing and I know so much. You should have seen me. You should have seen how wisely I proceeded -- with what caution I went to work. During those days of planning, I was never kinder to my fellow workers and to the customers. I was more than kind; I was charming. Yes, cunning and charming.

During the whole week before I dissembled the shuffler, I kept reviewing the procedure in my mind -- my now heightened and aware mind. I knew just how I would go about capturing the shuffler and terminating its whining ways.

Oh, you would have laughed to see how cunningly I arranged things. I contrived to move surreptitiously to the end of the room where the offensive device was installed in the poker table. It would happen at night, or rather, early in the morning before dawn. I would move slowly, oh so stealthily, under the table and then extract my screwdriver cautiously, oh so cautiously, and slowly, but calmly. I would undo the plate that held the whining offensive shuffler. I would then snip its connection to the power source. I rehearsed the procedure in my mind every day for a week before coolly undertaking the daring deed.

Even so, when the time arrived, I was ever more quiet and cautious than I had imagined I would be. (I ask you, is this the trait of a mad man?) I lay still under the table for minutes on end. Cautiously I undid the installation. As I snipped the power source and removed the shuffler, I could have sworn it spoke to me. I moved it to a heavy bag that I had ingeniously slung over my shoulder, so much the easier for ready use. But, as I moved the ugly contraption into the bag, it not only spoke, it began once more to whine. And, when I tapped it with my screwdriver in exasperation, it whined even louder.

Now you may think that I panicked, but I did not – more evidence that I am not mad. Instead, I talked to the machine. I talked to it calmly, softly, soothingly, much like I talked to my wife just before she drowned in shallow waters on our fishing trip.

"Who's there?" asked a pair of shoes walking by. Cleverly, I did not answer and the shoes moved on. Then, with extreme discipline, I lay motionless for nearly an hour, not moving much more than a few muscles, stroking the shuffle machine, not daring to speak to it above a whisper.

When I had waited a long time, I began to crawl slowly toward the door at the back of the poker room. Someone called to me but I feigned deafness. Instead, I leaped to my feet and kept moving steadily toward the door. By the time I reached the door and passed through, I imagined I heard someone once again call my name and I could hear laughter in the background. A matter of nerves, I decided; or perhaps someone had told a joke.

And now have I not impressed on you what you mistake for madness is but an over-acuteness of the senses? Now, my ears hear things they have never heard before. My eyes are more alert, and the awareness I experience has given me new life. You can see I don't really mind life in this place. The attendants are usually nice. The food isn't at all bad. And when they have my arms placed in this canvas jacket for receiving visitors like you, the attendants are kind enough to feed me.

During the drive on my way home, after taking the shuffle machine, I could hear the whining of the abysmal thing on the seat beside me. What did it want from me? I began to wish I hadn't released it from the bag. The whining was gradually growing more intensive. How can it do this without a power source? I could hardly wait to get home and forever silence this seemingly endless torture.

I rushed into the house to rip open the floor boards and conceal the offensive shuffler. But then I waited. I reflected, as a sane person will always do. Instead of rushing, I carefully took up three planks in the floor. Then I beat the shuffler thoroughly with a large hammer to terminate its loathsome senses. I then ushered its many parts into the darkness below. I replaced the planks oh so carefully, so craftily, that no one could ever detect that anything was wrong. No, no. I was too wary for that. (Do you still think me mad?)

The next morning two plain clothed policemen came knocking on my door. I opened the door with a light heart, for what had I to fear? I even invited them in.

They introduced themselves with perfect correctness, as investigators of the metropolitan police are want to do. People, they said, had seen me leaving the casino with property that did not belong to me.

I smiled. I bade the gentlemen welcome. The report, I said, must be a figment of someone's imagination. I took my visitors through the house. I bade them search and search well. The three of us settled, at length, in the living room where I showed them my collections from various casinos, thereby exhibiting my confidence and composure.

I arranged the chairs in the room, placing my chair directly over the resting place of the late whining shuffler. It was an act of audacity, I was pleased to think. How perfect a maneuver in my hour of triumph.

The officers were satisfied. I know it was my manner that convinced them. I was singularly at ease. I answered their questions cheerily and we chatted of many things.

But, before long, I felt myself getting pale and wished them gone. My head ached and I fancied a ringing in my ears; but still they sat, and still they chatted. Then the ringing became more distinct. I talked more freely to get rid of the feeling, but it continued and gained momentum until, at length, I found the noise was not within my ears; it was coming from elsewhere.

No doubt I now grew very pale. But I talked more fluently, more eagerly, and with a heightened voice. After all, what could I do? Yet the sound increased. The sound was now a high pitched quickening sound becoming ever louder. I gasped for breath, and yet the officers heard it not. I talked more quickly, more vehemently but the noise steadily became louder. I arose and argued about trifles, in a high key and with violent gestures; but still the noise continued.

Why would these officers not be gone? Why would not the horrid sound drive them from this place? I paced the floor to and fro with heavy strides, as if excited to fury by the smug observations of the men. And the noise continued to rise.

O God! What could I do? I foamed -- I raved -- I swore! I swung the chair upon which I had been sitting, and demolished it upon the boards above the noise.

The noise arose above it all and continually gained momentum. It grew louder and louder. And still the men chatted pleasantly, insipidly, and smiled. Oh, those smiles! Was it possible they could not hear it?

No, of course not. They heard. How could they not? They suspected. They knew! In their incessant pleasant conversation, they were making a mockery of my horror! But anything would be better than this agony. Anything was more tolerable than their derision. I could bear those hypocritical smiles no longer! Louder! Louder! LOUDER! the sound came.

"All right!" I shrieked, "Rip up the floor planks and rid us of this monster!"

The men only laughed.

The house blurred. My head spun. I collapsed in a shuddering heap in a bare corner of the room.

With the world fading, I could only whimper, "It is the whining of the hideous machine."

Discussion 360

The Folly of the No Limit Garbage Ace

It is recommended that the reader begin this series with Part 101.

Poker is not a card game played by people.

Poker is a people game played with cards.

Here's what's happening.

This happened recently in a no limit game. We have pocket aces in the big blind. The first to act before the flop is a young man who raises our two ace blind. There is one caller. We re-raise with our aces. The original raiser re-re-raises. The third player folds. Then we make the last raise because it's an amount big enough to put the re-re-raiser all-in. He calls with his two red nines, turns them over before we show our aces, and asks if they're going to be any good.

Amazing.

On the same day, another young man raises with ace / eight and is beaten by ace / king and describes himself as unlucky.

Later, on the same day, yet another young man raises from middle position with ace / jack and loses the hand. He recounts the play several times to everyone's silent forbearance, complaining about losing "with such a good hand".

It's happening in card rooms everywhere. And everywhere one of the most commonly misplayed hands is the small, embarrassingly fetid, garbage ace.

Let it be known. Hold 'em is a game of big cards. Please notice the plural in that old bromide. It takes two big cards to tango for value in the dance of no limit hold 'em.

What if we play the garbage ace?

There is the rare situation for garbage ace play. We've all done it, and we'll do it again.

We're waiting patiently for a hand we can launch and that hand simply refuses to arrive. The big clock is ticking in 4/4 time. The good poker pockets never come. We're blinding our money away. We're losing the image of an action player. Things are so bad we're almost bored. Suddenly, we look into the pocket and we have ace / four suited. What a bonanza! We're in an early position but, at last, we have something to play. Well, not much, but we'll play.

In truth, we're holding a bomb.

We have a hand that can get us into big trouble. What's the best we can expect from this flaccid starter? Well, barring such bizarre and wonderful things such as two aces or two fours, or three of our suit on the flop, we can't expect much. Even with one of those rare flops, we wouldn't win much money because we're viewed as tight. But we're underway, carrying the garbage ace bomb to somewhere.

Now we're into the hand. We have called the big blind, just to be active, and there have been no raises. If there were a raise, we'd have mucked the ace / four, for sure, as we've done many times in the past.

In previous Discussions we've talked about playing *something* once in a while to stay active, and that's why we're playing this piece of refuse.

Now the flop comes, ace, nine, seven.

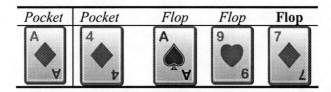

Pocket	Pocket	Flop	Flop	**Flop**
A♦	4♦	A♠	9♥	7♦

We're to act first. It's up to us. What do we do with this hand?

We have to check. That's the bad feature. We've made top pair and it probably isn't good. We're also UTG. We have to check.

As an aside, we nearly always check from that awkward first position, anyway. An exception to checking would be holding two middle pair after the flop, because the two pair have to be protected. In that case, we might take the lead by over betting the pot substantially. But such a bet would be made only against certain players and only when we have something invested in a pre-flop raise. We have nothing invested in the above hand and we could very well have the second best hand or worse. So we check.

Another aside. If there is a middle card flop, we could possibly bluff and take the pot. But, in this case, we wouldn't be sure we'd want to waste the risk of being discovered bluffing when there is so little to win and we have so little invested.

If there is a bet from one of the other three players, even if it is the button stealing the blinds, there is no reason to violate the prime directive; we don't ever call. And we can't raise. We throw the hand away. This is the usual fate of ace / x.

Okay, now let's say the hand is checked around and we get to see a free turn card.

If the board pairs, it is no help at all; the board pair is everybody's pair. We have no kicker because the four won't play in a showdown, and so we check once more. Again, we are prepared to throw the hand away.

If we happened to get a four on the turn to help our pair of aces, we could probably bet, but our decision depends on who the opponents are. We're still cautious.

In other words, it's nice to be active, but we can't get excited about ace / junk. It nearly always places us on the defensive. And we are by nature and by education, aggressive players.

Now let's change positions.

We're on the button. Same hand, ace / four suited. We wanted to really show some action, so we have raised the two limpers and the blinds. We have three callers. They've called because they aren't used to us winning a hand and it's the perfect place for us to steal the blinds. Their calls are born of suspicion.

We get the same flop.

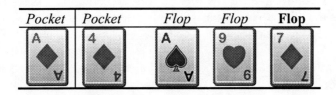

Pocket	Pocket	Flop	Flop	**Flop**

If one of the opponents bets, we can't call. Our hand is mucked.

If the action is checked to us, we can bet unless one of the players is known for his slow play. If there is a slow player in the pot, we might want to check along so we can see what he'll do after the turn. Also, besides not taking a risk with our weak hand, our failing to bet helps disguise our pair of aces.

But, still, if the action is checked to us and we bet, we could take the pot. So, to make this decision, we have to play our players. If we do bet and we are check / raised, we have to throw the hand away. The reason to muck is big slick could be out there and wasn't deemed big enough for a re-raise before the flop. (This big slick check / raise is common and a good play, one we often use, and one we are sometimes victim to.) So, after the check and raise, we end up with another instance of throwing our hand away. Please note, this time it was expensive with the pre-flop raise and our bet after the flop.

If the hand somehow continues, watch out for the straight. Because there are several players, one of whom probably has a better kicker with his ace than we do, we can't protect ourselves against the straight by betting. And another fine mess you've got us into, Ollie.

Conclusion: The weak ace will generally either win us a small pot with an unusual flop or, more often, place us on the defensive with a bad, or not so good, flop and an eventual loss.

In other words, all the ace / junk does for us is complicate the hand. It is not an aggressor's hand and it doesn't belong to the power player. The hand is intended mostly for the inexperienced player so he can lose his stack to us and explain how unlucky he is.

Should we ever play it?

Here's a common error. Ollie is near the button. There are enough limpers to call it a family pot. Ollie has ace nine, so he limps in with the others; he likes the odds.

Now, with seven players, where does Ollie think the other aces are? Even if an ace is in the flop, he likely has the worst ace of the bunch. Ollie is now hoisted on his own petard.

On those occasions when we have to play ace / nothing, we'll try to play it heads up or three to the pot. Being on or near the button will give us more of a chance. As we have discussed, we will elect to play it sometimes for the sake of playing. But we won't get pushy about it and we'll plan on throwing it away. We just wanted to be active.

Usually, the winning ace / garbage hand is a suited hand that makes a flush. And that, friends, is how unusual a winning hand it is.

Sometime, some day, on a poker table far, far away, we'll play it just to stay active and something more unusual than a flush will happen. But most of the time, we'll go all day without playing ace / garbage.

Discussion 361

Playing Less than Brilliant

It is recommended that the reader begin this series with Part 101.

Poker is not a card game played by people.

Poker is a people game played with cards.

Let's consider what to do with a suited jack and ten when <u>our opponent has a pocket pair</u> and the flop brings us another jack and ten. The question is, how aggressive should we be?

Pocket	Pocket	Flop	Flop	**Flop**
J♦	10♦	J♣	10♠	3♥

This would be a fairly rare circumstance. I'm trying to reconstruct how we might have gotten into the situation of believing our opponent has a pocket pair with us still in the pot, pre-flop, holding suited connectors. Maybe it happened this way:

Let's say we opened the pot with a raise, second to the button. We thought we had a good chance to steal the blinds and limper money because the button player, the player to our left, is tight passive and would likely muck his hand. We've done this with him before. But this time he calls us with something and it has to be fairly strong. Since he is passive, he did not re-raise. We therefore have placed him on a pocket pair.

Most any player, passive or not, would re-raise with queens, kings or aces. So we'll place him on a pair lower than queens, a middle pair.

Since the odds of the opponent having the case tens or the case jacks are pretty small, we could come out betting after the flop.

The odds of the board's three of hearts making a set are pretty small, too, because we see him as a tight player who wouldn't call a raise with a pair that small. Nor would he call a raise to play a two card drawing hand.

203

There is a better chance he could have one ten or one jack with and ace. If he's holding ace / jack, ace / ten, or big slick or similar, our initial thought is not to let him make any draws; those aces have a habit of falling at the wrong time. The safe play is to come out betting.

But let's try to be smart about this. There is an even stronger play awaiting us. If we check to our button man, we'll find out how good he thinks his hand is. Remember, he's tight passive and not likely to bet if he doesn't have a very strong hand. Checking our two pair will help us place him more squarely on a hand. But we're offering him a free draw, also.

If he bets, he has a pair. If he doesn't bet, he could have ace something. If he bets, we will raise him about a ton and win his pre-flop call and his after-flop bet.

If he checks along with us and there is no scare card on the turn such as an ace, we make a big bet or move all-in if he's short stacked. (Tight passives are frequently short stacked.)

To do all that, we have to be reasonably sure of our tight passive player. If we're not sure, we make the safe play; we don't check after the flop; we come out betting.

The bet before the flop, or the re-raise before the turn, or the extra large bet after the turn, should win the pot. We have a very good hand. We should also remember that the opponent has no idea what we really have. He probably thinks we raised with big cards and the flop didn't help us. We could win some money with a sizable call.

If the ace shows on the turn, we have to check to see what he wants to do. He's tight, so if he bets with the ace, he may have two pair. He's passive, so if he checks with the ace, he may have only one pair. In any case, if the ace shows on the board and he bets, we have to fold.

If, after a scare card like an ace, he checks with us after the turn, we're bound to make a full house on the river. Paco, impish god of poker, says that's the rule after we offer a free draw.

Enough. Let's change to some pocket queens.

We're holding pocket queens and we have a caller after we raised the pot. He sits directly to our left. The flop comes jack, nine and four.

Pocket	Pocket	Flop	Flop	**Flop**
Q♦	Q♠	J♣	9♥	4♣

Our opponent has been losing. He has been playing a long time. He's a little short in the stack, but not much.

We bet. He surprises us with a call. Now we think he's either sandbagging or he's desperate. We think about him a minute and we decide to be cautious; he might be sandbagging, maybe a set.

The turn brings the five of diamonds.

Pocket	Pocket	Flop	Flop	Flop	**Turn**
Q♦	Q♠	J♣	9♥	4♣	5♦

We check to him. He checks along.

The river brings the deuce of diamonds and we move all-in for his short stack. There is no call and we take the pot.

Now, a play like that bothers us because we didn't get full value for the hand and we allowed some free draws. The opponent called our flop bet and got two more cards for the price. Either he had a middle pair or a draw to a club flush with an ace / king of clubs in the pocket. At this late point, we think he had the club big slick. We won the hand, but we begin to think our hand was played a little sloppily.

After thinking about it, the opponent was losing pretty badly and we realize we should have read the desperation in his play. He might have called another bet after the turn. And if he didn't call after the turn, we would have gotten the pot one card earlier. In any case, we would not have given him a free look at the river. It's important to learn each time we do something less than brilliant.

Discussion 362

Check & Call and Pot Odds

It is recommended that the reader begin this series with Part 101.

Poker is not a card game played by people.

Poker is a people game played with cards.

We check and raise when we want a bigger pot and we feel the opponent who is to act behind us will make the bet. We also check and raise to bluff. (A section on bluffing appears in the Dominator section of this book. But please wait.) Is there ever a time when we check and call?

Of course. The empirical reason is we would not rule out any maneuver in poker. The plays are as numerous as there are infinite personalities in players and combinations of 2,869,685 possible hands. Those intertwining personalities and hands are what make poker a holy game and the most fascinating wagering contest on the planet.

There is a place for check and call in both no limit and limit games. We'll discuss limit in this case, just to drive home the principle of the draw out.

The most common place for a check / call would be with a drawing hand in a limit game with multi-way action and good pot odds. That's a given.

But let's say we're in a jammin' limit game with lots of family pots. (My god, Paco, it sounds like a power player's nightmare.) Let's say we're in it out of some kind of default; we thought the game at the table was different when we entered it, or we thought we could change it or we're just waiting for our no limit game to open a seat for us.

We'll say we're in a $10 - $20 structured game. We have a good hand and we have made our way past the turn, betting along with the rest of the six players with the maximum number of raises before and after the flop and turn. Well, that would be a pot of over $960. We're pretty sure we're beat after the turn, but we're drawing to a nut flush. At this point we're going to call every bet of $20 that's made, to the river, so we can be in the family drawing for the big pot. And, the survey says: It's okay to check and call for those tremendous pot odds.

The extreme example, above, and all its cousins, is a hold 'em game for gamblers and is for the power player to scoff at and stay away from before we call off our money. Anytime we're having a nightmare and we can get out alive, we take advantage of the escape plan.

Now and then we hear a player say he was "pot committed". The expression is a good measuring device for the power player. Anytime we find ourselves "pot committed", we are either in the wrong game or we're playing the right game wrong. The power player knows his bets must control the game and when those bets are ineffectual in gaining control and implementing the power player's expertise in risk management, he is simply gambling along with the others. Of course, we may elect to call a weak bet toward a monster pot and, in the long haul, we'll win. But usually we will be in control of the betting and those situations won't happen.

With the above observations, we know and acknowledge the power player's advantages in no limit poker.

The above limit example is made as an extreme demonstration that it is okay to call when there are pot odds in our favor. We know we are not likely to win the hand, but the odds will pay off in the long run in a series of similar situations.

Of course, the only time we need to calculate pot odds is when our hand is behind. If we have the edge, there is no calculation; we bet to win the pot.

It is much harder to find a situation in no limit poker when the power player is justified in checking and then calling

Of course, there is the unusual situation in no limit, which is much like the limit illustration, above. A novice player makes too small a bet for the size of the pot after we've checked our hand and we have to call for pot odds. It happens often in beginners' games, but not often in good company. Again, we realize the call has to be financed because we are not likely to win the hand but we'll win one along the way and it'll bring a return on our financing in the long run, hopefully not too long a run.

We'll just make sure we have the correct odds. These are the odds for drawing one card to make a complete hand:

Four card hand, one draw	Odds
Open end straight flush	2.13 to 1
Inside straight flush	2.92 to 1
Flush	4.22 to 1
Open end straight	4.88 to 1

All other combinations will fall in the ten to one or more categories and will not be discussed here because those odds are almost impossible to attain in no limit.

In review, the definition of a complete hand is a hand using five cards with no kicker, although four of a kind is considered a complete hand.

If, in play, the pot odds (the ratio of our bet to the pot) match the odds of our making a complete hand (the above chart), we can call the little bet and see how it all comes out. Better yet, we should have more than an even match of our hand to the pot to make sure we're getting our money's worth. We'll make a hand with the straight flush draw about once every 2.13 times, the open ended straight about every 4.88 times.

In the case of the straight flush draw, is the amount of the bet less than the size of the pot? If it is, the pot plus the opponent's bet gives us 2 to 1 in money odds.

In the case of the open ended straight draw, will the amount of the opponent's bet plus the pot give us 5 to 1 in money odds? It would have to be a very small bet.

But wait a minute. First we must be sure of the complete hand we're seeking. If we make our hand, will our opponent make a bigger flush – or a bigger straight?

We'll repeat another word of warning because it is important: The odds above set out how many times we will win with a draw out. Each loss must be financed by us until we get the winner. We therefore must be ready, both monetarily and mentally, to accept temporary losses until one or some of those pot odds long shots pay off. Sometimes a draw out win takes awhile and, sometimes when we make the hand at last, the win still hasn't caught up with our draw out losses. If we're not ready for this kind of financing, we should stay away from pot odds calls.

Discussion 363

Weird Flops

It is recommended that the reader begin this series with Part 101.

Poker is not a card game played by people.

Poker is a people game played with cards.

How do you play a weird flop? Does anyone really know? Weird flops often are checked through to the river and the hand is won in a showdown. Betting could be a big risk with so little invested. On the other hand, if there has been a lot of action pre-flop, a bet in the right place could mean adding a few more checks to our stack.

Let's suppose the weirdest flop of them all - three aces. It happens now and then.

Three aces on the board almost negate the rank of aces. Almost. There is one ace left. Nevertheless, kings are now very important and all the other cards move up a notch in importance. Any pocket pair is huge.

This three ace flop is going to be checked all around the table of let's say three players, because everyone is afraid of the fourth ace. The trouble is, after checking, no one knows if one of his opponents has the ace because the ace holder would have checked along to set the trap; he can't win more money at this point by betting. Additionally, anyone with a pocket pair would have checked too, even if the pocket contains kings, for two reasons:

- An ace in an opponent's pocket is not only possible, but probable. People customarily begin with aces.

- A two king pocket will also want to set a trap.

Now comes the turn card. It doesn't matter what the card is; everyone will be afraid that it paired someone's pocket card. And, if it did, the new full house would be afraid to bet. And so on through the river to showdown.

But let's look at the bright side. Suppose we hold the case ace. (We're in the pot so we must have raised with *something*.) We have the ace and any bet from us will end the hand. So we check hoping someone (with a pair of kings?) will take a stab at the pot.

We play the same way with a large pocket pair. But not a small pocket pair; a small pocket pair just died with the appearance of a medium to high turn card.

How about our high pocket card paired on the turn or the river? We still can't bet because the ace might be in someone else's pocket waiting for us to venture out, just like we would do if we had the ace. Ah, the limitations of no limit.

Want to be tricky? If there is no case ace or pair in anybody's pocket, any large bet from any player will win the pot. Is there a neutral type card on the turn?

We could wink at Paco, the poker god, and take a swing at the pot, if it's big enough to take a swing at. If the pot isn't big enough to bother with, we'll check as fast as we can so we can start another hand. But, if someone else takes a swing, any raise might win the pot, now a bigger pot.

It's time to consider the tempo of the game and the players who are in the pot.

If we have been trading pots with someone, waiting for the hand that will trap our pot trading adversary, there may be something we can do. It will, however, depend on what has transpired between us and our adversary lately. But, mostly, we won't risk money on these weird situations.

Weird flops in small no limit hold 'em are fun. Every time a weird flop hits the table, all the players go "ooooooooo".

This time we'll look at middle triplets on the flop.

While three aces made a top straight (and, to a much lesser degree, the wheel) a remote working possibility, the eights make five different straights a working possibility. They are four through eight, five through nine, six through ten, seven through jack, and eight through queen.

The hand will probably be checked through to the turn, probably through to the showdown river, just as with aces. Everybody in no limit is afraid of the trap, and no one has much invested. However, if there are pocket cards connected to the eights, making the four card possibility of a flush or straight on the turn, there could be a flurry of betting after the turn. Then there could be big betting with a good river after the cards are out. It happens sometimes and the outcome is usually a surprise because there is so little to read.

How about three deuces?

In most no limit games, no one is holding a lone deuce, although it sometimes happens. With this bizarre flop, the betting may open up after the turn, especially if the turn card is a high card such as ace, king, or queen, suggesting a full house. Again, we'll consider the players.

Let's say a king lands on the turn and there are three players. There could be a bet-and-take-it wager from any of the contestants, although the late position would be favored after the others check and there is actually no king in anyone's pocket. If the hand is checked through the king and an ace lands on the river, things could get interesting if the king was sandbagging.

In no limit, the lower ranking trips on the flop often bring a little more action than three aces or even three eights.

Discussion 364

Useless Flops and Useful Traps

It is recommended that the reader begin this series with Part 101.

Poker is not a card game played by people.

Poker is a people game played with cards.

We looked at weird flops in the last Discussion.

This time we'll look at something truly troublesome. We'll look at the three rag flop. (Cha, cha-cha.) The three rag flop consists of three relatively low, disparate and useless cards. The only apparent difference between this flop and the triplet flop is no one at the table goes "ooooooo", but one or two players might go "awww".

Both flops are interesting to play. Assuming the flopped rags are neutral to all opponents, we are, like in the trip flop, essentially back to square one, pretty much at the same point we were before the flop.

The three rag flop is more cumbersome to play than the trip flop because there is more to think about. With the triplet flop, we know what we must do; we must check no matter what we hold, at least initially.

In another aspect, the three rag flop is much like the triplet flop in that it places undo emphasis on the pocket cards. However, in the three rag flop, the opponents may not seem as dangerous because their small pocket pairs, if any, or their connected cards, if any, don't appear to be as threatening. Still, as in the flopped trips, we have three useless cards on the board.

We'll play a hand.

We're two from the button and we've raised with big slick, suited.

The button calls.

The flop favors us with three rags in various shapes and colors of the rainbow.

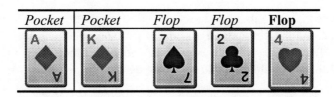

Pocket	Pocket	Flop	Flop	**Flop**
A♦	K♦	7♠	2♣	4♥

What do we do with this weird and troublesome flop?

Of course, we check to see what the button wants to do. He can bet and take it, as far we're concerned, because we have little invested and we're not eager gamblers. If he checks, it probably means he has no pair. But he did jump our raise fence to call, so he's proud of something.

We should always consider a set from this flop when there is a bet from our pre-flop caller.

In the meantime, if he has no pair and doesn't bet, we're fairly proud of our hand. The turn will tell us what to do.

A New Position. Changing the story to a new position, if we are to act second, instead of first, we could bet the hand after the flop and probably take the pot. The best position with a pre-flop raise strikes again.

But this is a weird flop that apparently helps nobody and the pocket cards should win, the same as in a flop of three cards of the same rank. It's just as weird as the trip flop, but the big difference is that it doesn't have the striking appearance of a stark three of a kind on the board. It also happens much more often.

The Real Hand. The above type hand is dealt many times in all hold 'em games. The following story is told here, not because it is unusual, but because it is very usual and needs to be underscored.

This time, Murphy will play the hand.

Murphy was two from the button, raising, and the button called. The caller was a very good player and, between Murphy and him, they dominated the table. He was a young man and played in the style of Doyle Brunson, with all the "Dolly" chatter and diversions, and he did it well. Murphy tried to avoid him when he could because there were softer spots to wait for and those spots didn't require a lot of patience.

213

But, since he was only two chairs behind Murphy, they were heads up now and then, and the young man asked and gave no quarter. Murphy has been waiting for a chance to change seats and place him more on the right, where Murphy could avoid a few of the harder decisions.

In this hand, after Murphy raised and the young man entered the pot, Murphy wondered why he hadn't been re-raised. The young man's calling action was different from his usual aggression. Anyway, after he called Murphy's raise, they got the above three rag flop.

Murphy checked to him and the opponent checked along.

The turn brought the king of spades.

Because Murphy was the raiser, and the young man a mere caller, Murphy bet the size of the pot.

The opponent called. If he also had a king, Murphy reasoned, Murphy had the best king because of the ace kicker.

The river was the nine of hearts.

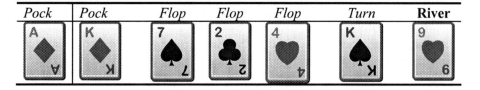

Murphy checked and the young man moved all-in. After not enough thinking, Murphy called. The young man showed a set of deuces.

This is the classic hidden set trap and it was unusually bad play on Murphy's part. He didn't pay attention to any of the clues, which were ordinary and not too hard to catch. Among the clues:

- Mainly, the young man was a very strong player and, in this hand, he played like a call boy. That should have raised a red flag. The rest of the reasons are related to this obvious change in pattern.

- The opponent didn't raise before the flop.

- The opponent checked along after the flop when he could have bet and taken the pot.

- He called Murphy's bet after a big turn card. Ordinarily, he couldn't call if the king didn't help him with a big kicker. If it did help him, he would have raised. In any case, his call was a departure from what is a normal procedure for his strong play. In this case, the call showed a tremendous amount of strength.

- His all-in move after a garbage river card showed big strength after weakness and was a conclusive clue. Actually, all his moves showed strength after apparent weakness, the usual mark of a set.

Murphy called because he sensed the opponent was ready to bluff. That's not a good enough reason. Murphy fell for what should have been an obvious and classic trap.

The river draw out is not the usual downfall of no limit play; hidden sets are the most common traps in no limit. We have to look for the signs. The above trap and its symptoms are not unusual; they are typical.

It's also important to keep our cool after we have made a shameful mistake. Murphy will not target the young man in future play, but he will be conscious of the man's attitude toward him; Murphy has a good picture of his image in the young man's head.

After the hand, Murphy was able to change seats to a position across from his embarrassing mistake. Sitting across from the same strong player, he picked up a dependable tell, which was this: When the young man had a solid hand, he stared in silence at no particular thing across the room. When he bluffed, he stared at his opponent - and talked to him.

In a later hand, Murphy knew the young man thought Murphy was ripe to be bluffed because of his last win with the set. It was opportunity time. Having picked up the tell, Murphy called a very sizable bet and got more than his losses back.

This true example is a reprise of earlier Discussions concerning no limit traps and how to avoid them. We mustn't let our guard down.

This is also an example of catching tells. It's easiest to catch tells when sitting across from the target player and harder to catch tells when sitting next to him. We are fond of saying we want the good players on our right. I personally want the best player on my far right, across from me, where I can see him at all times.

This story is also an example of keeping our cool for future profits. It is a lesson in patience and focus and it is a true story of how to capitalize on our mistakes.

Discussion 365

Flopped Straights

It is recommended that the reader begin this series with Part 101.

Poker is not a card game played by people.

Poker is a people game played with cards.

Steamboat George tells us about a hand he played and asks how we would have played it. He is in a no limit game and holds ace / queen suited on the button. Three players ahead of him have limped into the pot. Steam raises on the button and gets two callers.

The flop brings a king, a ten, and a jack.

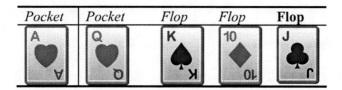

Pocket	Pocket	Flop	Flop	**Flop**
A♥	Q♥	K♠	10♦	J♣

The first player bets, the second player calls, and Steamboat calls; he doesn't want to lose anybody. At this point he knows he has made a mistake, but it's too late. (What was his mistake? Why?)

The turn brings a ten.

Pocket	Pocket	Flop	Flop	Flop	**Turn**
A♥	Q♥	K♠	10♦	J♣	10♠

The first player checks, the second player checks and Steamboat George bets the size of the pot. The first player thinks awhile and folds; he must have had middle connectors.

The second player calls. He has something better than middle connectors.

The river brings the deuce of spades. The opponent checks and Steamboat moves all-in. He is promptly called and the opponent shows a ten and a jack of hearts to take the pot with a full house.

Steamboat's question: How would we have played it?

We'll assume the table was right for him to raise pre-flop. Not a bad raise in any case with nothing but limpers in the action. We'll say it's a good raise. We'll also assume Steamboat's raise of the size of the pot was at least three times the big blind. Good raise.

There were two very large mistakes in his play, however. The first was not raising after the flop, and this mistake was acknowledged by Steamboat. There were two bets ahead of his time to act. A raise probably would not have gotten a call (we're surprised there was a bet) and he probably would have taken the pot. With a bet and a call ahead of Steam, there had to be some high cards held by the other players, and/or a drawing hand in the action. It was time to get rid of those draws with a very large raise. Better yet, if the stacks are right, go all-in. This is not hind sight; it is standard power player procedure.

With a bet and call in the face of the nuts in a no limit game, it sounds like a game we would all have liked to be in.

The only mistake on the turn was that Steamboat was in a spot where he shouldn't have been. But we've already discussed that.

At this point, Steamboat George tries to make up for his mistake by betting. We hope the bet was substantial. The remaining opponent only calls, thereby setting our hero up for the all-in bet after the river. At this juncture, it was a nice play by the opponent.

The river brings nothing. We'll have to acknowledge there could have been a back-in flush, but it doesn't matter because it wouldn't have made any difference to Steamboat.

After a check from the opponent, our hapless hero moves all-in. Really, now. In the face of an open pair? From an opponent who has shown no fear? This mistake was disastrous.

To directly answer Steam's question, we would have raised more than the size of the pot after the flop. (All-in would have been okay against short stacks.) If our big bet had gotten a call, we would have checked the hand through after the board was paired. There was no flush to draw to after the turn and, assuming the opponent wasn't trying to make a straight, only three cards could help the opponent's hand, another ten or one of two jacks.

If the opponent can make a full house by catching only a ten or a jack after calling our big raise after the flop, then his foolishness wins him the pot. And, of course, it did win because there was no big raise by Steamboat.

There is no second guessing on our part here. If the opponent is trying to make a straight, the worst we can do is tie. If the opponent is drawing to a full house or quads, he has only three cards in the deck that can help him. But we think we shouldn't give him the chance to try any of that nonsense without paying the post-flop full price.

Whether we'd call the opponent's bet after the turn would depend on the opponent but, in good company (which evidently this was not), we would let him have the pot. Again, the decision to call after the turn would depend on what we know about the opponent.

Smaller straights usually win bigger pots because there is more brinksmanship.

The rules are simple and mostly objective:

- If we have the top two cards in our pocket and a straight, we have the nuts. We must protect our nut hand against draw outs such the full house against Steamboat.

- If we have both the top and the bottom card in the pocket, we must find if one of the opponents has the two top cards of the straight in his pocket. We do that by raising and playing our opponent.

- We are wary of having the two bottom cards of the straight. Bottom straights win big pots, especially when the opponents don't think we would play such low cards. But we have to test for this winning bottom straight by raising and betting in the right places. And, in this case, we must really play our players.

219

Discussion 366

When Do We Quit for the Day?

It is recommended that the reader begin this series with Part 101.

Poker is not a card game played by people.

Poker is a people game played with cards.

One thing we've learned: Players who can't wait are there to gamble. Those with patience are there to win.

But here's a question: When do we get up from the table and quit for the day?

Some of the possible answers:

- When we have won enough.

- When it's time for dinner. It could be time for anything, but at least dinner is a scheduled time and we shouldn't play hungry.

- When we have lost our limit.

- When we believe we are not playing up to our usual capabilities.

- When the game is not our kind of game.

I like them all but the first one, so let's take it first.

We've all had those many days when we couldn't hold enough cards to win a pot now and then. Discouraging, those losing days. Then there are the days when the cards keep on coming, the game is cooking and we're on top of it all. We wonder how we could ever have lost.

On one of those winning days, we should stay to win more. The power player knows of no winning limit; he plays until he knows his game is no longer his "A" game.

220

While we're on this big win tour, we will guard against losing the rhythm of the game and playing hands too often and not too well. When we slip in any category of our playing acumen, that's when we should leave. But, when we're a big winner, things are good and we still have a winning attitude in our kind of game, we should stay to win more.

A word of warning. If any of us feels he has won enough and, in staying, he will lose interest in the game and the loss of interest will diminish his ability to play, he should leave – promptly. Don't wait for the button to come around; you've already left the game. Go!!

In this part of the decision to stay or leave, we must not confuse luck with good play. Beating a bunch of good players because the cards have run over us is not good reason for being pleased with ourselves; we should just be grateful. But, as long as we're under no restraints of any kind, time or otherwise, still making superior decisions compared to our opponents, we'll stay in this favorable game and add to our win.

Some players arrive at the game with a target amount to win. When they get there, they leave. To each his own method. I, personally, have found the target win amount to be dangerous. Many players have a tendency to push for that target, and that's not good. Also, when the target amount is stacked quickly in front of them, many of those target type players can't leave. So what's the use of a target win?

Here's a little self tell that many good players enforce: When they wonder what time it is, they know they're losing interest in the game and are on the verge of thinking about other things. They may place a time limit on themselves at that moment, so that they won't wonder how much longer they're going to play and, during that time period, they are likely to continue to play their "A" game. The time period is strictly enforced and they don't extend it because, when they extend it, they know they are reaching.

Of course, when any of us stops putting people on hands when we're not directly involved in the pot, we know it's almost time to leave, then we should place a time limit on ourselves while we concentrate on correcting that error. Whether we are loser or winner does not enter into this kind of decision; the decision rests solely on whether we're playing our "A" game.

Long, long ago, in a Discussion far far behind us, we established we should not lose any more than we can win back in the next day's play. Those one day losses aren't so bad to take; it's the losses that need more than one day to overcome that are discouraging.

Anytime we are not playing to our potential, we need, yes need, to get out of the game. Do we know ourselves well enough to do this? Do we have the courage? Remember, it is one long poker game day after day and, when our game falters, we'll be able to play better and like ourselves better, on another day. More than money is involved in this decision. Our self respect is at stake here, as well.

Another thing. Any time the game is not the game in which we, as power players, are Dominant, we leave. Sometimes we're among a bunch of hard rocks who just don't suit us and we leave. Sometimes we can't be Dominant because the cards aren't coming our way and we leave. And, what's more, any game that deteriorates into a family limper game that can't be reversed should be quickly placed in our rear view mirror.

The power player has learned to play with his instincts. The math and the maneuvers are second nature to the experienced power player. Our instincts in playing our players are what guide us now.

When we first get a nibbling urge to consider leaving the game, we should probably do it. We are beginning to lose interest and often that is enough to make the wrong decision in the next large pot. It could be the pot of the day – win or lose.

Know when to walk away. Those saved dollars are important.

The

Dominator

The Proposition

by Sam O'Connor

"Son, no matter how far you travel, or how smart you get, always remember this: Someday, somewhere, a guy is going to come to you and show you a nice brand-new deck of cards on which the seal is not broken, and this guy is going to offer to bet you that the jack of spades will jump out of this deck and squirt cider in your ear. But, son, do not bet him, for as sure as you do, you are going to get an ear full of cider." - Sky Masterson in "Guys and Dolls"

Waitressing in 1960 at The Boulder Club required a special kind of woman and a special kind of patience. Some of the patrons could get a little rough, although they could usually be kept at bay by the waitresses calling them "honey" or "sweetie". Good waitresses, hearts of gold. You know the kind.

Such an accomplished tray jockey was Darlene Jenelowicz. Darlene was the consummate sawdust joint waitress but her most unusual characteristic was that she was a close friend of Suitcase "Call me Bobby" Sellers. They were an unlikely couple. And they never got together at the Boulder Club because sawdust had no place in Suitcase's dapper image, or in his outlook on life.

Darlene worked the night shift at the Boulder. She liked it that way. The entire club was her wait station and she took care of things pretty much in her own brusque, yet somehow breezy way. Her regular customers were waitresses from neighboring casinos, dealers and other such employees getting off work at different night hours in various parts of downtown Las Vegas. She knew most of the customers by their first names. The atmosphere at the Boulder Club was usually relaxed and friendly, and the money was good enough for Darlene.

No one called Suitcase "Bobby" and no one ever would. It was too easy to call him Suitcase because the name fit him like the fine clothes he wore. He was said to have a whole suitcase of imported clothes. His shoes were alligator, his gait was easy and careful and he inspected the seat of every chair before he sat in it. Suitcase looked like a million dollars but he had hardly even one dollar of his own. He wasn't employed. He busied himself with looking good and with playing poker with Darlene's money.

224

Every morning after a night of work, Darlene would meet Suitcase around the corner on Second Street. She'd brush the sawdust off her shoes, throw her arms around Suitcase, and then they'd have breakfast at Binion's Horseshoe. Sometime during the morning ritual, she'd slip Suitcase a sawbuck, pay the breakfast bill, and then take her tired bones home for a well deserved rest.

Suitcase, emerging from the Horseshoe breakfast, bright eyed and resplendent, would glide to the poker room at the Golden Nugget and, almost every day, he'd lose Darlene's twenty dollars. Someday, he reasoned, his luck would change.

Actually, Suitcase was lucky to have Darlene.

In 1960, The Golden Nugget card room was the classiest card place in downtown Las Vegas. It was directly across Fremont Street from The Boulder Club and The Horseshoe, just as it is today. The Nugget ran six card tables in those days, the largest number of poker tables in town, with Bill Boyd as its capable manager.

Bill Boyd was one of the good guys in poker. He introduced the center deal and he was the first manager to spread a Texas Hold 'em game.

Bill had an easy manner and a way of engaging in brief, good conversation. He wore a sports jacket with duck vents and, when he was standing, he would rock forward on his tiptoes, trying to be just a little bit taller. Bill gave everybody a friendly smile and a firm handshake, employee and customer alike.

One of the Nugget's customers was Titanic Thompson. Titanic was just getting by in those days but he was later to become one of the top contenders in tournament poker, an event yet to be promoted by Benny Binion.

No one knew why Titanic Thompson was called "Titanic". Maybe he was on the ship that went down on its maiden voyage, maybe not. Maybe he just told one of his Titanic stories a few too many times and picked up the nickname. But what everybody did know, was that Titanic was tricky. Sure, he was one of the better card players, but he was much more famous for his patented specialty - proposition bets.

For instance, there was the time Titanic bet he could throw a melon over a somewhat average sized house. He got several takers on that one. After everyone agreed on who was to hold the money, Titanic placed the melon in an oven, dehydrated it to the size of a softball and threw it over the building.

Now, a scientist might argue that, without juice, it wasn't a complete melon. And an attorney might argue that there was no meeting of the minds. But I guess there were no scientists or attorneys in the group, because they all paid Titanic. And then they laughed about it.

On one fair desert morning, Suitcase Sellers found he was alone in the Golden Nugget poker room with Darlene's twenty dollar bill still burning his pocket. While he waited for Bill to arrive and open the poker tables, Suitcase occupied himself by watching the poker people brush the tables and open the chip racks. Someday, he told himself, he'd have money to open his own card room, so he'd better keep an eye on the preparation.

Finally, Bill Boyd came through the Second Street entrance and into the card room. Bill had an anxious look on his face. "Morning, Suitcase."

"Call me Bobby."

"Have you seen Murphy this morning, Suitcase? I'd like to avoid him for awhile."

"Haven't seen him. Darlene said there was a good game that went through to the wee hours at the Boulder last night. Guess you're safe. What's up?"

"Doesn't matter, I guess. Eventually I'll have to tell him about my two thousand dollar bet with Titanic."

"Yeah. He might want a loan," offered the sarcastic Suitcase.

"It was a proposition bet."

"No! You made a prop bet with Titanic? You?"

"Me."

"Why do you want to avoid Murphy?"

"Murphy knows Titanic and I went to Tonopah together. He'll hear about the two thousand dollars and I'd rather tell him myself than have him get it from somebody else. I don't want him to think I'm dodging him."

"Now, why would he think that?"

"Maybe, instead of two thousand, I could tell him the bet was for only one thousand dollars – or maybe five hundred. Do you think he'd believe five hundred?"

"He might. It's the two thousand that's hard to believe."

"I think I should try two hundred."

"What's the story? Two thousand dollars during a trip to Tonopah sounds good."

"I'll tell you what happened", Bill said emphatically, "Titanic can't read signs while he's asleep."

"And he bet you he could?"

"No. No. Hang on, I'll tell you what happened."

Bill paused while Suitcase waited patiently.

"Four days ago I asked Titanic to keep me company when I went to Tonopah. We drove there yesterday."

Suitcase nodded and said something about making it back okay.

"On the way back, I could see the city lights in the distance."

"Yeah, nice view from up there."

"Titanic couldn't see it because he was asleep. We passed a sign that said Las Vegas was twenty three miles. He woke up just after we passed the sign. He rubbed his eyes and said, 'Oh, is that Vegas?' I told him it was and that it was about twenty miles away. Titanic said it looked more like fifteen miles. I said that I didn't think so, more like twenty miles if he'd care to bet on it."

"Good. You've got him."

"It gets better. He said he'd bet me a thousand dollars Vegas was closer to fifteen miles than twenty miles. I said I'd take the bet if he'd make it two thousand. He agreed, we shook on it and said we'd watch the odometer and mark it at the city limits."

Suitcase was laughing. "Glad to hear someone finally put a bad beat on Titanic."

"Yeah, I had him where I wanted him. Then I started laughing. I couldn't help it. It slowly became too big a laugh and I figured I'd tell him there was no need to clock the miles because I'd seen a sign two miles back that said twenty three miles." Bill looked at the beaming Suitcase. "Right?"

"Right", echoed Suitcase, visibly pleased. "You had him where you wanted him and now he owes you two thousand dollars. I like it."

"No, I owe him", Bill said sourly. "The day before yesterday Titanic went out and moved the sign."

Discussion 400

Bullies and Calling Stations

It is recommended that the reader begin this series with Part 101.

Poker is not a card game played by people.

Poker is a people game played with cards.

Are you ready to DOMINATE?

By now the reader, the new and improved no limit player, has had some experience. He has been keeping an accounting and he has found he is in the winners' column quite often. He may even have a net profit over a month or so.

The new and improved player now also knows that no limit hold 'em is a repeating game of brinksmanship. The dominant brinkman will carry the day.

If the reader has followed the progression as outlined in this book, he has played a lot of Tight Aggressive, some Tight Passive, some Loose Aggressive, and some Loose Passive.

If he has followed instructions, he has played in each of the above categories so that he knows how the players who play in those modes think and what they are concerned about. He knows their patterns and their techniques. If he's good, he knows them at the table better than they know themselves.

There is no substitute for experience and the reader now has enough knowledge and experience to be a winner. As he continues to play, he gains more knowledge and more experience. He is ready to Dominate the game.

Let's see what the reader might be doing at this point in his progression. He is sitting at the table fingering his players' checks, counting them now and then, keeping track of whether he is winner or loser and by how much. He likes to play and quit winner. We all do. And now, it's time to move on to the bigger and more consistent win.

229

Are you ready to DOMINATE ??

If you have figured out that the win or the loss of the day in no limit is contained in two or three pots and that the other small pots don't make nearly as much difference, you are ready to Dominate. You have arrived.

You now know the small pots are just the dallying maneuvers to learn about the opponents and to set up the opponents for the bigger pots. And maybe you've discovered that the big pots are usually not won with the big hands, but won with ordinary hands that have a slight edge. We will now be looking for that edge.

The pressure will be on you. When some people are squeezed they fold. When others are squeezed they excel. The Dominator MUST excel.

Now we will explore the Dominator Section. Domination is the fifth player category, after TA, TP, LA and LP. It is the superior category and few people who play in the small blinds no limit games are qualified to be members of this exclusive club. But we're prepared to join. We like the idea of playing for a few large pots and then having a nice dinner. We know the opponents belong to us.

Playing the Table.

The secret to domination lies in the ability to recognize player types, game types, the momentum at the table and the image we, the power players, have in the eyes of our opponents. It also lies in our ability to adjust our play to those games and players and mix our play accordingly. When we can do that, we have the ability to Dominate.

Playing the Bully.

Perhaps the reader had in mind, when he started this book, he was going to learn to be the table bully. Well, dear reader, the true Dominator is more than that. He knows how to Dominate the bully! And we'd rather be the Dominator than the bully.

The bully is loose aggressive, and he often is one of the best. He is in and out of pots. If he's good, he doesn't lose many of the big ones. And, when he loses the small ones, he's merely preparing the table for the later big hand with the bigger win. He has a line of patter that is often infectious.

No one really dislikes this affable bully. He buys in with more money than anyone else and, often, we watch his tall stack grow even taller. He's everybody's target and we're the ones who can hit the bull's eye.

The bully is successful in a tight game. Actually, he's playing the game we should play at a tight table. We don't have to talk like he does, or con like he does, but we can play his loose aggressive game just as well as he can because we've been there before. At this point he's playing over the top of everybody and bluffing and winning a lot of pots. He's making sure the rest of the table is playing tight in comparison to his play. He knows everybody at the table is waiting for the hand to win against him. And he doesn't care. He is winning or losing the small pots to merely set the table up for the big pot.

Here's the key to the bully. The bully isn't the dominator; we are.

Like the players at the table, we are waiting for the right moment against the bully. But, in the meantime, we are playing loose aggressive against the others just as the bully is. We stay out of the bully's way unless we have a very good hand.

If the bully is good, he knows what we are doing. In only a short time, he knows who we are and what we are about. We're glad he's tightened up the table and we'll take advantage of it. The good bully will know that, too.

Should we try to play over the top of the bully? We can if we want to, but it's a lot of trouble and pretty hard to do. We'd need a lot of bankroll to try and, if we're unlucky, we may not be successful. It's usually better to share the table with him. We'll usually play the bully style but not against him. He'll recognize the arrangement; all good players do. If he isn't good enough to recognize our ability and the arrangement, then he's ours even more easily when we get the hand.

Sometimes there are two bullies at the table who are playing against each other. When it happens, it's an ego thing. They consider the rest of the table theirs, but they haven't settled down to sharing. Our bully could view us in that manner.

This situation is fun. We sit and make the good hand while the bullies do battle with each other and ignore us. When we win that big one, they are always surprised. We also know we don't have complete domination of the table and we may want to leave.

We play the bully or bullies solid. Let them do the betting for us. They love to set traps. We all do. Just remember that many times when they are checking, they are trying to set traps. We'll bet when we are reasonably sure we have the best hand. And we make all the opponents pay to draw to their marginal hands.

Playing the Calling Station.

You have to have a hand against the calling station.

The calling station doesn't play his opponents' hands; he plays only his own.

The calling station doesn't pay much attention to how much is bet. If he has a hand to draw to, he'll call. You bet twice the amount of the pot? It doesn't matter; the true calling station will call and draw to his two pair.

The calling station subconsciously wants us to do his betting for him so he can call. When he has something to draw to, he'll call anything we put out toward the center of the table. It follows, then, when he does have to lead in the betting, he tends to under bet the pot. This gives us the chance to look things over and perhaps to call for some good pot odds. Of course, when we do that, we have to complete a hand now and then or it can get expensive.

The calling station is ours. We simply have to have a good hand against him.

Sometimes it's hard to get those elusive cards. And then there are those times when he calls our big bet and improves his hand in a lucky draw for the win. Get ready. One day the draw outs will happen several times in a row. Calling Station river completions can be tough.

Because betting large amounts doesn't defer the true calling station, it's a lot like playing limit poker, except for the amount of our bets. Whoever has the best hand after the river wins.

We don't want too many of these types at our table; having more than one calling station drawing against us, no matter how much money, brings more draw outs and a bad run can get very expensive.

While it is practically dogma to have loose players on the left and tight players on the right, it is my personal preference to have the dyed-in-the-wool calling station on my right. That way, when he makes a bet, I know he has a good hand and will give me pot odds. And when he doesn't bet and I don't have a hand, it's easy not to do his betting for him.

In fact, this preference is born of liking all troublesome players that I have a hard time dominating, to be on my right. I'll only send my best against them.

True Domination.

- We play each of the players the way we've learned. We play them strong; we play them with power.

- We have to have a table we can dominate. This means we have to make a hand now and then in order to be feared. And we have to be strong. We can't play the limping game; we have to display power. When we find we aren't getting the hands to raise the limpers, we have to quit the game and play another time when we can truly dominate.

- We will play the opposite ends of the playing spectrum, the bullies and the callers, with patience and with focus. That, coupled with power, will make us Dominators.

Now, on with the refinements.

Discussion 401

The Difference between T A and Dominator

It is recommended that the reader begin this series with Part 101.

Poker is not a card game played by people.

Poker is a people game played with cards.

Murphy says, "A tight image is the best image you can have. As long as you have it, you have great opportunities to bluff."

If the reader has noticed the overlapping theories and contradictory explanations and examples, then the reader has followed well the theories and examples of this book. The bottom line is there are no strict rules concerning no limit hold 'em. The answer to almost anything poker is that we must play according to the experience we have gained.

However, there are differences between the definable player and the Dominator. Here's the story.

A few days ago, Murphy joined a no limit hold 'em game and it turned into one of those days in which he was a bit luckier than usual. Murphy was able to establish a tight and aggressive image early in the game by catching a couple of hands and getting called at the river. He was then able to bluff the next pots he was in and not get called. Additionally, Murphy was able to raise a few times on or near the button and harvest some blinds, some limper money and a couple of flop bets. He did all this with his tight image still intact.

Murphy had been playing for about an hour and a half in this game, without revealing a weak hand, when he raised on the button with an eight and nine suited. Murphy got a call from a limper type.

On the flop Murphy caught another eight, making middle pair. When the limper checked, Murphy made a continuation bet the size of the pot. The opponent surprised him with a call.

On the turn Murphy made another eight for trips. When the limper checked, Murphy bet enough to move him all in. Murphy was again surprised with a call.

As the rag on the river was being dealt, the two players showed their pocket cards. The opponent's chair went backwards, he stood and said in a loud voice "You can't have three eights. What're you doing? You play nothing but big cards!"

But there had been a change. Murphy now was glad to have the pot but, at this point, his tight aggressive image had been blown. Along with the tight image disappearing would be many of his intended string of bluffs to come. The entire table moved Murphy from tight aggressive status to the category of a player who will play a marginal hand. (Can you feel it when there is a change in attitude toward you? An honest "yes" answer is an important part of being a Dominator.) Now, the opponents will be more active against Murphy. And Murphy's game will change.

The tight image, an image the power player can normally start with, had lasted longer than usual for Murphy. And so now it was time to shift gears. Murphy now had to play as a player viewed as aggressive and who sometimes plays a marginal hand.

Now, Murphy will get more action with the occasional good hand. The biggest adjustment to make will be in picking his spots more carefully. It won't be hard to do; Murphy knows the players well at this point. He won't be able to bluff as much and he'll be ready to be called more. A more complicated game is afoot and Murphy has shifted gears.

The strong play made with a tight image and the ability to change and play well with a new image, are things that make the power player Dominant. When he or she has accomplished this, he or she is a Dominant player.

This Murphy story illustrates the difference between a tight aggressive player and the dominant power player. A TA in Murphy's chair never would have played the hands that were used to bluff, nor would he have played the hand that resulted in trip eights. And - this is important - he wouldn't have won as much as Murphy won on the trip eights and hands after the trip eights. Additionally, the true TA is not capable of shifting gears with each new and different image. Of course, by definition, a true TA won't ever have a new image to adjust to.

The tight aggressive player will do okay with novices when he gets good cards and the plebes and beginners pay him off.

The TA won't lose much when he has bad cards. But he will never win like the Dominator. In summary:

- The tight player is *waiting* for the hand that he *hopes* will be paid off.

- The loose player is *looking* for the hand that he *hopes* will be paid off.

- The Dominator is *playing* his hands according to his current image. He's playing the strong hand, the bluff and the trap that he *knows* will be paid off.

- The Dominator plays the table and responds according to his current image.

We will now proceed into the payoff section of this book. We will learn when and how to break most of the rules we have established for ourselves. We will learn to break them at the right time and for the right reasons.

But it is important once more to state that we should have played each of the four categories of playing: Tight Aggressive, Loose Aggressive, Tight Passive, and Loose Passive.

The experience is necessary in order to know the minds of the players in each category. The most valuable of these, and the one we should have the most experience in, is Tight Aggressive.

It would not be unreasonable to spend a year or two acquiring this experience with our new found knowledge. (I wonder how many readers are willing to do that.)

In any case, we must, in reaching this page, have all the disciplines deeply hypostasized. They must be a part of us and an automatic part of our play because we cannot break those rules until we know their value in the fullest sense.

In the following Discussions we will learn to shift gears, mix our play, confuse our opponents and use our power and be the table Dominator.

Discussion 402

The New No Limit and Domination

It is recommended that the reader begin this series with Part 101.

Poker is not a card game played by people.

Poker is a people game played with cards.

Opportunity for those who are not afraid.

Are you ready to DOMINATE?

By now you should be playing some good poker. You have become the dreaded Hustler. You win impressively. You win often and steadily. You lose now and then and sometimes you lose a large number of dollars. But you remain optimistic and you are ready to win bigger and even more often. If all these things are true, you are ready to be a Dominator and there is no better field of battle than $1 and $2 blinds no limit hold 'em.

The Weekend.

Just last weekend in Las Vegas there was a convention attended by an association of new business management hirelings. It was a convention of MBAs. These young people were just out of college and about a year or less in their new jobs. They eagerly marched on the no limit hold 'em games like columns of slide rule soldiers, ready for the battle of computation poker.

The de-briefings held by these young warriors after each hand played was, at first, kind of interesting, then funny, and at last absurdly long, repetitive and boring. Their analyses were full of percentages. The conversation was constant and predictable, and it was all about what would have happened if .... and who should have won if .... and so on. They didn't mind asking what opponents had when they quit a hand. I suppose, in their naiveté, their kind actually told the truth about what they had. The rest of us just told.

Place one weak player at a table and it doesn't take long for the experienced players to zero in on that player's main weakness and then start adding his other areas of vulnerability. Place one young business analyst at the table and there are many weaknesses for the experienced player to prey upon. Now multiply that by four, sometimes five or more, brave novices at the table, unwittingly ready for sacrifice, and we have an experienced players' feeding frenzy.

For the Dominators, there was that kind of opportunity for an entire weekend.

Some of the pilgrims played too loose and didn't know when to quit calling. They are easy to deal with and we help them slowly commit stack suicide.

Others played too tight and were throwing away too many hands, which is worse. How can that be worse? After all, money is lost on inferior hands.

If the reader doesn't know the answer to the above question, he doesn't know the nature of no limit and the upshot of these writings. He isn't ready for the no limit battle. He isn't ready to be a Dominator. Not knowing the central characteristic of hold 'em, which is to be aggressively dominant, the reader isn't ready to go to no-limit war and is encouraged to re-read these pages and gain more experience before attempting the ranks of Dominator.

Any time we are facing weak and inexperienced players who can be intimidated, it is our holy duty to take advantage of these players. The duty lies in the very definition of sacred Domination.

In past discussions, we reviewed several features of no limit that are different from limit games. Two of the more important characteristics related to the tenet of not playing tight in no limit hold 'em are:

- A player can bluff at any time because he can bet any amount effectively.

- While big hands win more pots than small hands, more large pots are won on marginal hands with a slight edge. They are hard for an opponent to recognize. They are easier for the Dominator to disguise. The marginal hand with an edge is the life marrow of the Dominator.

Now let's discuss the kinds of hands that win large pots and have that slight edge.

The humongous pots are won by us with hands like:

- Our aces up over weaker aces up.

- Our six to the ten straight, over a five to the nine straight, when the board shows a six, a seven, and an eight.

- Our ace flush over a king flush.

- Our two small pair over big slick when big slick has managed to make only one pair.

- Our trip deuces over aces and kings.

- Our set that is larger than the opponent's set - set over set.

- Our betting big slick like a Trojan against a garbage flop and accidentally making a wheel (We're entitled to a bit of luck.) and other unusual hands.

It takes courage and a bankroll. And it takes a little luck, but less luck than the weak players need. And that's the secret.

We will play many pots that never get to the stages above, simply because we have the power image and our early bets are often enough to bluff the pots over to our stacks.

We also recognize, through information gathering, those situations where we don't have that needed edge and we get away from those hands early for little cost. That's important, too.

And, sometimes, opportunity just doesn't present itself and we have a dry day.

We play more marginal hands and it's important that we know how. We must be able to tell when we have that slight edge. When we do, we'll bet that edge with confidence.

All this takes experience. We must play our players especially well and know when to make that big bet or all-in move. Experience can't be learned, it has to be lived.

We come to the table with an attitude of watching and learning. It isn't exactly like on TV; far from it. So we watch everything. There is much to learn, and we all learn something every time we play, even the most experienced.

We choose a card room that has no cap on the buy-in. Playing in a house in a $1 and $2 blinds game where we can only start with $100 makes no sense at all. We'll want to match the highest stacks on the table so that we won't get picked on and we can get value for all our hands and especially that one big hand. We want a stack big enough to Dominate the game.

We arrive at the no limit game with money we have set aside just for the game. We do that because we must be able to sit at the table and not be afraid of losing our money. An experienced player can smell the fear of losing. When he does, he'll bluff our stack away.

When we have the edge, we are very aggressive.

We protect our hand when we have the best hand. We get value for our winning hands and we know when and how to bluff. We, therefore, DOMINATE.

Now is the time to play the small games. There is a huge movement to no limit taking place right now. Most of it is in $1 and $2 blinds games. Many of the players are new which makes the situation fantastically rewarding.

Welcome aboard.

Discussion 403

The New Games in Town

It is recommended that the reader begin this series with Part 101.

Poker is not a card game played by people.

Poker is a people game played with cards.

The New No Limit Games.

Visitors to Las Vegas tell us no limit games are sweeping the country. They certainly have made their presence known in the card rooms of Tinsel Town. It seems no Las Vegas casino wants to be without one.

The exception now is the card room that *doesn't* have a small no limit game. We haven't been to all of them (a little hard to do), but we've been to a lot of them and the trend in poker is definitely toward no limit hold 'em.

The leading casinos in the low blinds no limit games have been $1 and $2 blinds with a minimum one hundred dollar buy-in and no maximum buy-in. And there is often a $2 - $5 blind game with a two hundred dollar minimum buy-in. We want the ones that also have no maximum buy-in.

By this time the reader should know the advantages of the no limit games that don't have a maximum buy-in (no "capped" buy-in). A game with no cap is the only true no limit game. The others limit the amount of money on the table and therefore affect the amount that can be bet and the amount that can be won.

It is also important to review something the reader already knows: The players in the no cap games determine the size and speed of the game by the amount they buy-in and the customary amount of the first raise. In this way, the casinos bend with the wishes of the players at the table. If that $1 and $2 blinds game is too big for us, we'll find one that's tamer. But most of the time we like the big small blind games because we can blind cheaply and play deeply. If there are some soft spots at the table we're in Dominator's paradise.

The good games are also nine handed, another feature favoring the players.

The only danger in the no cap game is the player who buys in for two or three times as much as the other players have in front of them and tries to bully the game. This type will again be discussed in these pages.

All games are designed by the house with the house in mind. Some of those houses have a buy-in cap of $200 or so which levels the playing field somewhat, keeps the pots small thereby keeping winnings low and the money in the game. Those games are a house delight; the players last longer and the rake is more constant. But we don't like them nearly as well as the no cap games.

The card room managers may tell us their capped buy-in rules protect the tourists by keeping the bullies from coming in. But we know the game is designed more to perpetuate the house rake. We're looking for no-cap games, thank you.

Sometimes the house's buy-in cap works against them. Some of the games will last for a long period of time resulting in a few winners with tall stacks. But the newly arrived players are prevented from protecting themselves with large buy-ins and the play becomes one sided. At that point, from the house's point of view, the game has gotten away from them and so has the rake because losers leave the game sooner and the game breaks up. Those things happen. Of course, if the house would lift the maximum buy-in, players could land in the game, protect themselves, and the game would keep going. But that's not in the house rules.

The difference between $1 and $2 blinds and $2 and $5 blinds.

Sometimes there is hardly a difference at all between the lowest $1 and $2 no limit blinds and, the next in line, $2 and $5 no limit blinds. The amount of the first raise and the aggressiveness of the games largely determine the size and type of action.

However, in general terms, the larger the blinds, the more action is encouraged. Also, when the minimum buy-in is larger, there is usually more action.

Probably the biggest difference lies in the larger game drawing more good players. We will usually find more soft spots in the smaller game.

Murphy played $2-$5 at Wynn last night, then $1-$2 at Binion's. Murphy thinks the apparent difference is not unusual. More experienced players are usually seen in the $2-$5 game, but last night brought an even more decided dichotomy.

When we can catch a $2-$5 game with a few pilgrims, we are lucky. However, Murphy's game had all experienced players, including a well known columnist for a national poker magazine. (Interestingly, he was one of the worst players, albeit the most vocal.)

Murphy played in the $2 - $5 game for two hours and got very few good cards, which kept his winnings low. But he finally managed a win of $145 when his pocket kings held up. He then made two check / raise bluffs (having few good cards, Murphy had a very tight image and made effective use of the check / raise bluff). Then he made a good call on an opponent's foolish Desperation Bluff. (Much more on these bluffs later.)

Under the circumstances, Murphy was happy with his small win. But the night was young and he decided to see what was happening at Binion's.

Benny's place was starting a $1-$2 game and Murphy sat with all new faces who were all beginners. Murphy played and won $437 in two hours in the smaller game.

The contrast in player profile was text book. It probably won't happen exactly like that again, but it was a good illustration in the difference between the two levels of games. The $1-$2 game is smaller, but softer. And it's a good place for the reader to start.

Let's Play a Hand.

We all know when we get sick; it's on the week end. We break our glasses or our legs on Sunday when the doctors aren't available. But, unlike other things in our lives, the best poker things usually happen on weekends and, if we aren't too dependant on those broken glasses, we have the best chances of doing well.

Here's a little weekend play. Nothing spectacular. But the hand demonstrates a few points.

The game was $1 and $2 blind and Murphy is in the number nine seat. A nice lady, an attractive lady he'd seen before, took the number seven seat. She's around sixty years old and she likes to play the game of hold 'em.

In the very first hand that Murphy played, he was next to the button and he held pocket kings. The pot was opened with calls from three early seats and a call from the new lady player. Murphy raised seven times the big blind because that's what Murphy had observed was required to take the limpers out. Two male players called Murphy's raise and so did the pleasant lady. With the pot four handed, Murphy decided next time to raise eight times the big blind.

The flop came with a queen, a four, and a five, rainbow.

Pocket	Pocket	Flop	Flop	Flop
K♦	K♠	Q♦	4♣	5♥

The first two players checked and the lady bet two thirds the size of the pot.

The two thirds bet told Murphy the lady was a little afraid of her money, especially in view of the fact that she held what was almost certainly top pair.

One of the early callers was in the small blind and he had been well established by Murphy as a call boy. Murphy didn't want him hanging around to draw to a small straight. Murphy wanted a bigger pot and he wanted to test the lady opponent on her evident fear of risking her money.

Murphy raised only the amount of her bet. It was a bet and raise large enough to drive out the call boy and probably the other player, and it was a bet small enough for the lady's two queens to call.

The two early players folded and the lady called.

Now Murphy felt confident his sole opponent had a queen and an ace in the pocket. And, by not re-raising, she was definitely afraid of risking her stack of checks.

The turn brought the eight of spades.

Pocket	Pocket	Flop	Flop	Flop	Turn
K♦	K♠	Q♦	4♣	5♥	8♠

The scared queens checked.

Murphy bet the size of the pot. It should be enough to discourage the frightened stack. On the other hand, the opponent could draw to her ace if she wanted to, but she would have to pay for it. She thought long and hard and folded her hand.

She then asked the dealer for a rabbit and the dealer, against the house rules which he broke for the nice lady, showed her the river would have been the ace of clubs.

Lessons Learned.

This wasn't a huge victory; and it's not something to be particularly proud of. But it points out a couple of things new Dominators should already know. It is the foundation of power play.

- Raise enough to drive the drawing players out.

- Play the players! In this case, find what the kicker to the queen is by raising. Murphy figured the opponent was scared of her money and wouldn't come back over the top with a bigger raise after Murphy only raised the amount of her bet. Also, she wouldn't have called a huge raise.

- Playing the players, Murphy thought the lady was a player who would call a raise that matched her bet, but only if she had an ace. Murphy could then place the lady on ace / queen.

- After determining the opponent had an ace kicker, Murphy wouldn't let the opponent draw without paying a good price. Sometimes, with some players, it has to be more than the size of the pot. (In this case, Murphy was glad she folded.)

Discussion 404

Gambler's Fallacy

It is recommended that the reader begin this series with Part 101.

Poker is not a card game played by people.

Poker is a people game played with cards.

Why is there a difference in betting an amount at one time and betting the same amount over several bets? It seems it's the same amount of money, after all. Why is there a mathematical as well as a *playable* difference in the two?

The answer lies in understanding **Gambler's Fallacy**.

My friend Christopher bounced around the card rooms of Las Vegas in the early 1960s. Always down on his luck, he nevertheless continued to be enterprising. He talked the manager of The Silver Spur, a small downtown casino on the northwest corner of Fremont Street and First Street, into leasing him space for a stud poker game. There was one table, one dealer and one Christopher wife as a shill who also observed the game and kept it honest. Meanwhile Christopher would take money from the stud game drop box and go three doors west to the Las Vegas Club to play the Faro Bank.

While Faro, along with poker, was a big part of the saloons of the old west, the game at the Las Vegas Club was, quite possibly at that time, the only Faro game left in the world.

Chris was glad the Faro game was there because he knew how to beat the game; he had a system. The trouble was, the system was based on Gambler's Fallacy.

Faro, or Faro Bank, is utter simplicity in its operation and betting. The players, gathered round the Faro table, could bet the house that a card, chosen by the player, would either come out of the box or stay in the box. That's about as complicated as it got.

The layout was a table with a likeness of each of the thirteen denominations of cards carved into its wooden surface. The dealer sat at the end of the table with a wooden box, slightly larger than a deck of cards.

The dealer would carefully shuffle and cut the deck without exposing any cards and just as carefully place the deck into the box again without exposing any cards. A house representative would witness the accuracy and integrity of the shuffle and placement of the deck into the box.

When the box was turned over, the players could see the bottom card of the deck because the bottom of the box was open, with a small frame around the edge. The frame kept the cards in the box.

After the box was turned over, what was the bottom of the box was then the top, with the top card exposed through the frame. The exposed card was the "cover card" and would be removed after the first betting.

The players were now free to bet which cards would come out of the box or stay in the box. They bet by placing their assigned color of chips (like the chips in roulette) on one of the carvings of the thirteen cards. If the chips were placed "straight up" on the carving, they were betting the card would stay in the box. If the checks were "coppered" (a small copper symbol, or a penny, on top of the chips), they were betting the card would come out of the box.

The dealer would then move the already seen "cover card" from the box by sliding it out of the side of the frame. Then he'd move the next card *out* of the box, leaving a card *in* the box, exposed through the frame.

If the card exposed through the frame had a bet on the carved table, the dealer would pay the player. If the bet was "coppered", he'd collect the bet for the house.

Likewise, if the card that came out had a "coppered" bet, the dealer would pay the player and, if the bet was "straight up", the dealer would collect the bet for the house.

If the bet was, say, on the five, and two fives showed themselves both in the box and out, the dealer would collect both bets for the house. The house took all ties, and that was the extent of the house advantage.

Faro devotees all knew if they waited for the case card (last five in the deck, in our example) then they didn't risk a tie, because the other three fives had already been played. By waiting for the last card, Faro was the only casino game anywhere that could be played without a percentage for the house.

Our feckless friend, Christopher, had it figured out. He would play only case cards and only those case cards whose predecessors, the other three fives in our case, either all came out or all stayed in. If they had all stayed in the box, that meant, he reasoned, that the last five stood a very good chance of coming out. Betting the case five, and betting it to do what the other three had not done, meant he had all the best of it. Right?

Wrong!! While there could be no tie, the last five had a fifty / fifty chance of coming out or staying in, just like its litter mates.

Gambling in the west, and gambling in general, was built on Gambler's Fallacy.

Today, the roulette wheels accommodate players by posting, above the wheel, the most recent history of the numbers chosen by the little white roulette ball, so the players can choose the numbers that haven't appeared recently. Similarly, in craps, if there hasn't been a field roll on the dice in five rolls, someone will make a field bet because the field "is due". If 79 and 80 haven't appeared on a Keno ticket all day, someone will bet 79 and 80 because they "are due". If someone at the craps table has hit the big six twice in the same dice hand, he'll take his bet down because he thinks the six has less chance of repeating.

All the assumptions in the above paragraph are dead wrong. In probabilities, where there is no outside physical influence, the past has no effect on the future.

Mismanaging the bankroll.

How did Christopher lose the money so quickly that he made by running the stud game at the Silver Spur? After all, his bets could never tie and so he had a 50 / 50 chance to win.

He lost by being so confident in his system, based on Gambler's Fallacy, that he over-played his bankroll. And that is the second most powerful item going for the house – players' mismanagement of their bankrolls.

It has been proven over again that, in a 50 / 50 situation, the house will win in the long run because it has the most money and the gambler will over-play what he is prepared to lose.

In that sense, Gambler's Fallacy gives the player an excuse to bet too much, run out of bankroll, and make the house happy.

However, if anyone can find a Faro Bank somewhere, he can play with an even chance to win, if he stays disciplined, in control, and exercises good management. But, watch out. A progressive betting system may be the loser if it is under funded.

Better than even.

On the other hand, the poker power player doesn't want an even chance; he wants more than an even chance. The experienced poker player doesn't want the best gamble; he wants the least gamble.

In playing hold 'em, dividing the bet we might make after the flop into two bets, flop and turn, or three bets if we include the river, is not the same in mathematical probabilities as making the sum of those bets in one bet after the flop, because each player must pay for each card after it is dealt. Not only does dividing the bet fail to protect our hand, it gives the opponents multiple chances for the same amount of money with an increase in pot odds with each card. Each event - flop, turn and river - is a separate event with its own probabilities, none of which is influenced by the other except for the fact that there is one less card in the deck.

Gambler's Fallacy is a weakness found in many players in hold 'em. The lower blinds no limit games are especially ripe with this type of thinking. It is born from tagging along with the betting in low limit games and is one fallacy the Dominator of $1 and $2 no limit games can take advantage of.

Many players will call raises with a small pocket pair because they are "due" for a set. Some opponents will call any bet for a draw to a flush on the river because they are "due". We're quite sure the "live straddle" player thinks that way; he wants to make his raise first before he sees his cards that are "due" and to act last for the same reason. While we occasionally may be drawn out on because of Gamblers' Fallacy, in the long run the power player takes good advantage of the fallacy thinker. Like the casinos, we're glad to have him around.

Discussion 405

Pot Odds, Real and Implied

It is recommended that the reader begin this series with Part 101.

Poker is not a card game played by people.

Poker is a people game played with cards.

Pot Odds.

While pot odds opportunities are often available in limit poker games, they are found less frequently in no limit games because of the many choices of betting levels and techniques.

Limit? It's easy. If the only bet available is 1/6 of the amount of the pot, we can often make the drawing call because the ratio of the pot to the bet is better than the ratio of the outs to the remaining deck. The same kind of call can be made against us. So no limit easily becomes the game of choice for protecting one's hand.

No limit? It's harder to find a favorable ratio. And we, as power players, never give those kinds of odds. However, because there are so many weak players in the lower blinds no limit games, others often make the opportunity available to us.

On the following page is a chart that makes the calculation of pot odds much easier than most writers and technical type players would have us believe.

In the thick of poker contests, all we need is a simple chart for easy calculation. The following is designed for those times when we're in the heat of battle and the bullets are flying.

The percentage column shows the approximate chance of helping a four card hand with a one card draw. The "chances" column gives that approximation in ratio, something the player can easily apply when under pressure. The column in red (last column) MUST be memorized for each of the five situations.

250

The chart is for drawing one card only because there is usually a bet after the one card (turn) creating yet another pot odds decision for the river. A similar calculation must be made for each time a card is to come. However, if we are in a situation where our opponent is all-in or other like condition where we can get two cards with only one bet, then the odds can be divided by two. For instance, B. will rise to better than 1 chance in 1.5 when we are assured of two draws for the price of one bet.

Chances of Helping a Hand after the Flop – One Card Only		
	%	*approx*
A. An open ended straight, a four card flush and an existing pair.	46.8	1 in 2
B. An open ended straight and a four card flush.	36.1	1 in 3
C. A four card flush and an existing pair.	36.1	1 in 3
D. Completing a four card flush only.	19.1	1 in 5
E. Completing an open ended straight only.	17.0	1 in 6

Any time the money odds (the ratio of the amount of our call to the money in the pot) are better than the odds for drawing, in the chart above, we have the financial opportunity to make the call.

Hastily, it should be pointed out that, even though the money odds are in our favor, the odds of completing our hand are against us in each case. Therefore, the failures to make the hand must be financed until we can complete one of our draws in a later hand and win the big bucks. However, in the long run, we make money by taking advantage of the imbalance of pot odds to hand odds. We often miss a few (which must be financed) until we hit a winner. And sometimes we hit two or even three winners in a row. If we're able to keep books on these events, we'll find we're on the plus side at the end of a given long period of time.

Implied Pot Odds.

Now comes an opportunity presented to us quite often but infrequently described or explained by writers and seldom taken advantage of by the average player. The opportunity is best illustrated in the following hand played by Murphy.

Murphy is on the button in a $1 and $2 dollar no limit hold 'em game. He holds a queen and a nine, suited in clubs. Several dinking players have called the $2 blind and Murphy makes his button raise of $15, making it $17 to play.

Surprisingly, the small blind calls. A player also calls from middle position. The others fold. The blind is an ordinary player, tight passive, and the middle player is a man who is not afraid of his money but is weak in strategy. He is losing and trying to double his stack.

With three players contributing the big blind and limping money, the pot now amounts to $57.

The flop is all red, bringing a deuce and two queens.

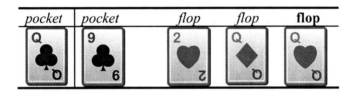

The blind timorously ventures a weak bet of $15 in his usual passive style. The middle player calls.

Murphy was expecting a bet from the opponents and, before the bet and call, Murphy had been ready to fold his hand because of his weak kicker and no clubs in the flop; almost any other trip queens would have won.

But the weak bet and call makes it interesting. A weak bet and a simple call of less than one third of the pot deserve a test raise.

Murphy raises $60.

The blind unhesitatingly calls and so does the middle man. The middle player's call is especially interesting to Murphy. The pot is now $282, less a $4 rake, for a total of $278.

Murphy, at this point, places the blind on three queens with a poor kicker and places the middle man on deuces full, trying to set a trap. The intended trap explains the middle man's unhesitating calls, pre-flop and post-flop. Murphy also sees that the blind is short stacked with less than $100 and the middle player has about $800.

252

The turn card is the five of diamonds.

pocket	pocket	flop	flop	flop	**turn**
Q♣	9♣	2♥	Q♦	Q♥	5♦

The blind goes all-in for $97.

The middle man calls the $97, not wanting to lose Murphy.

The action is now on Murphy.

The pot totals $472 and Murphy can call with $97. However, Murphy believes he is beat by the middle man's deuces full and may even be beat by the blind's three queens. What should he do?

Murphy knows that if no helps comes, the deuces full will win the pot. Likewise, if the board pairs a deuce, he's finished.

Murphy also knows that, if the board pairs the five of diamonds, he will split the main pot with the blind and win any side pot with the middle player for a probable large amount. Additionally, Murphy knows that, if he pairs his pocket nine, he will win both pots for an even larger amount.

And what else does he know?

Murphy knows that, if he calls the $97, he will have only $172 invested in an existing $569 pot.

Now, it's time to compute the implied odds and Murphy will take his time doing it.

Murphy knows, with almost any river card available, the middle man plans to go all-in with his deuces full of queens. Money odds from the almost certain future money to go into the pot is what makes the implied odds.

The people game has brought Murphy to this point and now that he knows the how the opponents are likely to act, it is no longer a people game and the play is reduced to mere arithmetic.

253

When the all-in happens, the two pots will total well over $1,250 with no additional money at risk from Murphy, other than the $97 call.

We need only to compute roughly. Murphy has approximately one chance in fifteen of helping his hand and splitting the pot. And he has about one chance in fifteen to win the pot with a nine on the river. So, barring the unlikely appearance of a fourth deuce, Murphy has about one chance in seven and a half of winning something.

The money odds, existing and implied, are 97 to about 1250, or almost thirteen to one.

The calculation of calling with $97 for a seven and one half chance of winning something to a possible thirteen to one in money odds makes Murphy call the $97 all-in bet.

This hand was actually played and we all know how it came out – Murphy got a nine on the river. How could this have happened? Luck of the Irish?

The middle player with the deuces full will undoubtedly go somewhere and tell his best friend, probably many friends, how he flopped a full house, went all-in and was drawn out on at the river for one of the worst bad beats of his life.

The middle man will be right in that he was drawn out on, but it was not a bad beat - his hand was woefully misplayed. (His friends will never hear that part.) In his eagerness to double his stack by not losing Murphy after the turn, he sent an invitation to be drawn out on.

After the turn, the blind went all-in for $97. At this point, the deuces full can't afford to take a chance with what are obviously three queens in at least one place, maybe two places; logically, he has to make a big raise against Murphy to reduce the number of trip queens drawing for a full house. But he fails to do so.

You see, in computing the implied odds, Murphy computes only the remaining stack in front of the deuces full player because Murphy will never have to risk his money if he makes a full house with his queens; he'll have the nuts for at least a split main pot with the blind or all of both pots if his pocket nine pairs. If he doesn't make a full house of some sort, he folds and he has had his chance at a $1,250 pot for $97.

254

If the deuces full had not misplayed his hand and he had gone all-in after the turn instead after the river, Murphy would have had to commit around $800 to see the river card. This would have been an impossible pot odds decision. Murphy would have had to fold and be disappointed when he saw the nine arrive on the river.

One of the huge advantages of no limit hold 'em over limit play is being able to make the proper large bet at the right time to protect a winning hand and reduce the number of bad beats. Unlike Murphy's middle man, we will never give an opponent the opportunity for such tempting pot odds, existing or implied.

And we will take advantage of pot odds when offered to us.

Discussion 406

All-In with Big Slick

It is recommended that the reader begin this series with Part 101.

Poker is not a card game played by people.

Poker is a people game played with cards.

The Dominator with Big Slick.

A good reader asks if we should go all-in before the flop with pocket tens when the blind has moved all-in with pocket ace / king.

The answer to his question is, "Of course not." That part is easy. The hard part is in knowing how our reader knew the opponent had exactly ace / king.

We'll suppose our reader is asking a mathematical question and wants to know the odds of the tens holding up through the river. The answer is the odds are so close to even, it is a gamble for both players and that isn't what we're normally looking for. There are exceptions and those are addressed elsewhere in these pages.

In fact, in good company at a full table cash game with no one short stacked, we don't go all-in pre-flop very often with anything but aces. In good company, the all-in move comes after a couple of raises and, after those two or more raises, anything less than pocket aces are not worth the risk of an all-in move.

Yes, it's true. There are <u>often</u> occasions when we should throw pocket kings away in the face of an all-in move.

Stated again, if our kings don't get the last raise after our initial raise, they usually aren't good, in good company. But when the game is loose or even wild, we will play our players and sometimes play our kings.

256

There are circumstances, naturally, when we have moved the right player all-in when we had pocket kings, and sometimes with pocket pairs of far less distinction than the noble kings.

The math is easy. The harder part of mucking pocket kings or moving all-in is picking the right time. The Dominator knows picking the right time depends, not on the science of mathematics, but on the art of playing the player.

Sometimes a player will be short stacked and make an all-in move and our Big Slick will call with confidence. There is little to risk, the opponent is probably reaching with a so-so hand. If we sense desperation, we'll move the short stack in every time with Big Slick.

The fascination with Big Slick continues for good reason. While the big guy, when unsuited, is ranked number ten in our starting hands, which is based on the number of pots and money won with starting hands, Big Slick looms larger than his ranking. It is because he is comprised of the two largest cards in the deck and because of the occasional need for such plays as an all-in move before the flop.

Obviously, the best all-in pocket starter is two aces. The second best all-in pocket is two kings. But if Big Slick is up against either of those, two of his matching cards are holding temporary residence with the opponent. With most of his mates already gone, Big Slick is drawing from a short odds deck. He's in a world of hurt, especially if the opponent is holding aces, because his kings aren't any good even if he pairs. Therefore, we can't send Big Slick into an all-in draw against the type of player who goes all-in before the flop with only ace pairs and king pairs.

But what about pocket queens for the opponent? The chances of Big Slick winning the draw against pocket queens, as with the tens above, are against him by a ratio of about five to four, or close to even. (Further math refinement is unnecessary. Totally, young dude. Approximate odds are all you need.) But, when we include the blind money, all limper calls, and money from first raise calls, pot odds level the risk reasonably for big slick. (It's massively obvious, dude. You know, approximation is way cool because the crux of the game lies in playing the players.) The decision to go all-in will depend mostly on the type of opponent we're facing and what he's likely to be holding.

The lower the opponent's pocket pair, the better the chances for ace / king. Not so much because of the power of rank, but because of the chances for the ace / king to make a straight. Even better for king / queen because it is open ended. And the same kind of small advantage for a flush is true if Big Slick happens to be suited. But the odds are still around 5-4 plus pot odds, or about even.

The opponent's pocket pair is far less likely than Big Slick to make either a flush or a straight, and straights and flushes will not often be the main concern. The main event for Big Slick on the board is simply catching an ace or a king. And, because we are all-in before the flop, we have five cards to look at without paying a high price for the view.

Again, we don't often go all-in, pre-flop, with Big Slick in a cash game. Usually, we don't have enough invested in the hand to risk a showdown play. That rule changes if the opponent is short stacked and desperate. On those occasions we have less to lose and we may quite possibly have the best starting hand. The rule of thumb should be to go all-in pre-flop if the all-in amount is limited to pot size. Early in the hand, it's usually a small pot. The rule is only a rule of thumb to be tempered by the profile of the opponent.

Side bar. Many players may not realize, in a showdown hand against big pocket pairs the middle suited connectors are better than a small or a middle pocket pair. The odds still aren't good, but they are better than the chances with a middle pair.

Discussion 407

The Tightest Player at the Table

Poker is not a card game played by people.

Poker is a people game played with cards.

It is recommended that the reader begin this series with Part 101.

Playing tight.

How do you know when an opponent is playing tight? Be careful with your answer.

Griff ("The Grifter"), a good and experienced player, was playing in a $2 and $5 blinds in a no limit game and it was just one of those days when good cards were hard to come by. The Grifter was down a few hundred.

There were some good players in this game. They were waiting for the $5 and $10 game to start and were biding their time in the smaller hold 'em game. In fact, all the players were good players except two. The first of those two was situated to The Grifter's right and the second one was a player was to Griff's immediate left. The one on the left was a knowledgeable but inexperienced young hot shot, one of the new breed.

Griff was able to win a pot after a while and then was able to bluff a couple of small pots. But, other than that small action, he was busy throwing bad pockets away.

Not that he threw every hand away, of course. When he was near the button, he would raise with marginal hands, not get rewarded in the flop, and then he would muck the hand.

Griff knew he had to stay active. As a result, he didn't show any of his hands and a quick stack count showed he was only slightly in the losing column.

Being on the losing side didn't bother Griff. He knew that one good pot would move his ledger balance to the plus side and two good pots would place him solidly among the winners.

The young hot shot to Griff's left was named Todd. Todd was cocky. He believed he knew so much more than the rest of the players at the table. He was slick. He liked to set traps. He confidently displayed a pile of $100 bills that was way more than what Griff had on the table.

The Hand.

In this particular hand, Todd was on the button which meant Griff was next to the button. There were two limpers in the pot and Griff raised $25 with his ace and three, suited in diamonds. Todd immediately called. The blinds and the limpers folded. It was now heads up, Griff and Todd on the button.

The flop delivered deuce, queen, six.

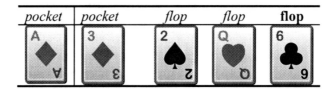

As usual, Griff got none of his diamonds and his luck seemed to have wasted another pre-flop raise. Griff checked his garbage hand to young Todd who had eagerly called the raise. At this point, as far as Griff was concerned, Todd could bet and take it.

But Todd checked along. Maybe Todd believed Griff would know the queen hadn't helped.

But the Grifter wondered about the check-along. Pocket jacks?

The turn brought the five of hearts.

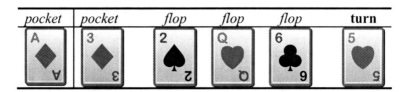

Griff again checked. (Go ahead, Todd, bet and take it.)

Todd checked.

The river was the four of clubs. (The Grifter never did get a diamond.)

pocket	pocket	flop	flop	flop	turn	river
A♦	3♦	2♠	Q♥	6♣	5♥	4♣

Griff decided to over-bet the pot to make it look like he was trying to steal it. He bet $100.

Todd jumped. (He was young.) Todd raised $200, making the bet $300 total.

Now Griff had to decide whether Todd had a three and a seven to make the higher straight. No, that wouldn't be at all logical.

How about a seven and an eight? More likely, but improbable.

Todd had eagerly called The Grifter's pre-flop raise, so there shouldn't be any small cards in his hand, unless it was a small pair. Ah, yes, a small pair. Twice Todd had been in a position to bet and take the pot when there was minutia on the board but he hadn't taken either opportunity. With a seven and an eight, it would have been bet and take it time for Todd.

So, it was easy to see, Todd was sandbagging and trying to set a trap - with a set of queens? No. Pocket queens in the hands of Todd on the button would have been reason to re-raise before the flop.

Could he have a set of another kind? Yes, he could. But then, was Todd such a bad player he would actually call a pre-flop raise with a small pair?

Maybe Todd's after river raise was a bluff. If Todd had put Griff on a bluff and now was coming over the top with a weak hand, the young upstart **couldn't** call a re-raise from Griff. And, if he had less than a straight, he **shouldn't** call a re-raise. Was the action over? The Grifter decided to do a little selling.

"Well let's see," he began mumbling, just loud enough for the kid beside him to hear.

"You called my raise before the flop, so you must have big cards. You couldn't bet after the flop because of the small board cards. You didn't bet after the turn because your big cards still hadn't been helped."

After a pause, Griff continued, growing slowly more audible. "You might have a pair of queens with an ace, which would make my two pair good." Griff looked up at the dealer. "I'm all-in," he said with emphasis.

"I call," was the quick response. Todd was eager to show his hand. He smiled directly at Griff and turned over his cards, showing a flopped set of sixes.

The Grifter showed his straight and began counting his paper and checks to indicate to the dealer how much Todd owed him.

Todd squirmed. "You had a three? A three?" He seemed to writhe in anguish. He looked at the other players for understanding and sympathy. His voice grew quite loud. "He's the tightest player at the table. How could I think he had a three?" The others merely smiled.

Todd removed his dark glasses, stared at the floor and then pushed his chair back. He took out his flip top cell phone and made a call. "Man, you won't believe this bad beat. I just got a set of sixes drawn out on. He was all-in. The guy drew to a straight against my set and he's the tightest player at the table."

When Todd's attention focused once more on the game, he took a moment to glower at the Grifter. "Nice hand. Keep playing that way and I'll get it all back."

Griff looked at him evenly. "You have a lot to learn."

Lessons illustrated:

- There are young inexperienced players even in the sophisticated games, losing their money while they slowly learn how to play better.

- Because a player isn't seeing hands through, is folding in the face of flop after flop, is raising before the flop and is throwing the pockets away after a re-raise, does not necessarily mean he's a tight player. It just could be he's not getting any good cards. Seeing the hands he shows is the only sure way to determine whether a player is playing only premium cards. Todd thought he was playing his player, but Todd didn't have a clue.

- Play your players well. Todd misread Griff in a serious way. Griff had Todd pegged all the way down to the hidden set.

- Small pocket pairs should not call a lonely pre-flop raise. The math just doesn't work.

- Then there is the pre-flop raise with many callers creating a big pot before the flop. In those cases there is a big pot to be won and those odds plus the implied pot odds are astronomical. Not only are the pot odds and implied pot odds good, most of the premium cards may be held by the many other players making big cards largely unavailable to them in the flop. So, in those situations, we'll see the next three cards and be prepared to throw the pocket pair away when they aren't helped. If they are helped, we'll play strongly and wisely, not like Todd.

- Once a set is flopped, we'll be careful of the possible flushes and straights. Young Todd was in last position and should have bet a big amount after the turn in order to stay in control. But Todd wanted to win a bigger pot; he wanted the trap; he wanted Griff to bet first - so Griff finally did. From the start, Todd went to a lot of trouble to call a pre-flop raise, draw to a weak hand, luckily flop a good hand and then lose control of the play. He didn't just let Griff stay in the hand, he invited him to stay.

- Redux. The inactive player may not be a tight player. We have to see some of his cards to be sure.

Discussion 408

The Importance of Defense

It is recommended that the reader begin this series with Part 101.

Poker is not a card game played by people.

Poker is a people game played with cards.

Question: What day do we decide to play poker?

Answer: On a day we know we can win.

Oh, Oh. Let's be careful with this one.

We have to make sure feeling wonderful is not the wrong time to play.

It's a great day! We wake up feeling like the day is ours. We take a little more time with our appearance. Today is the day we can make an impression. Today is the day we will make our presence known at the poker table.

We feel our game has reached its pinnacle in strategy and execution. The poker table is ours. We will win because we have it figured out. We will make those winning hands, the ones we have seen in our imagination. They are big pots. We'll play like we did last time we made that monster win. We have the knowledge and the knack. We can hardly wait.

We arrive at the casino and report to the floor manager like a warrior ready for battle. We're full of confidence; our weapons are at the ready and are ours to decisively wield. We're ready for our chips and our chair.

We go to the table. We greet the other players with whom we are familiar. We chat a little. Why shouldn't we? We're confident. We're there to win and we know we can.

Anything wrong here?

Probably. We evidently, from the usual point of view, are not ready to play our "A" game. We're not confident; we are cocky. We're not sure; we are vain. We aren't seeking a win; we are seeking approval. We're here to make the mark we deserve.

Of course things at the table aren't going to happen just the way we hoped and, with our cockiness and our ebullient optimism, we are set up to be too pushy and to make a lot of wrong moves and be taken advantage of.

There are good players at that table who are waiting for the overconfident player. We're going to be caught by these barracudas every time we're cocky enough to swim in the wrong waters.

Ever been there? Ever feel that way? Ever lose for being overconfident?

We all have. When we play with an overconfident attitude we are playing our "B" game at best, possibly our "C" game. Either of those is a losing game. And then, when we start to lose, history shows we will want to plunge deeper into those waters, too anxious to re-gain that fleeting approval we thought we should have and are still seeking.

Let's look at what we're doing when we take those kinds of losses. What's missing in our approach on that wonderful day of brilliant bullishness?

The biggest answer: Defense.

Although we are aggressive power players, we have to protect our flanks and our stacks. When we fail to do so, we invite the enemy to raid our spoils.

First, when we approach the table, we must recognize we are not visiting our friends. Those people are our adversaries. They are there to take our money. We must not only know that fact, we must treat those adversaries accordingly. We should be polite because we are ladies and gentlemen, but our courtesy must be like that of duelists in the morning fog, far more cordial than friendly.

Next, we must take the attitude that those adversaries will not, cannot, get our money. We must be fully defensive toward our stacks. Make objective starts in the hands. Get away from the hands at the right time. Raise judiciously. Watch for the traps. Never, ever, count on the draw.

265

We will not overlook two holed straights on the board.

We will not forget to put the opponents on a hand, a specific hand.

We will not overlook the calls which may be signaling a good hand.

We will watch for strength from apparent weakness and hidden set traps.

We will study our opponents and look for patterns and tells so that we won't be put to a guess when are faced with the opponent's sudden big bet.

If we can apply a good defense to go with our original General Patton attitude, we will win the day.

Defense is part of a winning attitude that an entirely offensive attitude can't provide. If we watch our flanks, don't get in too much hurry, don't worry about image other than our poker playing image, we are capable of playing our "A" game and taking home the money.

A quiet confidence is better than a cocky overconfidence.

And so the question is begged once more: How well do we know ourselves?

Are we really there for the winning? Or are we there to make our mark, to prove our superiority? Knowing ourselves really well will help here.

Have we ever said to ourselves, "Look here, Self. I don't quite feel like you could have a balanced game today. You're too moody and a little off center. I think you and I will skip a day at the table and wait for a better time."

When we can do that, we know ourselves well enough to be consistent winners. We're ready to Dominate the game because we know, recognize and control our weaknesses.

Discussion 409

Shifting Gears and Mixing Play

It is recommended that the reader begin this series with Part 101.

Poker is not a card game played by people.

Poker is a people game played with cards.

Shifting Gears.

Shifting gears means the power player changes style and image when necessary, sometimes in mid-hand. Shifting and mixing are crucial to Dominating the table.

What does shifting gears mean? It simply means we change our style of play. Shifting gears should not be confused with changing the amounts of our bets or the method we use to make our bets or any other thing except changing from our current style of play to TA, TP, LA or LP. (These styles have already been discussed by us many times.) We make those changes as the situation calls for the change.

The power player can make those changes at moment's notice, with the rattle of an opponent's checks. In doing so, we are mixing our play, which helps to keep adversaries off balance. And the power player is aware which style should be used at any given time.

Example.

Murphy has established his power image and he is the aggressor at a small blinds, no limit table. He now has the image that will take advantage of strong play.

Murphy is in late position and everybody has folded and the player on his right, Mr. Loose, raises the pot.

Murphy has noticed that Mr. Loose likes to bet the size of his hand, a large bet for a good hand and a small bet for a small hand. (This is a common pattern tell in small no limit poker.) Murphy also knows this player will raise near the button with a weak hand.

Murphy is holding a king and queen suited.

Mr. Loose has raised and it's up to Murphy. My girl friend says don't ever call, but let's look at this situation. If Murphy raises, Mr. Loose will call his raise, just to see the flop. When Murphy makes that raise, he will be building a pot, but he won't learn anything about the opponent's hand because he knows he will be called, regardless – more money, nothing learned. And, after all, the Dominator's biggest reason for a pre-flop raise is to gain information.

So Murphy will mix his play. He'll call this time. Mr. Loose won't notice that Murphy digressed from his usual raise because Mr. Loose concentrates mostly on his own hand. What happens next will depend on the cards that fall and the action supplied by Mr. Loose.

The flop brings a jack, an eight, and a six.

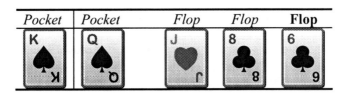

Mr. Loose, first to act, makes a bet that is about half the size of the pot, a weak bet. Still, as small as his hand may be, he has taken the initiative, possibly with the best hand. Many players in Murphy's place will fold at this point and they wouldn't be wrong; it's the safe play.

However, because Mr. Loose has made a small bet, Murphy now has some useful information and he'll put the opponent on an ace / rag until there is more evidence.

It's a raised pot with an additional bet. At this point, Murphy could try to raise him out of the pot. If Murphy raises Mr. Loose, Murphy could take the pot. But a raise would be chancey because Mr. Loose, as evidenced by his name and Murphy's study, likes to call and he undoubtedly has the best hand at this point. He may have a small pair, maybe top pair.

Since Murphy knows Mr. Loose to be a caller, Murphy will call the weak bet for fairly good pot odds and see what the turn brings.

The turn gives the players the deuce of diamonds.

Pocket	Pocket	Flop	Flop	Flop	**Turn**
K♠	Q♠	J♥	8♣	6♣	2♦

The turn helped no one. Or did it?

Now Mr. Loose checks his hand.

Murphy bets more than the size of the pot. Murphy wins. The deuce helped.

The deuce was not what Murphy wanted, but that's not the point of the play. Murphy was playing Mr. Loose's hand along with him and the hand wasn't helped by the deuce. The loose, calling player plays mostly his own hand and, in this case, he didn't make one.

What did Murphy risk by calling after the flop? He risked Mr. Loose getting a favorable turn card and he risked the amount of the small call.

If the turn shows a jack, an ace, another club or a connector to the eight and six, Murphy may have had to throw his hand away when the opponent bet. Murphy would have had to guess but, instead, he could make a big bet.

This technique works well against opponents whose pattern of play we know well. When we know our opponents, we can help them play their hands. Every Dominator does it often and with impunity. The Dominator's biggest secret is the ability to play the other player's hand.

The Dominator can win with either his own good hand or the opponent's poor hand.

Discussion 410

More Calling Stations

It is recommended that the reader begin this series with Part 101.

Poker is not a card game played by people.

Poker is a people game played with cards.

Pocket Aces.

First a word about pocket aces. A little review.

We nearly always raise with pocket aces in order to gain information, to build a pot and to protect our hand. We want value for our hand. We also raise to get rid of the limpers. We don't want a bunch of cheap shots taken at our aces because, surely, one of them will connect. Less than five players (that means four or less in the pot, which in turn means three opponents) will be satisfactory. Two opponents would be better. But the odds are usually good enough for our aces to hold up with three opponents and the size of the pot will give us good value for our hand. We raise an amount calculated to leave us with two opponents but if three opponents happen to call, it will be just fine.

The exceptions to the above general rules would be in a tournament where we could eliminate an opponent by placing him all-in before the flop, or in a cash game when we might do the same thing with a player who has an affinity for the pre-flop all-in play.

Murphy's Hand.

In a no limit hold 'em cash game, Murphy had been playing in the number three seat for about fifteen minutes. He had most of the players lined up to some extent and the number six chair, in particular, was easy surveillance. He was a calling station and, this time, a thinking calling station.

The gentleman (truly a young gentleman) was from California. He had the garb and the attitude of today's in-touch poker player.

The Californian wore the little dark glasses, dressed in polyester, displayed a big gold watch, and he had the customary slouch of the calm poker chemist. He was quiet, analytical, and he played the odds. He raised when he had high pocket cards and he limped in when he had connectors. He was an easy read. And he had a bad habit of calling.

Murphy was dealt pocket aces.

The calling station was on the button. The number nine chair was under the gun and opened the pot. The next player raised. The player to Murphy's right re-raised.

That was enough players for Murphy and, not wanting to drive the opener out, Murphy merely called the re-raise. Please note that Murphy is not slow playing the hand by slow play definition; he has the information he needs and he has just the number of opponents to make it worthwhile. He isn't interested in the trap nearly as much as he's interested in a nice, protected pot and value for his hand.

The Calling Station jumped the two raise fence with ace / king suited in spades.

The opener folded. The raiser called the re-raise, leaving a total of four in the hand. The situation was close to perfect with two of the players to act before Murphy. The calling station was to act after Murphy. There was a good prospect of having only two adversaries, or a heads up situation, in the near future.

The flop brought a five, a seven, and a king.

271

The two players checked to Murphy. Murphy bet the size of the pot. With two previous raises, four handed, it was a nice sized pot. The Calling Station called. The other two players folded. Now it was heads up.

The turn brought the king of diamonds.

flop	flop	flop		turn
5♣	7♣	K♥		K♦

Murphy knew if he checked, the opponent would bet; it would be an open invitation to steal the pot and Murphy wasn't ready to give up to a bluff. So Murphy took the initiative and control. He bet the size of the pot.

The Calling Station called, of course; he very seldom raised. But now Murphy knew, because the Calling Station was a passive caller, he probably had three kings and Murphy was ready to muck the hand after the river.

The river gave the gift that keeps on giving, the case ace.

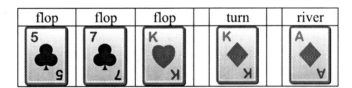

flop	flop	flop		turn		river
5♣	7♣	K♥		K♦		A♦

Murphy bet the size of the pot. The Calling Station raised the amount of Murphy's bet. Murphy moved all-in. After a long, long time and a lot of analysis, the Calling Station called. No surprise in the call.

Besides the opponent's habit of calling, what happened here? Yes, we all know, Murphy got lucky. What else? Here's what else happened.

The opponent reviewed, in his mind, how the betting went, and that's what he's supposed to do. He remembered Murphy didn't raise; Murphy flat called two pre-flop raises.

But the Calling Station had read Murphy as a raiser and so surely Murphy would raise with pocket aces. Also, Murphy bet into the board kings after the turn and, by just calling, the Calling Station had Murphy set up for the big bet after the river, a bet the Calling Station didn't want to miss out on. The ace, he reasoned, gave Murphy aces up, either that or Murphy missed his flush. The Calling Station was sure his trap had worked.

Surely, it must have worked, he felt; he worked so hard at it. His analysis told him either Murphy was betting aces up for value or Murphy was bluffing. Either way, the Calling Station could call with his kings full of aces.

Lessons learned:

- Don't be a Calling Station.

- Don't jump two raises with king / queen suited. (In this case, the king / queen player was lucky and it worked out. He just didn't take advantage of it by making a sizable bet.)

- When we have those trip kings with someone betting at us, we'll move him in before he makes something!

- We're constantly ready to shift playing gears.

- We won't be afraid to bet for information. It won't be a weak bet because a weak bet is a tell in good company and it also encourages a call that will bring little information. We'll make our usual kind of bet, the size of the pot. But the information better be worth it.

- Full house over full house is usually a very big pot.

Discussion 411

The Importance of Stacks

It is recommended that the reader begin this series with Part 101.

Poker is not a card game played by people.

Poker is a people game played with cards.

The size of stacks becomes very important to the Dominator. It is item number four on our big list.

First, as we all know, we play our players.

Second, as we all know, we try to find some good cards.

Third, as we all know, we play our position.

Now comes number four, the size of stacks

Many inexperienced players will look at the tall stack across the table and think to themselves, "I'm going to play nothing but strength against this player so I can be sure of having a chance of beating him instead of losing my stack to him." For the Dominator, this notion is entirely wrong.

Short stacks.

First, we must once more establish that we are never short stacked. We can't win much with a short stack, so we make sure we have as much, or nearly as much, in front of us as the highest stack at the table. When we have the tall stack ammunition, we're ready to play well and win that big hand; it may be the amount we win for the day. Above all, we are experienced and we are confidant.

In Domination poker, the opponents' stacks become important because they affect all the other appearances in the game. For instance, poor players generally will be the ones who are short stacked. On the other hand, good players know enough to have ammunition for their pocket guns.

274

Another thing. Because most short stacked players are weak, those players often will be the ones we can't bluff too well. For that reason, we will usually need a good hand against the short stacked players. Tall stacks, however, can often be bluffed.

But there are more reasons for playing the good hand against short stacks. Because there is less to win, we can't take the chance of playing the marginal hand; there just isn't enough money to make it worthwhile.

Let's look at our button position with pocket sixes.

If there are only a couple of limpers along with the blinds, we might like to raise with this innocuous little pair; maybe we could take down the money then and there and, if not, we have a good chance of winning a larger pot with just the two sixes because we were first to raise and we have position after the flop.

But let's say the pot was raised by a middle player who is short stacked. We have approximately one chance in eight of helping our hand in the flop. With the short stack player as an adversary, we have little money to win and a slim chance of doing it. So, we throw our tiny sixes away and hope it won't be long until the next hand is dealt.

In conclusion, playing against the short stack requires a good hand on our part unless we sense the short stack wants to lose and be through for the day. In that case, a marginal pair or big slick with an all-in bet may be just the thing to put him out of his misery.

Tall stacks.

Let's take a look at the tall stack who is a good player.

In many situations the table will be composed of weak players and a tall stack that knows how to play, or plays well enough that we would rather share the others with him instead of playing him heads up at needless risk. If that is the situation, we'll simply stay out of his way and share the spoils of the weak players with him. The tall stacked player, if he is a true hustler, knows that is what's happening; it's a silent arrangement.

Now, let's consider the tall stack across the table from us who only thinks he knows how to play.

He likes to play against us. So far, we've been playing a cat and mouse game with this tall stack gambler. We're trying to develop a hidden or unexpected hand of some kind so we can move some of that tall stack to our end of the table.

We're on the button with those pocket sixes.

Now our story will slant another way. In this version, we have action from our tall stack across the table. He has about $1,300 in this $1 and $2 blinds game, and we have the second tallest stack with about $1,100. Our opponent mouse (we're the cat) has raised from under the gun and he has a caller. It's now up to us to act. If we re-raise this hand, the action will likely be heads up, cat and mouse.

We still have only one chance in eight of another six appearing on the flop, but now there is something to win if we make it. We hear the siren call of implied odds in this three way action. (See Discussion 405 for a review of implied odds.)

In this case, we can consider calling. If we call, our action will be as powerful as raising. Our mouse knows we are aware of his early raise and its representation of a strong hand. Our call, then, will be a surprise to him and a powerful move on our part if we have shown nothing but power recently. Our call will also keep the third player in the hand which will be nice if we make our hidden set. My girl friend would approve of calling.

We'll place our opponent mouse on high cards, maybe a high pair. If there is a low flop with a six in it, we might have him where we want him. If there is a neutral flop and the hand is checked to us, we might be able to bluff and take it. Do we have the image?

How we play the hand from here has been covered many times in prior Discussions and generally revolves around playing the player, the possible connectors on the board, our recent history with the mouse and the rest of the table, and how he views us at this point in the game. But in most cases, whether slow played or not, we are set for a possible large pot and a big win.

Even a small win will likely win back all the sacrifices we've made to marginal hands in trying to set a trap against the mouse. But, reader beware, if we never build that trap we could lose the amount of sacrifices paid trying for those traps. That is what we would call a bad day.

Will we make the hand? It's still one chance in eight on the flop and not much chance at all on the turn. The hand could be checked through. Again, if we don't make the third six on the flop and the mouse checks to us, we might be able to bet and take the pot thereby limiting our cat and mouse small losses. And we hope to pick up some more of those losses from the other players by playing our usual Dominator game. We're in a new area of mixing our play.

The point of this Discussion is we can play weaker pockets for a chance for a surprise hand against another tall stack. It may be one of the few ways to make his stack ours. Our hand, of course, doesn't have to be a small pair; it can consist of suited connectors or anything that seems to be in the rhythm of the cat and mouse game and will be a surprise for the mouse. Meanwhile, he sees us playing nothing but power cards against the other players.

Lessons learned:

- Watch the stacks. In cash games, we won't play much with the short ones; they aren't worth it. We'll play tight hands unless we sense exasperation in the short stacked opponent.

- Watch the stacks. We're after the tall stacks and we'll sacrifice small losses until we can set the trap. That is, if we really want the big win.

Typical Opponents

Gamboling at Binion's

By Sam O'Connor

Clemmens made his way through Binion's Horseshoe casino to the poker room in the back of the casino. He was motioned to seat number four. He locked up the seat and went to the window to buy casino checks. They were still "checks" to Clemmens, although he would sometimes say "chips" to satisfy the younger players and the hold 'em movement which was being called the "new poker".

There were nine seats at this no limit table.

An obvious novice player sat down in seat number six. He was a young man who feigned confidence but, to Clemmens, he was clearly nervous. He was one of the new breed, just in from California for the weekend.

Occupying the eighth seat was an opposite type, a young hustler named Wolfgang, from the east coast. Wolfgang was a very good player and he warned the table about it. He operated in a style reminiscent of the great Doyle Brunson. The Wolf had the presence and patter of The Texas Dolly, perhaps even a little more garrulous. And he almost always walked away with the tall stacks.

The Wolf was about thirty three years old, medium height, soft and round. He had small eyes and features that almost drowned in his fleshy face. His mouth was a Donald Trump mouth that pursed and puckered when he spoke, which was most of the time. His line of chatter was always about himself and was spoken in east coast American English, spattered with slight German lapses from his childhood days in Austria.

The novice player, two seats to Wolfie's right, found himself almost immediately head to head with the formidable Wolfgang.

The Wolf's blather accompanied the play of the hand. "I'm livin' in town wid my girl friend. I'll call your raise. She wants to marry me some of dese days. Dose days are comin' soon, too. Deal da cards. Let's see da flop. She's tall and smart but she doesn't know anything about my biznuss. Maybe she just likes my money. Did you bet? I don't know, I guess I'll marry her. I raise $1,000. Do you see any reason why she wouldn't marry me?"

279

"Maybe because you talk too much?"

"So I talk. What's wrong wid dat?"

"It's boring."

"Okay, den, I won't talk." . . . . "You're betting? Can you beat a pair of kings? I didn't marry my last three girl friends. Dey were beautiful, too. I'm going to call if you can't beat kings. Can you beat my kings? Yeah, dose girls loved me, but I didn't marry 'em. I'll raise."

"I'm going all-in."

"I t'ought you couldn't beat my kings. You sure you can beat my kings? But dis girl friend has been around a lot longer dan da udders. Okay, I call."

The novice showed a pair of aces. Wolfie showed aces and kings and took the pot.

"I told you I had kings. 'Course I didn't say nuttin' 'bout da aces."

The novice left the table to join his friend who was on the rail watching the hand. Both boys were laughing. Clemmens could overhear something about not lasting very long.

The novice's place at the table was taken by a nice appearing woman who wanted to know the rules of the game. Could she buy her chips at the table? If she checked her hand, did she have to throw it in?

Clemmens liked having a lady at the table, although beginners were kind of cumbersome. They slowed the game and they sometimes acted on their hands at the wrong time. But this lady was bound to quiet the players' harsh remarks, soften the atmosphere and add a little interest to the conversation. When there was a lady at the table, things were just a little more pleasant.

This particular woman was in her forties and reminded Clemmens of Annette Bening. He liked to label the players and maybe give them a name, so he thought of her as new player "Annette".

She bought a stack of checks and Wolfie helped her with the exchange.

Annette called the blind and the subsequent raise in all of the first three hands dealt.

The Wolf cautioned her to watch the game a little at first. It was best that she have some idea of what it was like before she ventured in. He'd be happy to help, he said, advise her a little. Wolfie was making friends.

The players heard a few words of "I call" from Annette as soon as one of the players moved her all-in. She lost the hand and the players feared that was the last "I call" they would hear from the sweet lady.

Annette managed a smile. She sat back in her chair, thought a minute, and then bought more checks. This time, instead of just one stack, she bought five stacks, a full rack.

The chip runner brought the rack from the cashier's cage and Annette asked Wolfie about the best way to arrange them. The Wolf said the best way to arrange them was just like his stacks. Like his eleven stacks, he smiled patronizingly.

The button was placed in front of Annette and the cards were dealt. She looked at Wolfie, "Does this mean I'm the dealer?"

"Yes, I have da small blind and you have da button. It's a good place to raise."

"Okay, I raise."

"Of course you should have a good hand. Can you beat kings?"

"Nope"

"I'll call," said the oily man from Austria.

The heads-up flop was no apparent help to either player.

"Dis reminds me of my biznuss in da east. I don't get any help dere either. I'll check."

"I'll check, too."

The turn was another rag.

"I'll have to bet. I have a manager for my biznuss. He takes care of the old biznuss, but he doesn't create any new biznuss. Know what I mean? I have to bet this time."

"I'll call."

"You sure you want to call? My biznuss manager doesn't like my girl friend. But you're nicer than he is." Wolfie turned his face toward Annette. "I like you. Can you beat pocket kings?"

Annette shook her head. "Nope."

The river card was yet another rag. The board showed no possibilities of a straight or flush and it showed no pair. It was a garbage board of the first order.

"I can't believe I got dat last card. Now I have to bet you some money. My kings bet dese two stacks."

"I'm going all-in," said the lady with the nice manners.

The Wolf jerked his head toward Annette, small mouth agape, and he stared for a few seconds.

"You know what you're doing? I have pocket kings. If you can't beat pocket kings, I'll let you take your last bet back. You deserve it. Can you beat kings?"

Once more Annette shook her head. "Nope."

"Okay, then. I have to call."

Annette looked at the dealer and smiled. "Is it time to show the cards?"

"Yeah, it's time," intervened Wolfie. "I called and here are my kings. I never lie."

"Here are my three sevens."

"You lied to me."

Then Annette looked directly at Wolfie and said something in German, something contrary to her usual manners, something that wasn't very nice and somehow sounded to the other players even worse in German.

The Wolf's beady eyes grew unusually large in his reddening round face. He stammered a German reply.

He got no answer.

Wolfie watched as Annette ordered some racks and asked the chip runner to take them to the window for her. As she turned her back and walked away, Wolfgang shouted, "Wer bist du? Mein Name ist Wolfgang!"

No answer from Annette as she joined the two laughing boys at the rail. They hugged a group hug and walked off together arm in arm.

Wolfgang looked bewildered. He turned his head and stared at the green felt table.

The Wolf was silent for three whole minutes.

Discussion 420

Rookies at the Table

It is recommended that the reader begin this series with Part 101.

Poker is not a card game played by people.

Poker is a people game played with cards.

Murphy found himself at the no limit table with four of the city's good poker players and four novices. That's a good mix.

When the game consists of all seasoned players, it dims the experienced player's margin of possibilities of a good win. When the game consists of all novice players, it makes it hard to exercise creative play. It follows that four seasoned players and four novices as opponents make the most interesting kind of game.

The four novices were at Murphy's end of the table to Murphy's right and the good players were to Murphy's left. That's not the best arrangement, but no one moved, so Murphy couldn't change his seat to a more favorable position.

Two players left the table for a few minutes and another player's cell phone rang. The cell phone player scooted his chair from the table to take the call. That left the game six handed for a few minutes and suited Murphy just fine. He was in the big blind with ace / king suited.

The player under the gun, a good player, opened the pot and the novice across from Murphy called. When the action came to Murphy in the big blind, Murphy raised substantially. Both players called.

The flop brought an ace, a king, and a nine.

Pocket	Pocket	Flop	Flop	**Flop**
A♦	K♦	A♣	K♠	9♦

Murphy bet more than the size of the pot. The good player dropped out and the novice called.

The turn showed the jack of hearts.

Pocket	Pocket	Flop	Flop	Flop	**Turn**
A♦	K♦	A♣	K♠	9♦	J♥

Murphy checked the hand to the possible straight. The novice bet an amount way less than the size of the pot.

Now, just for starters, many beginner players are hard to figure. If that bet had come from an experienced player, Murphy would have had to think about it in only one way. But a bet from a novice presents a whole 'nother set of cogitations.

The cards in question are a queen and a ten to make the straight. A good player would not have called Murphy's pre-flop raise with a queen / ten - well maybe if they were suited in a short handed game. The good player definitely would not have called the second bet of more than the size of the pot, just to try to catch a jack.

But what would this novice do?

Murphy decided a novice wouldn't try for the gut straight either. Even he knows it's too expensive.

So what was the opponent holding? He had an ace, for sure. And maybe the jack hit him. That's it, Murphy tentatively decided. Ace / jack.

The novice opponent also had the habit of betting the size of his hand, and the current bet, which Murphy hadn't acted on yet, was much less than the size of the pot. The small bet reinforced Murphy's "no straight" decision.

Murphy raised the small bet. He raised the size of the pot. (Both players were high stacked and all-in move in relationship to the size of the pot was not appropriate.)

The river brought the queen of clubs.

Pocket	Pocket	Flop	Flop	Flop	Turn	River
A♦	K♦	A♣	K♠	9♦	J♥	Q♣

Murphy checked to the novice opponent. The opponent promptly and eagerly moved all-in.

Murphy reviewed all the bets from pre-flop to now and he reviewed his own decisions. Murphy decided the novice probably held ace / jack – ace / something for sure. Holding a ten, in light of the betting, made no sense. Maybe it would be a split pot, but Murphy didn't think so.

Murphy called the all-in bet.

Immediately after Murphy's call, another novice on Murphy's right, who liked to show what he knew, announced "A queen and a ten." This third guy, the announcer, was kind of fun. He liked to do little chip tricks between hands. He had dyed black hair, cat-like dark glasses and a pierced lower lip with something silver in it. He said it again for emphasis, "Queen Ten."

Murphy's opponent had made his hand and that's why he made his all-in bet. He proudly turned his hole cards face up, an ace and a queen.

Rookies. They're hard to figure. And that's what makes them dangerous. But they are quite beatable. We want more of these precious little producers at the table, but not too many.

Discussion 421

Recreational Players

It is recommended that the reader begin this series with Part 101.

Poker is not a card game played by people.

Poker is a people game played with cards.

Some visitors are experienced and are playing for recreation. It makes a fun game and a profitable one because they are not necessarily bent on winning. But, much like the rookies, the recreational players are dangerous.

Murphy was in a no limit game with a nice mix of players. Murphy was in the number seven seat and a nice, round man, Mr. Jovial, was in seat number three. He was there for fun and he was having a good time.

Murphy was near the button with ace / eight suited in diamonds. The pot had been opened by Mr. Jovial. Murphy raised. One of the blinds called, and Mr. Jovial called.

The flop delivered a nine, an eight and a four.

The blind checked and Mr. Jovial checked. Murphy bet the size of the pot.

The blind folded, which was a relief. Mr. Jovial called, which wasn't a surprise.

With no initial bet and no raise, Mr. Jovial could have almost anything, but not a raising hand. Murphy put him on at least one high card.

The turn brought the three of diamonds.

Pocket	Pocket	Flop	Flop	Flop	Turn
A♦	8♦	9♣	8♥	4♣	3♦

Mr. Jovial checked and Murphy bet the size of the pot. The opponent called.

The river card that would have concerned Murphy would be another club but a six for a straight wouldn't have bothered him; there was no working straight because of the high card Mr. Jovial had in the pocket. Luckily, the river did not bring the third club.

The river was the six of hearts.

Pock	Pock	Flop	Flop	Flop	Turn	River
A♦	8♦	9♣	8♥	4♣	3♦	6♥

Mr. Jovial made a bet of about half the pot.

Murphy still had the opponent on at least one high card and high cards never made a board appearance. Murphy refused to entertain the thought of his going through all the betting with a five / deuce for a straight. A seven / ten combination was also unlikely.

Murphy, however, did think about Mr. Jovial playing a five / seven and then put it out of his mind. In short, Murphy rejected the possibility of a straight of any kind.

Mr. Jovial often underbet the pot. Murphy hadn't placed a pattern on that maneuver yet. But, likely, he bet the size of his hand like most weak players who vary their bets in small games. A parenthetical aside: (We also have to be wary of the underbetting player who makes the small bet just to get a few more bucks for a nut hand. This, of course, was not one of those situations.)

But Murphy did have a slight tell on this fun gentleman. The tell was a little sketchy because the opponent was always in good humor. But Murphy thought Mr. Jovial had a habit, when he bluffed, of offering a big, infectious smile for his opponent. He had one for Murphy with this bet and, in addition, he folded his arms, sat back a little, and continued the smile. For Murphy, that was enough to underscore the possible bluff.

In reviewing the betting, Mr. Jovial was not proud of his hand when the nine, the highest card in the flop, hit the board. He played a calling game after the flop and now, after the river six, he was leading the betting for the first time. So, Murphy could see only a slim possibility of a nine in his hand and his bet was definitely a bluff - in his mind, at least. He could still have the best hand with top pair.

At this point, Murphy had to decide if Mr. Jovial was bluffing with the best hand.

Are Murphy's pair of eights good? If Murphy decided they are not good, Murphy will move all-in. The opponent is in no position to call an all-in bluff.

On the other hand, if Murphy's analysis is wrong, and Mr. Jovial has an accidental two pair or a pocket pair, and calls an all-in bluff, Murphy's stack is toast. Meanwhile, if Murphy decides his analysis is correct and Murphy flat calls, there is only the underbet at risk.

Murphy has confidence in his analysis and he calls the underbet. Mr. Jovial shows an ace and a three suited in clubs. His smile turns into a laugh, "It's your pot, unless you can't beat a pair of threes."

There were compliments from the table for a nice call. Murphy thought it was simpler than that.

Lessons learned:

- We play the opponents' tells and betting patterns. We play the opponents' hands along with the opponent. This is one of the secrets of winning.

- Second pair is often best and it's good to know when. The above illustration is an example of knowing when.

Discussion 422

Playing with Tourists

It is recommended that the reader begin this series with Part 101.

Poker is not a card game played by people.

Poker is a people game played with cards.

Tourists can be different from novices, although we sometimes find them in the same package. Novices take the game seriously and are trying to advance to the next level, just as soon as they realize there is a next level. Tourists aren't trying to advance; they are simply on vacation.

Neither are the recreational players the same as tourists, although a tourist may be a recreational player. Recreational players are experienced but don't care. Tourists are on vacation, play infrequently and don't care.

Tourists, then, for our purposes in these pages are simply people who have seen hold 'em on television, perhaps played a little on the net and they have dropped by to play in a real and famous carpet joint so they can say they've been there and done that.

Sometimes, Too Many Tourists.

At the beginning of the year end holidays, the poker games are good. As stated here earlier, there is a nice mix of players. During the period between Christmas and New Year's, the valley is flooded with visitors, a large number of them from California.

On New Year's Eve, over 400,000 pilgrims appear on The Strip to see the spectacular fireworks displays that begin at the southern end of the Boulevard at Mandalay Bay and continue in sequence, hotel by hotel, to the northern end at the Sahara. And many of the "ohs" and "ahs" come from visiting poker players.

Many of the holiday visitors, the new kids on the block, are there with their calculations, odds quotes, advice to each other on how to play hands and how they played their last hands, dinking and limping into pots, betting one fourth or less of the pots, paying the high odds for draw outs, and generally disrupting the usual strategy of good and experienced no limit play. In that sense, the holidays are the best of times and the worst of times.

We like the visitors to produce for the games, but unless we have only a few visitors, or get an unusual number of good hands, the play of the game is destroyed by the amateurs.

The amateurs lose, of course, because we simply tighten up and play less frequently for smaller pots, slowly moving their beginners' stacks to our side of the table. When we make a hand, we get paid off. And, of course, the pilgrims are bluffable, too; they even tell the truth about their hands. Imagine!

The pots we win against the travelers are smaller because they end sooner. Our bets are bigger to help ensure we have a win and the new kids in the casino can't call with their limping hands.

Meanwhile, when we're not in the fray, the new comers have a good time playing each other, trading pots, feeding the rake, discussing the hand just played and discussing where they last played in a tournament on the internet and the bad beat that knocked them out of the running.

Our smaller pots are supplemented by a few bluffs in strategic places. The calculating beginner plays his hands much the same way bridge is played, by merely calculating the cards. Bluffing, therefore, is not easily in the tourist's arsenal and it follows he usually doesn't recognize a bluff when it is in front of him. Then sometimes, the pilgrim suddenly realizes we've bluffed him and afterward will call more of our bets because of dire suspicion.

In general, our usual win takes a little longer and the play, accompanied by callow conversation, is almost exasperatingly more boring. Playing with beginners requires an unusually large dose of patience.

Okay, that's the end of the whine. God bless all the producers everywhere and especially the new technical players. In the small blinds no limit games, we survive nicely when they're around.

Patience.

We all know, in poker, patience pays and impatience results in an act of charity.

The above thought is especially true in the limper type game, the pilgrim's preference. He's limping, hoping to make a hand and at the limper stage is playing only his hand, hoping for a favorable flop.

At first, we try to change the family style table into a playing table but, often, when we are far outnumbered and don't get good cards, the change just won't come and there are persistently six or seven players in every pot, even four or more after we raise.

Patience then becomes more important than ever. After each round, we must step back a little and think about how we played the last round.

Were we patient enough? Did we get too active? Are we starting to play the family style game along with the rest? Maybe we're starting to think, "If I could just get one of those family pots after the river, I'd be okay for awhile." That kind of thinking can turn us into just another family member, living and hoping for exceptional cards in the squalor of abject limperhood.

To play and win in the family style, we'd have to draw something really good and beat six opponents after the flop, then beat two or three opponents in an after river showdown, as if we were playing in a small structured limit game. We can spend a lot of money attempting that because we'd be just another odds player, hoping for our share. On balance, it doesn't pay. It is one of the main reasons we switched from limit to no limit poker and it's why we're involved in this book. We prefer to *play* and to Dominate.

It's best to play in our traditional no limit game at a traditional no limit table when opportunity presents itself. We'll lose fewer pots from draw outs. We'll read our players well and win more consistently.

Let's take a look on the bright side, our kind of aggression usually breaks open the limper action and soon the others will have to respond our way. Then the game can belong to us.

It's interesting to see the young producers' stacks slowly diminish. All of them diminish, to be sure, but some quite slowly. Sometimes it takes a lucky player a long time to go from winner to loser simply because he is getting good cards. But his consistent bad play will take its toll almost every time. Some of these players would do better in a structured limit game, although a little more concentration on playing people in all games would help them a lot.

Patience. It means <u>not</u> playing the marginal hand in the game of pilgrims or in the techie game.

Watch out for kickers. It's tempting to play an ace without a good kicker because we haven't played for awhile. But the limper game is not the place to be unnecessarily active; the limpers will stick around and pay us off even when they know we play the nuts. They want to see. They're funny that way.

We have to be careful; we are playing with people who don't notice our gear shifting and unusual play. They are playing cards, not people, and we need cards to beat them.

Here are some general rules, although there are exceptions to these rules:

- There is no need for mixing play with the odds player because he does not play his players well and generally does not pay enough attention to what we are doing in order for us to gain advantage in mixing our play. The odds player is simply playing the odds, trying to make a hand.

- He will, however, often bet our hand for us.

- We will move in with a big bet at the right time to protect our hand from this draw happy player. With us, he'll either fold or pay for his foolishness.

- Patience will have to be the focus of our play.

There are never too many opponents who are beginners and don't know how to play but, please Paco, we'd like to have them sprinkled through the games somewhat. In other words, it's good to have bad players at the table, but it's best to have bad players who think they know how to play. And we want a few good players who will allow us to maneuver.

293

Discussion 423

Playing the Maniac

It is recommended that the reader begin this series with Part 101.

Poker is not a card game played by people.

Poker is a people game played with cards.

A very learned and successful poker hustler once advised those who would listen to play when they had an edge in the overall game and quit when they didn't have that edge.

Another, more familiar, way to say it is cliché but also true: When you look around the table and you don't see the sucker, he is you.

Still another way: When you see you are not the best player at the table, quit and go home.

As poker hustlers, true poker hustlers with acumen for power play who Dominate the small blinds no limit games, we play where we have a decided and pronounced edge.

We have discussed LP players (loose passive), LA players (loose aggressive), TP players (tight passive), and TA players (tight aggressive). Those readers who have followed our Discussions, played by our Discussions and won by them, know that each of these four player profiles have sub profiles. The sub profiles are in more detail than the broad categories; they are more finely tuned and they develop as we play.

It has been suggested we are normally quite TA, when everything is on balance. But the Dominator becomes a player beyond TA when he mixes his play, shifts gears as the occasion warrants, becomes LA in the late positions as opportunity presents itself, and TP in the early positions as warranted. (See Discussion 409.) The Dominator becomes a check and raiser, a caller and becomes everything else that's needed for the occasion. And he is sensitive to the right occasion.

First the power player learns the values and how to play his players. Then he learns to mix his play and becomes a Hustler. When all that is accomplished and he has some experience, he learns when and how to break the rules and soon he qualifies for the fifth category: Dominator.

"Maniac" is becoming a common term used around the poker room. The maniac is a loose aggressive player who's style does not change. He's in most pots. He comes into the action raising an amount worth far more than the pot.

He wins a lot of pots early and he has a lot of the smallest denominator players' checks on the table ($1 checks) in his stacks. He is usually quite garrulous, sometimes offensively so. Although sometimes affable, his attitude is mostly one of disdain for all the little people at the table who are afraid to risk their money and don't know how to play their cards like he does. He is on his habitual poker ego trip and, win or lose, he is not likely to change.

At this point, we must make a distinction between the Maniac and the Bully. They are not the same.

The Bully finds occasion in a weak or limper game to take advantage of the timidity prevalent at the table. He "bullies" the table with continual raises, scooping up unlikely pots along the way. He does it until the players are playing a looser game. He is, therefore, extremely loose aggressive for a limited time. He gains a loose image. When the game loosens and he gets too much action, he changes tactics. He has mixed his play. The temporary bully is often a good player in the long run.

The term, "Bully", then, is a tactical term sometimes used by good players. Being a "Maniac", on the other hand, is merely a relentlessly bad habit.

Playing the Maniac.

Today Murphy played next to a man from Greece. When he made change for Murphy so he could post a blind, Murphy thanked him in Greek (it's the only Greek Murphy knows) and they were chatty for a moment in broken English. (Murphy doesn't let chatty happen for very long periods.) The Greek turned out to be the second best (!) player at the table. Unfortunately, the Greek was seated to Murphy's left, but things will work out all right.

The man from Greece was not the manic. The maniac was the player at the opposite end of the table.

How does Murphy deal with this playing maniac? "Patiently" is the key word. Very patiently.

All those who are experienced players at the table are waiting for the trap that will move some of the maniac's checks to their stacks.

Murphy finally gets his chance. So what happens when Murphy gets that high pocket pair?

First, Murphy makes the maniac the exclusive opponent. Murphy has to bet the Greek, to his left, out of the hand. When the maniac comes into the pot raising pre-flop, Murphy re-raises, thereby eliminating the other players from the pot. Murphy doesn't want them to draw out on him and take this future large pot; they can be beat some other time.

After raising the others out, Murphy only has the maniac's hand to beat.

The maniac will not be bullied, so Murphy is confidant the maniac will call a re-raise. If the maniac raises once more, Murphy will likely call because he has just now shifted gears to a tight passive player.

Let's underscore the last sentence: Murphy, after the last raise, has just shifted to a tight player, a tight passive player. He is mixing his play, the mark of the Dominator.

After the flop, the maniac will likely try to bully the pot because that's his style. Assuming the cards are falling satisfactorily, Murphy will call. The maniac will do Murphy's betting for him. If the maniac can't try to bully because of extremely weak cards, he'll lose interest. So Murphy will keep him interested by calling, not raising.

Naturally, if the board comes to a place where the maniac may be trying to connect a straight or flush, Murphy will have to move in with a big bet to protect himself. But, until that time arrives, Murphy will call the maniac's over betting and win a very big pot.

It's a repeating story everyday at the places where we play in small blinds. It's ours to take advantage of.

Now, we'll play the hand with Murphy.

Murphy started with pocket jacks and there was never an overcard on the board. The maniac didn't have much. So, he reasoned, with garbage on the board how could Murphy have much? He tried to bluff Murphy off the hand after the flop, after the turn and after the river. (With only one pair, Murphy wasn't strong enough to raise him after the river.)

Murphy liked the look on the maniac's face when the maniac's biggest bet was called after the river. The maniac tried to reason: How could Murphy call with one pair and such a weak hand? Actually, it was easy.

The maniac hates to quit a hand and hates to lose a pot. He'll try to buy most pots he can't win. He's ego driven; we know it and he's ours.

So we'll be patient. We'll wait for the good hand. When we get it, we'll let him do our betting for us. If the hand is getting dangerous, we'll make the giant oversized bet; even most maniacs will respect the giant play. We'll also throw the hand away when we think the maniac has a better one. If he's bluffed us, it'll only add fuel to the fire in the next hand we play.

If the maniac is half smart about his play, we may have to be active in some short pots so we can get his action when we want it. It takes discipline to keep our losses short but we'll get it all back when we have a hand against the maniac.

The maniac makes large contributions to our win when we are patient. He's a lot of fun to beat.

Discussion 424

Starting by the Chart? What Were We Thinking?

It is recommended that the reader begin this series with Part 101.

Poker is not a card game played by people.

Poker is a people game played with cards.

The reader, at this point, should have many months of practice at the Hustler level. He should have made the discussed starting hand exceptions and gained experience from those exceptions, losing and winning many times over and establishing a winning average. It's all necessary before he can successfully advance to Dominator status.

Experience is paramount. Facts can be learned - experience has to be lived.

From time to time, we have modified our selection of the pocket starters. Those modifications depended on the complexion of the game, the type of opponents, position, our current image and many more things.

In Discussion 202 and subsequent Discussions we learned which pocket cards were good for starting a hand and we've been talking about it ever since.

There are 1,326 possible starting pockets in hold 'em and the very tightest of players will start with only about 5% of those hands. And many of those won't be played past the flop. The Dominator must play more hands than that. Moreover, the hands we've called "marginal" are usually the hands that, when played well, will win the largest pots.

The chart's hard rules. What were we thinking?

In the realm of Dominator, the power player hustler can start with anything he likes. Oh, oh. Let's think about that and discuss it.

That does not mean the Dominator starts willy nilly, raising every hand and so on. That's what the maniac does and that's why he is one player we beat consistently.

But starting with anything does mean we can bend the starting chart more than ever when it suits our Dominator needs. There are those times when we get some good cards at good intervals and the rhythm of our play brings the opponents' stacks dancing to our side of the table. And there are those times when we need to manufacture our wins. This means that, in a good no limit game, with lots of action we sometimes have dominated the table to such a degree that we can play most anything and bring fear to our opponents. We must capitalize on that situation; we're obligated to as member s of the Dominator Club.

Realizing the situation and taking advantage of it means we will win far more money than only our proportionate share of good cards would bring to us. And that's why we learn the ways of the Dominator.

We can win some pots by moving through the opposition when the time, rather than the cards, are right. We'll do it until we make the mistake of letting someone catch us. When that happens, we'll shift gears once more. The Dominator knows what his current image is and he knows how to take advantage of it.

When we shift gears once more, where are we? We're at a place that confuses the table. We could have anything.

"The trouble is, when you raise, I don't know if you have ace / king or seven / six," a player once told me. I thanked him for the compliment.

When we're Dominators, we're at a place in play where some astute players at the table suddenly realize we're not just lucky; we're active and we're damned good. Now we're talking Domination.

Here's the pay-off. We know two, three, or more players who will, from this moment on chase us until we catch them. Because we are good at reading our adversaries, we know who these players are and we will play our game. We'll play only good hands past the flop against these chasers. If they don't chase us, we'll go back to raising with marginal starters until once again they decide to come after us. Then we'll shift gears once more. The diligent Dominator has fun.

Here's the big pay-off. While we're playing marginal hands, someone will chase us and we'll get a garbage flop the acrid smell of which can only match the odor of our terrible pocket cards. It'll be a match made in opportunity. The chasers will be surprised when we turn over our eights full of deuces. What happened to their two pair of kings and eights? We'll be the subject of a story they will tell their friends, over and over.

The pot with the lucky flop can be so large that it more than makes up for several small hands we lost in order to set the trap of the lucky eights full of deuces. And that is where the big money lies.

The Dominator loves to make that raise with the opposition not knowing whether the raise is because the Dominator holds ace / king or much, much less. The Dominator plays cat and mouse better than Tom and Jerry and there is far more than cheese in the trap.

Tom Hellmuth once boasted that he could sit in a small blinds game and win without ever looking at his pocket cards. It's probably true; he's one of the better cat and mousers.

Tom Hellmuth also once said that high stakes poker is all about bluffing. We'll put the whipped cream and cherry on that subject a little later in these pages.

Now, let's not get cocky. The cat and mouse game works when we get a few good cards now and then. Not many cards at all results in no winnings. We can, and do, lose. There is still gamble in the game and the gamble lies in whether we get a few good cards. And it lies in whether we get them at the right time. After all, we do have to show cards now and then. When we get our complete complement of good cards, it's even better.

If we can get one half the cards we're supposed to get and we get them timely, we'll win a good share of the money at the table. We'll enjoy the benefits of the Dominator's game.

So. What were we thinking when we made that chart and insisted on everybody learning it and making it second nature?

The chart for beginning hands is for us to know what's good, what's not so good, and what is terrible. Then we learn when and how to play them.

These things must be second nature to us now. That is the purpose of the chart and the purpose of months of experience playing and knowing the chart.

Learning it well means we can break the rules. Learning it well and experiencing it well means we will break the rules with aplomb. When we hypostasize all the rules, we know their value. Then, and only then, can we be successful at breaking those rules.

Be advised, it takes more than the objective knowledge of hold 'em; it takes experience, lots of experience. If you can learn it and experience it in less than two years, please write me about it; you'll deserve my applause. But make sure you've won as a Dominator for a period of time long enough to prove it to yourself. Proving it to yourself, after all, is what it is all about.

Discussion 425

When and How to be the Bully

It is recommended that the reader begin this series with Part 101.

Poker is not a card game played by people.

Poker is a people game played with cards.

Many readers have thought, before reading this book, "bully" was synonymous with being the Dominator. Synonymous is far from the truth, although we sometimes become the bully because the table is crying for bullyism and we are happy to oblige.

In our Discussions, we have touched on situations where, in order to control the table, we need to play a little looser and raise a little more often. The topic here is different because it involves much more. Now we're going to talk about raising twice as much and adopting the image that is not a tight aggressive image, but a big loose aggressive image, the image of the bully.

We can do it because we know the starting chart backwards and forwards, why the chart is made that way and we also know the starting card pitfalls. All the calculations such as odds for draws and pot odds tumble freely in our heads and are applied almost automatically. We have a knack for reading our opponents and we know how to apply the "intel" we have gathered.

In other words, we have the confidence to be the bully. Bully is not a reputation we seek; it is, however, a tactic we sometimes use masterfully.

The game that summons the bully in us.

Once again we're in a small blinds no limit game where all the players are playing like it's a limit game. They are limping in to make seven handed "family" pots, making small bets and drawing flop, turn and river cards as long as they have some kind of hand to draw to. After the river card, these players turn their pocket cards over and look up to see who won the pot this time. Then they usually laugh and talk about the hand until the next pocket cards are dealt.

It's all great fun and, as Dominators, we know the fun game has to change in order for us to have control and make it fun for us. It's time to be the bully.

Several things have to be in place in order to start our bully session:

- When we bully, we keep firing those raises into the pot with good to marginal hands. No, not every hand. But it's time to shake the table up a bit. We'll keep it up until we start getting called. After that, we'll pick our spots. Mixing our play is the fun part.

- We have to have a mountain of checks in front of us, lined up in numerous stacks. There is an implied threat in those imposing stacks and it is a lost opportunity when we don't use that implied threat in this kind of lack of action.

- We have to take an attitude that says we are not afraid of any thing or any body at the table. That does not mean we are haughty or condescending; it means that we simply keep firing from the shoulder.

- We quickly find who first catches on to our weak hand bullying and is waiting for that good hand that will beat us. When he catches on, he'll play us something like the way we play the maniac. (To review playing the maniac, see Discussion 423.) He'll try to play a tight game and we'll be ready for him. He can also be bluffed.

- As others catch on, we keep track of those types and play them accordingly, varying from our ready to fire bully play.

- As we accumulate players who are aware of us and are lying in waiting, we'll gradually back off bullying and win a few legitimate pots. And we'll know when to back off entirely. At those points where we back off from each determined player, we wait for the hand that will get the call for what is perceived as our "maniac" play. If we get a few cards, there should be a big pot or two as we back off. We know how to switch gears and we'll do it almost imperceptibly.

303

- When nearly all the opponents are at last playing our raising game, the game and the players are ours in a more traditional style, one where we can maneuver. We have Dominated during our bully session and we will now Dominate in a much better Dominator game.

The discipline of mixing our play is essential. The fear of raising a pot and having to abandon it must be non-existent, even though we have to abandon hands frequently. The fear of a slowly diminishing stack cannot be a part of our thinking; we know we'll get it all back and more when we win those bigger pots we're setting traps for.

But it is a mistake to bully the wrong table. When we try to bully other than the timid player, we can be in trouble. We know that maniacs who play aggressively, willy nilly, against us in other games are the very opponents we often take advantage of. (Discussion 423.) We don't want to fall prey to an experienced player when trying to bully him.

If we lose a few pots and our bully image is turning to a sucker image, we must slow down for awhile or maybe leave the table. The cash table hustler is not there to build a reputation or to make either friends or enemies; he is there to win. If the cards don't come, he can walk away without a further thought.

On the other hand, if we lose some of our stack and the table is still mostly populated with timid players, we can maintain our bully play. We'll be patient about the big win. No need to withdraw just because the last few hands didn't work out. Because we have lost a few pots, we have prospects of getting a good call with a good hand, perhaps the next hand. If we keep putting the weak players to a guess, we'll reap an eventual weak player harvest.

We must be more alert than ever when playing the bully game. We must be aware. We must know when an individual player's attitude changes toward us. In the bully game, we're into a new and intense mix of play. Our heightened awareness is vital to our win.

If the players stay timid and refuse to play the raising game, we can keep bullying our way to some good profits because they will eventually call that big hand when they think we're bluffing.

Discussion 426

Improving our Wins

It is recommended that the reader begin this series with Part 101.

Poker is not a card game played by people.

Poker is a people game played with cards.

Why you are a winner.

You do win, don't you?

A friend named Tom Brock used to play in one of my games some time ago in a desert town. He loved to play and he nearly always lost. One night, at the end of the game which always ended at 2:00 a.m. sharp, Tom had some money left. He looked hopelessly at his remaining stack and said, "You guys must not have played very well tonight."

Although no one could remember Tom ever winning, he must have won sometime because everybody wins once in a while. But let's not be too optimistic about whether we are real winners. Sometimes the cards just run over us; sometimes we're just lucky. There is a difference between being lucky and good play.

The good poker hustler keeps a record; that's how he knows he's a winner. He doesn't think to himself, "I won today because I'm a good player and those days when I lost, I was just unlucky." No, sir; he keeps a record so he'll have hard evidence he's a good poker player. Never mind those feel good days after a good win. Never mind the inevitable losses. In the long run, he knows he's a winner because he keeps the records that prove he's a winner.

How we win.

To demonstrate mathematically how we, the good hustlers and Dominators, are a cut above the rest, we have to make one big, broad and factual assumption. The assumption, for the sake of illustration, is that we get the same poker hands to play as everyone else over a period of time - one hundred years, if you like.

It may not seem like we get the same cards as everybody else in the space of a day or even a week, a month, or more. Everybody has those dry periods when the good cards just don't arrive. And it seems to happen regularly in time restricted situations such as tournaments when we are more pressed for time by the acceleration of the blinds. The fact that we make, cut short, or extend our own time limitations in cash games is one of the advantages of the cash game.

The truth is, in the long haul, each player gets his share of each of the fifty two cards.

Another truth is the power player, when patient and in focus, wins more than his share with those fifty two cards.

Here's why:

- <u>The players we play</u>, we play well.

- <u>The hands we start with</u> win more often than the other hands. That's because we pay attention to the players, the cards, the position we're in, and the amounts we bet. We do it better than the other players do.

- <u>The positions we play</u> are better played by us, from the blinds, to UTG, to middle position, to the button.

- <u>The amounts we bet</u> are designed to protect our hands, to give us information and to build the pot better than the betting techniques of other players.

- <u>The value we get</u> for a hand is more than other players get for the same kind of hand. And sometimes the value consists of making sure we win the hand by protecting it, instead of being drawn out on like other players.

- <u>We bluff well</u> and in the right places because we play our players better than the other players and we select our bluffing situations better than the others.

- <u>We call bluffs well</u> and in the right places because we play our players better than the other players and we are more aware of the types of bluffing.

Since we do these things better with the same cards that other players get, we win more than our proportionate share. That is the secret of consistently good wins.

Playing the table.

"Playing the table" is fast becoming a common expression. But let's make it clear that we, the Dominators, don't treat it as just an expression; we know what we're talking about.

The Dominator *plays* the game he sits in. He *plays* the players he sits with. He *plays* the cards he's dealt. And all these things are at least a little different every time he sits down. When the Dominator makes all the adjustments necessary with each play, he is playing the table.

Most of the decisions we make when playing the table are about the opponent. Only a small percentage of each hand played is about the cards.

When we can play the opponent's hand along with him, we know what it takes to win the hand. We know what the opponent is afraid of. We know which maneuvers can be made against each individual. We are playing the table.

This means we are mixing our play because each player is played differently by us. Sure, we have them categorized in the familiar four categories but, when we play the table, we know enough to play each player in a slightly different way.

Our pocket cards are only important if we have to show them. "If we never show a hand, we'll never lose" is a facetious statement we sometimes hear. But it applies in many ways to the Dominator.

The reader isn't ready to execute this advanced playing if all he is doing is reading and playing his own hand. He must be able to read the opponent's hand and capitalize on it. Additionally, by playing his hand only when he has a hand, he doesn't know how easy it is for his good opponents to read <u>him</u>.

307

It is assumed, at this juncture, the reader can pick the right time, with his current image in mind, and make the proper play. There is nothing magic in knowing good play but there is constant difficulty in the execution of good play. Knowledge and experience are the keys.

No one said that Domination is easy. We have to work at it. We have to be alert. We have to be diligent.

When we can do all those things, we can pick the spot to play any pocket cards and win.

When we can do all those things, we can pick the spots to play only good pocket cards and win.

We know how to get the most possible money for our play. That way there are fewer losing days and better winning days.

Some parts of the above strategies involve knowing the cards and the mathematics involved, the useful part of which we know better and calculate quicker than others because of the simplicity we've attached to them. (See Discussions 203 and 405.) However, all the above items involve playing our players better than the others, and that is the crux of the people game called poker.

We've discussed the first five bulleted items, above, at length. Let's engage in some more discussion on bluffing, the last two items. There are many days when the money from the bluffs successfully made by us, and the bluffs successfully called by us, will be most of our day's win.

Bluffing will be easier in the small no limit games than in the large no limit games because the players we play against in the small games will not be as knowledgeable nor as experienced as those in the big games. The art of bluffing is often new to novices.

When the skilled small blinds player learns bluffing, his wins can grow to twice their ordinary amounts or more. We will soon be discussing **All about Bluffing** in the coming pages. Bluffing is the biggest difference between the ordinary $1 and $2 blinds player and the Dominator. It's the mother lode.

Tells

The Bad Beat

By: Sam O'Connor

One of the early morning pastimes at the poker room at a local Hotel on the Strip in Las Vegas is watching the prostitutes walk purposefully through the casino after a night's foraging. These particularly beautiful young women are on their way from their place of work, past the poker room, to the parking garage where they will slide into their shiny new cars and go to wherever prosties spend their daytime hours.

Part of the entertainment was watching the poker players watch the parade.

At 5:00 a.m., Joseph occupied the first chair and was the chip leader at a no limit poker table nearest the rail. He was also the loudest talker and the foremost instigator. He sat as tall as he could in his chair and pointed a lot. Sometimes, when he felt he needed more leverage, he would stand behind his chair, grip the back of it, and flood the table with a cascade of boorishness.

In his defense, Joseph just wanted to have fun. He meant no harm to anybody, but he offended many.

The rest of the table consisted of four young players from Los Angeles, a reserved middle aged man from Las Vegas, a young man from Korea, a sandy haired man from New York City who spoke Cantonese with one or two of the dealers, and a mustachioed silver haired gentleman dressed in a western straw hat, boots, and a barley corn jacket.

Murphy was there. He was the quiet one who sat in the last seat, next to the dealer.

Occasionally, Joseph would call out to one or more of the working girls as they passed. Hector, the floor manager, had tracked the verbal assault to its source and had to tell Joseph to hold his voice down. Joseph would make an ignored remark and things would be back to normal.

Inevitably, the game came to a point when, after a few uneventful hands, Joseph was bored. He spotted two women passing by and decided he could talk to them on the other side of the rail, out of Hector's jurisdiction.

He approached the young ladies. One of the young men from the table went with him. Joseph bargained with the girls for a minute or two while the young man intently listened and learned a few things.

Upon returning, Joseph reported to the table that the girls had wanted two thousand dollars for their favors and the accompanying young man confirmed that accurate and altogether descriptive information.

Soon Joseph, peeking at his pocket cards, looked up to see a blonde young woman leaning on the rail, watching the game. There was no hesitation in his greeting.

"Hey, Beautiful, why don't you come join us? It's a friendly little game. You know, it's just me and my friends here. C'mon, we'll teach you how to play poker."

The blonde beamed a winning, confident smile. She took her time. "Well, I can't do that, can I? First, someone will have to leave the game before I can sit down. But then, after that happens, I'll be able to take a seat, kick your ass and take your chips."

Joseph let out a big guffaw. He jumped away from the table, spun around and bugled like a bull moose in rutting season. What a woman!

Hector promptly came to the scene and politely, but firmly, instructed Joseph to be seated. Joseph was told to hold it down, or else. Hector didn't want to do it, he said, but Joseph was getting dangerously close to the "or else".

At this point, the middle aged man at the table graciously said he'd really like to stay for the drama and entertainment but he had some sleep to catch up on. He ceremoniously bowed and offered the lady his seat at the table.

"Is it a lucky seat?" she asked congenially.

The newcomer got some players' checks from Hector and sat down. Then she looked Joseph dead in the eye, long and steady. Her voice lowered. "Pop another beer, big guy." She waited. "Are you ready to play poker?"

Joseph showed a flushed and unbalanced grin. "This is great," he finally managed, "maybe we can get some more Miss Americas in this game."

311

Joseph spotted Hector watching him and he decided to push his relationship with the now ever watchful floor man.

"I tried to get you a girl, Hector, but she wanted two thousand dollars. I don't think any bimbo is worth that much, do you?"

Hector was grinning, trying to be a nice, but firm, floor man. "No way. Always too much for me. Besides, I'm younger and better looking than you. I don't have a need for the ladies of the evening."

On another day, in another place, Joseph might've had something to say. But this time he merely forced an uneasy smile.

In the next hand, Murphy held pocket aces. After one short stack caller, Murphy raised four times the size of the pot.

Joseph shot Murphy a momentary hot glance and said in a big voice, "Raise!"

He then pushed a few stacks toward the middle of the table, three times the amount Murphy had bet.

The young man who opened the betting, and was short stacked, systematically placed the rest of his money in front of him. Murphy sensed the young man's desperation and knew the lad was not only short stacked, but short in his pocket cards as well. The young man sat with his right elbow on the table and his chin in his hand; he was ready to call it a day and night.

Murphy's first inclination was to re-raise Joseph but he quickly thought better of it.

If Murphy flat called the all-in and gave Joseph an opportunity to play, it could prove worthwhile. After all, the blonde put Joseph down, he lost in his negotiations with the working girl and Hector had been forced to develop a policy that might eject Joseph at any time. It would be a good time to engage Joseph in a hand. Joseph was on edge.

Murphy called the re-raise. He was gambling a little with two opponents instead of one, but not much. Also, there would be two pots instead of one and the side pot would be much larger. If the short stack drew out, Murphy might still get value for his aces.

By calling, Murphy kept Joseph in charge of the betting.

Murphy placed Joseph on big cards, maybe a couple of paints. After all, he must have come over the top with something in the pocket.

The flop presented the players with the three of spades, the five of hearts, and the ace of diamonds. It was a beautiful rainbow of cards with a rewarding third ace for Murphy.

Murphy checked his hand, placing the action with Joseph where it belonged. Joseph could take the lead.

Joseph bet half the size of the pot.

The bet caused Murphy to place Joseph on big slick, ace / king. Joseph's bet was small, but he was not afraid of Murphy's hand. It seemed to Murphy Joseph was, in fact, quite proud of his aces with a king kicker and Murphy felt Joseph was inviting him to do some raising. He wanted to see what Murphy was going to do about it.

Murphy thought a few seconds and "reluctantly" called. Joseph, the big charger, was still in charge with no dangerous cards on the board.

The turn was the eight of spades. Murphy checked once more.

Joseph was wary. He checked this time which told Murphy Joseph had only one pair.

The river brought the king of clubs, making Joseph aces and kings. Perfect.

This time Murphy moved all-in with the best hand and Joseph called so fast it sounded a lot like "all-in" and "I call" were in the same sentence, spoken by the same person.

Murphy, never one to slow roll, immediately showed his pocket aces for the winner.

313

Now about that bull moose. Ever hear one when it's wounded? It must sound a lot like Joseph when he's been hit cold for a monstrous pot.

Joseph bellowed a second time, then grimaced and flung his cards toward the middle of the table. Joseph had lost his cool.

Conscious of what he perceived to be his table captain image, he tried to regain composure. "That's a bad beat. A goddamned bad beat!" Then he finally cooled down.

Still wanting the image of the understanding table captain, he looked up at Murphy. "Nice hand, sir, very nice hand."

"Thank you," offered Murphy, "It was a lucky flop."

"Yeah," Joseph simpered, "now I've lost with the hooker, I have Hector leaning on me, and I lost a big hand in a bad beat."

Desperate for new attention, Joseph glanced toward the blonde at the table. "Two thousand dollars is what that bim wanted. Would you charge that much?"

The entire table of players suddenly stopped watching Murphy stack his checks. They looked first at Joseph, then at the attractive blonde. Loud Joseph was gazing at the lady intently, bent on following up on his way-out-of-line question.

The lady was unflappable. "I'd do it for half that," she laughed. Her off handed reply was met at first by mixtures of surprise from the table, but ended in nervous laughter. The laughter brought a clear sign of relief.

Joseph now had the bawdy levity he needed. "Hey, Hector," he called across the room. "I've got a half price deal for you. You gotta like this. Only half price for a good lookin' broad. Tell you what, you take the one thousand dollar deal and I'll pay for it. Out of my pocket. On me. Whata ya say? We'll be friends."

"Sorry, not interested. Better yet, you put up the thousand and I'll play a heads up freeze out with the lady, starting with five hundred each. That way, we'll all be happy. And, lucky you, with my deal you'll be allowed to watch."

The blonde stood slowly, but easily. Everybody watched in silence. The young man who went with Joseph to listen to him talk to the young lady in the hallway moved to her side.

The blonde looked at Joseph. "I can't take your thousand in any case, Joseph. You're under arrest for violation of Section 201.3 of the Nevada Revised Statutes. Pandering. Clint, here, will read you your rights."

There was no smile from the blonde this time as she showed him her badge.

"Now that," murmured the newly arrested Joseph, "is a really bad beat."

Discussion 430

Intuition

It is recommended that the reader begin this series with Part 101.

Poker is not a card game played by people.

Poker is a people game played with cards.

Star Trek.

All Trekkies are familiar with the opening poker scene aboard the Enterprise.

Geordi, Data, Troi and Will Riker are seated at the poker table. They are ready for action. Deanna is looking coy. Data is wearing a green eye shade which compliments his yellowish pallor. Geordi is looking like he still can't act. Will Riker . . . Wait a minute. Will Riker? Number One? The mawkish flesh from Alaska? Why is he in this scene?

Then the situation becomes obvious to enquiring minds. The game is set-up for a bust out and Number One is the mark. Only a sucker and a fool would sit in with a blind man who can see the human aura, a three million gig walking computer, and a ship's cheerleader who can read minds.

In the truly wonderful and entertaining universe of Gene Roddenberry, Deanna Troi is an "empath". But the counselor stretches far beyond the empathy ranks because she does magnitudes more than experience empathy.

Webster says empathy is the intellectual identification with the feelings of others. In other words, an empathetic person vicariously experiences others' feelings. But the empathetic person falls short of being able to read minds or to transmit and receive thoughts like Deanna does, depending on the script of the day.

Deanna Troi, then, is no "empath". She is, however, some kind of amazing Betazoid clairvoyant.

Are there true "empaths" at the poker table today?

YES! Even as this is written, there are "empaths" jousting on the green field of honor in the holy game.

We will assume that an "empath" (not really a word) is a player who experiences empathy, something all of us harbor and use to some degree. A talented "empath" - not a Deanna Troi clairvoyant - at the poker table is able, in effect, to place himself in the chair of his opponent and sense, to some large or small degree, the angst or eagerness of his adversary. Just as important, he can look back at himself and see himself as his opponents see him.

Empathy is used extensively, constantly, every day by people who are not on the Enterprise or at the poker table. It's used in huge dollops by salesmen and politicians (is there a difference?) and empathy is the most vital and commanding talent of method actors. (Geordi could use some of that.) Empathy is all around us and it is a worthwhile and rewarding gift.

Many of our poker champions employ an abundance of empathy. Bluffing, calling, dodging and usually being right are acts that are more than luck to the "empath".

Does every good player rely solely on empathy?

Of course not. An empathic player who does not constantly exercise analysis and discipline, together with empathy, will be a losing player every time.

Does every good player have an abundance of empathy?

Nope. The analytical player, who habitually and objectively reviews his opponents, their habits, betting patterns, mannerisms, and methods, can substitute those talented and acquired habits for much of what comes naturally to the "empath". Moreover, players who depend too heavily on empathy often tend to get lazy and become quick, easy prey for the habitually disciplined analysis of the power player.

If you have been endowed with a good supply of empathy, it can be employed to overwhelming advantage. Use it well. Deanna Troi would be proud. And, at the poker table, you'll never have to explain dylithium crystals.

317

Empathy as a part of Intuition.

Players who are fond of people are the most likely to become the best players.

Why? Well, because poker is a people game. Those who like people have an understanding of people. (It's hard to dislike something or someone we understand.) And understanding the opponent is what separates winners from losers at the poker table.

When the empathic player places himself in the opponent's position, he is a long way toward knowing that person. He experiences what makes the opponent tick and what makes him bet. But empathy is only a part of making the right move.

When we combine empathy with the repetition of the holy game, the familiarity fills our subconscious. Our minds fill with repetitive information and we become intuitive. Intuition is simply our subconscious telling us something. Experience-fed players are more intuitive than the beginners they play against because of all the information their subconscious has amassed. It is one of the Dominator's heaviest advantages.

"I had a gut feeling he was bluffing, so I called him. And, you know, I was right. From now on I'm going with my gut." Those are words we frequently hear and maybe we've sometimes said them ourselves.

The "gut feeling" is what we are calling intuition. It's based on experience and many previous decisions. That experience and those decisions are locked in our subconscious and are instinctively applied to each poker decision we make.

"I had a gut feeling he was bluffing, so I called him. And, you know what? He had the nuts." Oh, oh. What happened in this case? Well, no one said intuition was perfect.

When our intuition leads us the wrong way, our subconscious data base has one more entry it can use to help us decide what to do the next time. There is always time.

Learning to use Intuition.

Can we learn to use our intuition? Oh, yes.

First, we need material to feed our subconscious. That means we must pay attention; we must focus on the game and the players. Everything we see, everything we experience, everything we feel about the opponents is registered by our psycho-cybernetics. The more we play and the more we pay attention, the more is placed in our brains and the more information our intuition can access.

Then comes the time to access.

"My first inclination is the one I always go with." Many players believe that is true and many players are right, but not necessarily every player every time.

Each of us, as an individual, learns how best to use our intuition. The more empathic of us will learn to read the psyche of the opponent and place the emphasis in that kind of read. The more objective of us will process the information more slowly and go with the first inclination when those circuits have fed our decider what we want to know. All of us will do some of both, some quickly, some more slowly. In high stakes stages of poker, bluffing and tells ARE the game. The players all know about the "little voice" that talks to them and suggests what to do. These players know themselves and their opponents. And they are so familiar with that little voice, they can call it by its first name.

Guessing is not intuition. Anyone can guess. Intuition is the honed skill of tapping our subconscious for that bit of extra information when we need it.

$1 and $2 no limit games.

Intuition is a huge weapon for the experienced player in $1 and $2 blind no limit hold 'em. To gain experience, we keep playing and practicing. No limit hold 'em is a complicated game. We learn through experience and we never stop learning. In playing, we build our intuitive knowledge. The noble game is made to order for people who have mastered the objective side and savor the subjective game of people, with all the familiar patterns.

In the small games, $1 and $2, the money earned from intuitive play is much easier than playing down the block with the older boys.

Discussion 431

Spotting and Using Tells

It is recommended that the reader begin this series with Part 101.

Poker is not a card game played by people.

Poker is a people game played with cards.

Suitcase Sellers spent a portion of his youth hustling the game of Razz at the Golden Nugget.

Razz is a lowball stud game. Objectively, there is little margin for playing it well, but there is a large margin for playing it badly. So it isn't a likely game for a hustler. Just like draw poker, a power player had to rely heavily on his people skills. For most hustlers to sit in a Razz game there had to be at least two players who were loose producers, throwing off their money by playing badly. And, while the Razz hustler was waiting for bad play, he had to play the good players without making mistakes.

Suitcase neither played games with bad players nor played any of his players well, so he had little chance in the game. And, of course, he thought he was merely a victim of bad luck and his luck would change one day.

Sometimes Suitcase would have extra good luck, which meant he would play the twenty dollars his girlfriend gave him for a few hours instead of playing for only a short while.

Suitcase had a buddy named Charlie Shadad. Charlie hustled the same games that Suitcase did; only Charlie won. He played in the right games and he played his players well. And, it follows, the whole time Suitcase thought Charlie was just lucky.

Charlie Shadad graduated from the small downtown games and started playing at the Stardust, moving constantly higher until he reached the biggest game. Charlie was in the money.

Suitcase couldn't figure out why his old buddy didn't stake him to some higher games. He knew he'd stake Charlie if the situation were reversed. Sometimes Suitcase would shake his head. "There he is playing in bright colored checks and here I am talking to lamp posts."

Suitcase had long ago been told of a tell in Charlie's play and Suitcase had always kept the tell a secret. He was told when Charlie went back for another look at his hole cards before he bet, Charlie had a solid hand.

One day, Suitcase was in a snit about his predicament and he decided to tell the other players at the Stardust about the tell on Charlie.

As a result of Suitcase's information, suddenly Charlie was losing money. Charlie asked a friend what he might be doing wrong and the friend told Charlie it was common knowledge that his second peek at his hole cards before he bet meant Charlie was there like a bear.

Then, just as suddenly, Charlie started winning again. Charlie was playing over the top of the tell. Charlie reversed his habit and started taking a last look at his hole cards when he was bluffing and never taking a last peek when he had a good hand.

When the opponents caught on to the reversal, Charlie started mixing his signals. Charlie recouped his losses and remained the king of razz for a long time.

Suitcase is still talking to lamp posts.

It's important for us to know what our image is to the other players. Remember, draw poker and hold 'em get more calls than all other poker games. It's hard to bluff and, before the power player starts to bluff, he must be very sure his power image is intact.

To prevent tells, we must try to be a mechanical player. We'll try to have the same look whether we have caught good cards or bad cards. We reach for our players' checks with the same speed, with the same expression. We'll make them guess by always playing the same.

An alternative is table talk and a loose appearance while playing a power game. Some players are good at this kind of tactic. They've made table talk work for them. The good table talk guy could be you or it could be the other player. We won't coach much on this subject.

Beware that table talk is a dangerous game. We may gain more from our table talk, but there is also more for the opponents to read. Most good players prefer to listen rather than to participate in table talk and they have benefited heavily from talk that some very good players have thought was deceptive.

There are many little tricks played by affable hustlers at the table. Buy the next guy a drink, then bluff him next hand. Compliment him on a good play, bluff him next hand. Pick up a good hand; insult your opponent so he'll call you. Tricky. It's not usually the power player's method, but it is possible to be a talking trickster and be a power player.

However, it's easier to listen and defeat the talking player. When we watch and listen and observe carefully, those chatter tricks become tells.

Tells are abundant at the hold 'em poker table. And their abundance is a good thing, because we don't have many cards to give us clues. The power player must find the tells for each individual opponent. But there are some common patterns:

- Weakness is strength. Shrugging his shoulders, the "weak" player reluctantly shoves his checks toward the pot. He doesn't seem to be interested in his cards and his eyes wander around the room. He's uttering some complaining table talk. These things could mean he's strong and is inviting us in.

- Strength is weakness. The "strong" player splashes his chips toward the pot. A look of satisfaction with his hand, which he closes tightly. A verbal announcement of confidence when he opens the pot. These things could mean he's weak and doesn't want a call.

The above "Weakness is strength and Strength is weakness" could sometimes mean just the opposite. It all depends on the player opponent.

The best tells are patterns of play by the opponents. What does he do in certain situations? Open from what position? Raise with what kind of pocket cards? From what position? Bet or check with what kind of hand after the flop?

We must be observant. We have to play our players. Also, this should not be confused with our prior discussions concerning players who bet strength from apparent weakness; we're talking about actions here, not the cards on the board.

We mustn't overlook the Charlie Shadads of the game who will tell us whether they are strong or weak by their facial expressions, the way they hold their cards, the way they go for their checks, the way they make their bets. When we pay attention, it's easy to pick up those kinds of tells.

One of the most common tells is used in predicting what the players who are to act after us are going to do. Watch the player on your immediate left. He might be telling you whether or not he's going to come into the pot. He's holding his cards one way to get to his checks. He's holding his cards another way to muck his hand. Then notice each player behind him in turn. Soon you may know whether the half of the table behind you is going to play or not going to play.

This is important. Always watch the eyes of your opponent. His eyes, when the cards hit the table, will often tell you plenty. Next in importance are the hands that hold the checks and arrange the pocket cards.

Tells are everywhere.

Here is some general stuff we know:

- Well dressed people are usually conservative.

- Good luck charms have a big meaning (liberal). Same for religious medallions.

- Stacking checks carefully almost always indicates a conservative player. Sloppy checks usually mean sloppy play, very liberal.

- Women players call more than male players. Please don't look for sexism here; it is a dependable statistic.

- Players who constantly quote odds usually don't play their players well.

- Players who look away from the table after a bet usually have a solid hand.

- Players who show their hand to a friend who is standing behind them usually have a good hand. The exception is the show off player who wants to make a grandstand bluffing play.

It is important to point out that many of the types of players described can change during play. The tight player can loosen and the loose player can tighten, depending on what their fortunes at the table have been and the changes in their temperament. The power player is sensitive to these changes and plays accordingly.

There are many players who don't like to call when they are winning because they might lose their profit. Usually, these players will sit back, sometimes literally sit back, and wait for the good hand.

Then there is the type who always calls when he's winning because he's uncomfortable with his win. Yes, uncomfortable with his win! Many players come to lose a certain amount and go home. We must know which of these players is which and play them accordingly. Picking up this information is securing a bounty in tells.

Any player who has something else to do at the table will play nothing but a good hand. Sometimes one of these things is happening: He's talking to someone who approached the table, his chair cushion isn't right or he's just won a pot and his checks aren't stacked yet. Usually, this player can't be bothered with anything but a strong hand.

Frequently, the hand being shuffled by the opponent needs help. He's thinking about it while he shuffles his pocket cards. Watch his eyes when he looks at the board; they may tell you a lot. Then there is the player who always shuffles his hand and does it the same way each time and is a little harder to read. But he is offering us some tells also.

Here's a contradiction. When a player bluffs, he usually acts very calmly. When he has a strong hand, he may be nervous.

The reason the bluffer is calm, is that he knows he must be calm in order to bluff. However, the player with the big hand is excited. If he's a relative beginner, his hand may visibly shake. It happens often with new players.

On the other hand, the player who is normally acting nervous and is suddenly calm usually has a very strong hand. The same goes for the player who slouches and suddenly sits up straight and pays unusual attention to the action.

What about eye contact? It's hard to interpret. Some players stare at the opponent almost mercilessly after betting. Most stare at the pot. There are few clues in those two instances, if they always do it. However, there is one eye contact that is almost always a dependable tell. If a player bets, looks at you briefly, offers a thin smile, and then looks nervously away, he is usually bluffing.

Remember Charlie Shadad? Charlie always went back for a second peek at his hole cards to make sure he had the hand he thought he had. But Charlie was playing low ball stud. He wanted to make sure he wasn't paired with a low card in the hole before he made the big bet. In poker, as opposed to low ball, the second peek player is looking to see if he made a hand or has a hand to draw to; he usually hasn't made his hand yet.

Example: Three spades are in the flop or in front of the opponent and one of them is a queen. The opponent looks one more time at his pocket cards. The first thing we know is that he doesn't have queens. We also know he doesn't have spades. What we strongly suspect is that he has one spade in the hole, which hasn't made a big impression on him until the flop and he wants to make sure he's drawing to a spade flush that might win. It can happen more often when he's making sure he's drawing to a straight, because the straight is often harder to read and needs another look.

Remember, tells are different with different players. We have to be observant to benefit.

Discussion 432

Basic Tells

It is recommended that the reader begin this series with Part 101.

Poker is not a card game played by people.

Poker is a people game played with cards.

White Haired Murphy was one of the greatest poker players of the forties, fifties and sixties. A lot of draw poker was played in those days. Murphy would sometimes watch a low level player start to bet his hand, then draw back, then stumble his checks toward the pot. Murphy would watch in amusement, making no move toward his checks or toward his hand. By the time the bettor had completed his demonstration, Murphy often would have a broad smile on his face. Then Murphy would throw his hand toward the dealer, look at the opponent and say in a loud voice, "Well, you bluffed me."

What Murphy said didn't mean much to the bettor, but the seasoned players at the table knew what Murphy was saying and there would be a round of chuckles and knowing glances.

<u>Weak or Strong?</u> There is a general rule that the weak and hesitant act from a player is the sign of strength. It's only a general rule, but we can use it until we've find out otherwise.

Part of the work of the power player is to find out if weakness shown means strength or a display of strength means weakness. It's one of the easiest tells to establish simply by watching a few hands. After we have established whether a player is strong when he displays strength or weak when he shows weakness, or just the opposite, we can usually count on the player continuing that tell and that method of play, maybe for the rest of his life. There are a few players who will mix their actions but, still, there aren't many of those in the lower blind games who can mix their show and tell.

<u>Acting too soon.</u> When a player has made a bet and another player acts like he will call, the betting player may look like he's going to spread his hand, or turn his hole cards up. This is designed to show eagerness to display the winning hand. Most often when this happens, the betting player has a weak hand and doesn't want a call. Consequently, the maneuver should make us call with a degree of confidence. However, there are a few amateurs who might actually have a good hand in that spot. It's up to us to see which applies to which opponent.

Likewise, any opponent reaching for his checks before it's his turn to act, probably has a weak hand. He wants to change somebody's mind. So does the player who "accidentally" exposes a card.

<u>When the act changes.</u> Example: In a hold 'em game, our opponent has been calling our bets. He seems only vaguely interested. Then on the turn his demeanor changes. We can usually assume he just got some big help from the turn card.

If he was looking at his hole cards a lot and acting like a call boy, all he had was a hand to draw to. Now, after the turn, he's alert and no longer needs to look at his pocket cards. He probably has a made hand of some sort. And our information came entirely from the tell on the turn.

<u>The force in betting.</u> The stack slide or splash is the easiest tell studied by most players at the table because players tend to watch the betting action as it happens. Therefore, the most evident action to study is the bet coming from an opponent.

Does the stack slide-toward-the-pot show strength or weakness? The base rule is that it shows strength, although a good player will use it as a bluff. And the forceful-splash-toward-the-pot bet usually means weakness. But these very general rules deserve a few general words of caution. The bettor knows we're watching and could be very careful of the impression he's giving; the tells we pick up when he doesn't think we're watching are usually more revealing.

A power player may change his betting style from time to time through the year, but he should always keep his betting the same way he made his first bet at the table. The power player doesn't mix the way he makes his bets; he mixes the hands that he is betting.

Meanwhile, after we've watched the eyes of the opponents as the cards are dealt, we will watch the way the bets come in. Those that vary their methods of betting are supplying us with tells; we merely have to find those tells. The less experienced players with a forceful bet are telling you they are weak. As for the rest of them, we'll stay observant.

Reaching too soon. We've gotten the flop and the turn. The dealer is burning the top card for the river. Our opponent is already reaching for his checks. Rough analysis: he's weak. Even more likely, he was still drawing to make a hand and now wants to represent something that we know he doesn't have.

If we are the one to act first, the weak hand hopes to prevent us from betting. If he bets, he's probably bluffing. But if it's his second bet and he's lucky, he may have made the hand and he's eager to say, "I told you so".

However, if he is the one to act first, we'll have the semi bluff raise ready.

If it is after the turn, we will not call this person, unless we have put him on something we are fairly sure of and we feel we have him beat. In calling him, we will be encouraging another bet on the river. No need to raise after the turn because our raise won't mean anything. The only way he can call us is if he has us beat! That would be a waste of good raise money and the waste of a possible good future bet.

Anytime our opponent has reached for his checks too soon and he doesn't follow through with the bet, he hasn't made the hand and the power player can take the pot with a big bet and/or a decent hand.

Conversation at the table. Never mind the guy down at the end of the table who talks loud and plays a lot of hands aggressively and laughs when nothing is funny. We all know him. We don't play against him unless we have a better hand.

Generally - you guessed it - mournful or disappointing talk shows strength and cheerful talk shows weakness. There are sounds other than the sound of clear words that can help us. A warning sound like "ohhhh" is probably weakness. A "tsk tsk" sound of disappointment is probably strength. Sounds, like gestures, usually signify the opposite of what the opponent wants us to believe. But it all has to be verified.

Discussion 433

Common Tells

It is recommended that the reader begin this series with Part 101.

Poker is not a card game played by people.

Poker is a people game played with cards.

The Indian from the White Foot tribe always tells the truth. The Indian from the Black Foot tribe frequently lies.

Heard after a bet on the river card on a reservation far, far away:

"So, are you a White Foot Indian or a Black Foot Indian?"

"I'm a White Foot Indian."

"But wouldn't you say you were a White Foot if you were a Black Foot?"

"Nice try. But if you want me to take my moccasins off, you'll have to call my last bet."

Our Native American brother, a power player, is making a good bluff. He is steady and has little expression. He isn't trying to talk his opponent into calling or trying to talk him out of calling. He is a power player with a good image. His white eye opponent must guess the condition of the power player's hand (or foot).

When our native friend was placing his money in the pot, was he smiling? No. Smiles can be easily read. The natural and confident smile indicates an opponent who is quite comfortable with his hand. At this moment our Indian friend could discuss world affairs, if he wanted. Or his mind could be a blank. He's a good bluffer.

Looking at the other side, a bluffer with a thin, forced smile is nervous and hopes he won't be called. He doesn't want to discuss anything and replies to any conversation with short, choppy sentences. He wants his opponent out of the pot.

329

On yet another hand, an opponent who initiates the conversation and who may be over friendly is probably bluffing. But we're not sure. We must know our opponents.

While these are good guidelines, they are generalities. There is no substitute for knowing the individual players and any one of them could be good at reversing these signals.

Comfort zones. When we wore younger men's clothes, we thought that smoke and poker could never be separated. Now there are smokeless card rooms in most poker areas. But we'll use the cigarette example for the comfortable player. If he has just made a bet, looks away, and reaches for his smoke, he has a good hand. We could also say he reached for his sandwich but, you know, a sandwich at the table is almost as rude as a cigarette.

The player who can divide his attention between the cards and the pleasures at hand, usually has a winning hand. Conversely, the weak hand just wants to know the outcome of the action.

Checking the Checks. When do you count your stack? Probably when you stack those checks you just won. Or maybe between hands, you take a quick count.

But - this is important - if you have never addressed this issue before, you probably glance at your checks when you get good pocket cards or a good flop. This is the most common tell in poker.

When a player gets a card or flop that doesn't help him, he isn't interested in his checks. When he gets a good card or flop, it is instinctive for him to glance, just briefly, at his stack. It's an automatic reflex. Bad players do it all the time. Most average players do it habitually. Even expert players sometimes do it.

Here's a discipline every successful power player knows and uses: When the cards are being dealt, whether it be a card to each player, or the flop, or any board card, the power player is the last to see those board cards, because he is watching the players during the deal. He sees the expression on the opponents' faces and he sees whether or not they have glanced at their stacks. He often learns more from watching the stack glance made by the opponents than he does from the cards that were just dealt.

The cards aren't going anywhere soon; they will be there when we get around to looking at them. But, if we miss the opponent's split second stack glance, the opportunity to catch one of the most dependable of tells is gone forever.

<u>Sudden posture.</u> Sometimes we watch a player sit back and wait for a hand. Many times it's because he's winner and has vowed that no one is going to get his checks. If that's the case, we've vowed not to give him any action. But what if he's sitting behind us in the play order? Usually, we'll want to stay out of his way if he's coming in and we must do our best to find the tell that signals he's going to be in the pot.

When mister sit-back-and-wait suddenly sits a little straighter, or adjusts his chair cushion a little, moves his elbows on the table, or is now somehow more attentive, he's ready to play. You can't beat him with an ordinary hand and you can't even begin to think about bluffing him. This sit-back pot is probably his.

<u>Taking time with betting.</u> Limit poker is a hurry-up game. Because the bet, in relationship to the size of the pot, is usually small; the decision to bet, call or raise is not as momentous an occasion as it might be in no limit poker. Limit play depends more on the cards than does no limit poker. Still, it is important in any game to play each hand and make each action with the same rhythm.

But, even if we know what we're going to do as soon as the card or flop is dealt, we should take as much time to fold as we do to call or raise. And we should do it each time. This constant rhythm keeps the opponents from reading something into what otherwise would be varying intervals.

The rhythm also helps create the illusion that we never play a bad hand and there is always something in our hand for us to think about.

Discussion 434

General Tells

It is recommended that the reader begin this series with Part 101.

Poker is not a card game played by people.

Poker is a people game played with cards.

You've seen them, the odds makers. Let's see, what hand to play, which hand to throw away. What hand to continue playing or throw away. Some players are looking at the value of a hand at any time during the action by calculating the odds and the odds are their main concern.

While some players will devote full poker time and effort to these objective goals and consider themselves poker players when they have mastered them, they will be less than half accomplished in their ultimate goal. That is because the numbers and the odds are only the rudiments of poker. We, as power players, know that the numbers game is only the beginning.

Winning poker, played by the power player, depends largely on the *play* of the hand. It depends on our knowledge of the opponents and how that knowledge affects the value of the power player's hand. As stated on previous pages, a large part of the play of the hand lies in tells and another large part is in making and catching bluffs. Combining all elements of playing the player makes the power player Dominant.

Things we have learned about tells.

- Players who dress and otherwise appear conservative are conservative players. Players who stack their checks neatly are conservative players. It's hard for a conservative player to act and to play any other way. The only thing left to figure out is whether the opponent's version of conservative is the same as ours.

- Players who dress messy and stack their chips in messy heaps, nearly always play a messy game, which doesn't necessarily mean a bad game. Sloppy people find it impossible to act in a neat manner. We're sure messy play is really what they are doing.

- The shaky bet is a strong bet. The trembling bettor has a big hand. There is seldom an exception to the rule, but it is possible for an experienced player to reverse the symptom in an over-the-top bluff. We won't worry about it because it is rare; this character has to be a real actor.

- A smile from an opponent must be analyzed. A warm and genuine smile is probably an honest smile and the opponent who makes a bet while wearing this smile has a strong hand.

- We must find the smile that is thin and forced, followed instantly with a look away. This is likely a bluff. Those who have landladies know the thin smile we're talking about.

- A player who receives a card that helps his hand will glance at his checks for a split second. He's ready to bet and he has a strong hand. We'll be sure we watch the eyes of this telling player when he receives his cards and looks at them.

- A player who bets and then shares his hand with another person is usually not bluffing. The exception is the show-off who is trying to impress his buddy.

- The over friendly player at the table bluffs a lot.

- Opponents who act with strength usually have a weak hand. Players who act with weakness usually have a strong hand. But we'll be careful with this rule. We'll make sure our opponent actually falls into these categories. Two or three hands should tell the tale.

- Any player who acts promptly when receiving the flop, turn card or river, is probably representing an honest hand. If he looks and promptly checks, he is probably equally as honest and didn't help his hand. If he looks, thinks, then bets slowly, watch out!

- An opponent who looks away from the table probably has a dangerous hand. A player who stares at his cards for a period of time is looking for something that isn't there. He's usually weak and is looking desperately for something to draw to. The exception is the person who is just slow at reading cards.

- A player acting out of turn is usually weak. He may show that he's ready to spread his hand or he may be reaching for his checks too early. Or he may look back at his hand as we start to make our call. All these usually mean he's bluffing.

- When an opponent bets with a hard splash of players' checks, he is usually bluffing. Likewise a gentle slide of a stack of checks usually reveals the quiet confidence of a hand well made.

- Woeful table talk is usually a sign of strength. Too gleeful? Usually a sign of weakness. We can usually listen to the "oooohs" and "aaaahs" and other sounds and often treat them the opposite of what they are intended to indicate.

We must use the above general rules of tells only as guidelines. It's a good start because weak to medium class players will fall easily into those categories. But we must polish those observations in order to reap the profits. And we must pay special attention to the experienced opponent who plays well; he'll be trying to send mixed signals.

The power player knows that each opponent is an individual and each has his own idiosyncrasies. The more experienced the opponent, the more study is required by us.

In watching the World Series of Poker in 2003, I found an old opponent's tell was still a good one. He is a very experienced and successful player; some would call him the king of poker players. I tested the tell continually as I watched and found it still to be close to definite. Soon after, I watched Phil Ivey lose some small pots to him and then beat him in several large pots with some very good calls. That's when I knew that Phil had found the tell, too.

In long intervals between hands, we will go mentally around the table and recount, in turn, all the things we know about each player. On our checklist should be all the tells we know and some things that aren't classified as tells, such as background, whether he was on the golf course today, and other such trivia which is sometimes quite helpful.

When we find we are a little short in knowledge about one of the players, we concentrate on him for awhile. After all, he may be in our next pot.

Bluffing

Poker Fever

By Sam O'Connor

"Now and forever, it's a sad day when another tired man lays down his hand and quits the holy game of poker."

Poker – what a blessing on the human race.

Poker was popular in the barracks and recreation rooms in the armed services during each of the wars. Funny, how the poker winners on payday became the money lenders until the next payday. And they say government employment isn't a form of free enterprise.

Las Vegas should build a statue to Senator Estes Kefauver, the senator from Tennessee. His Crime Commission of 1950 effectively closed almost all the little gambling places in the U.S. and sent the operators and patrons scurrying to the glitter city of Las Vegas.

Kefauver was hero enough to run for Vice President in 1956 against Eisenhower's second term, but Kefauver had taken away the people's fun while Ike had given the people their country; it was no contest. The public likes the positive which made Ike the clear winner. Still, the Senator remained the decided, albeit unheralded, hero of Las Vegas by concentrating gambling in Nevada where it was legal. But, as Red Buttons would say, they never gave him a dinner.

Today, gambling has moved back to the little towns, to the Indian reservations and to the river boats. In the USA, gambling in general and poker especially have come full circle. Only now it is legal.

In 1960, all of Clark County numbered less than 70,000 people. The area in the population count included Las Vegas, North Las Vegas, Henderson and Boulder City with Las Vegas accounting for only 47,000 of the total 70,000. Locals, including us poker dealers, could drive downtown, park anywhere off Fremont Street where there wasn't a parking meter and leave our cars there all day and all night. There were small shops east of Second Street where there are now huge casinos. Across the street from the Golden Nugget, where the Four Queens now imposes, was a drug store that served a blue plate special for 89 cents. Next to it was a news stand with a shoe shine chair.

All dealers knew their way around downtown in 1960 and that included the side door to the Mint, later to be gobbled up by the Horseshoe Club. That door was something I was to use forty three years later to see the World Series of Poker.

Benny Binion invented the WSOP in 1970 and it had evolved to this circus event of 2003, ably promoted by his son, Jack. I was thrilled to be back in Vegas to see it. Downtown, during the WSOP, the atmosphere was electric. Excitement was through the roof.

With a little help from my friends, I was ushered once again through the old side door and up the stairs to the main room where I was able to elbow my way to a vantage point somewhat near the tournament action. I stood next to a man about my age named Pete.

He spoke first and extended his hand, "Hi, my name is Pete."

I grasped his hand and nodded. "They call me Sam", I said warmly. "How's the game coming?"

Pete filled me in on the final table. It consisted of Farha, Lester, Moneymaker, Vahedi, Benvenitsi, Singer, Harrington, Pak, and Grey. Pete declared with some emphasis, "My man is Sam Farha. I like his style."

Pete went on to tell me his wife, Mary, always went to the WSOP with him but she had recently passed away.

"Sorry to hear that," I offered weakly.

Pete kept on talking. He said poker was important to Mary and him. They looked forward to the big event every year and they cheered for Sam Farha when they could. Pete informed me I was standing in his wife's place that day but that it was all right with him; he was glad to have my company.

There was no doubt Pete understood the hold 'em game. And he knew a lot about Sam Farha. Pete told me about Farha's lack of pattern in his bluffing. Pete liked the high stakes tournament play and could talk at length about the WSOP and Sam Farha.

Soon Farha was in a heads-up pot with Lester. There had been raises before the flop. Farha had an ace and a rag. Lester held a king and a ten.

On the flop, Farha's ace got no help and Howard made kings and tens. There was a bet and a call. Still no ace for Farha on the turn. Check, check. The river brought neither player any help and Sam Farha, with no pair, moved in against Lester's two pair.

Pete informed me, "Sam has a good read on Lester. He knows just when to bluff him. Watch this."

Lester looked a long time at the open cards and at the pot. Lester was cool. He took some time. Then he slowly mucked his hand.

Just as Pete had predicted, Sam Farha had bought the pot on a stone cold bluff!

Pete's arms shot in the air barely missing me. As I stepped back, he looked like a referee signaling a touch down. "Woweeee, Sam! That's my boy! I wish Mary could have been here. She would have enjoyed that play."

We watched some more of the contest for awhile while Pete tried predicting most of Farha's bluffs.

At last, I said I had to go and that I hated to leave. "My best to you, Pete."

But then, I thought of Pete's wife just passing away. "You know, Pete, you really should have gotten someone to come to the tournament with you, to sort of take Mary's place. Maybe a relative or a close friend."

"Oh, I couldn't do that," he said quickly. "They're all at the funeral."

Discussion 440

All About Bluffing

It is recommended that the reader begin this series with Part 101.

Poker is not a card game played by people.

Poker is a people game played with cards.

The reader now knows that the secret of the Dominator's play is in shifting gears, playing position and being in and out of pots – you know, slippery, like a bar of soap in the bath tub. Now we're going to discuss the sudsiest tool of them all.

Many famous professionals will tell us that, after the game is learned, it becomes a game that is all about bluffing. While we find many of the small blinds players making beginners mistakes, it is bluffing best and catching bluffs best that make us winners in any hold 'em game.

This section should set the reader to constantly thinking about bluffing. Even though he may not elect to do any bluffing for a period of time at the table, he should constantly be thinking about it. It is where the additional large margin lies in winning. And, of course, we have to do right.

After we are steeped in the knowledge of cards, position, stacks, players, tells and the ability to mix our play by shifting gears, the game boils down to bluffing.

Once again, because it is important, the largest advantage the Dominator has in any level of no limit hold 'em is his skill in bluffing well and in catching bluffs. Every Dominator is constantly on the alert for a place to make a good bluff or to catch one.

While in the lower blinds games, we may win a little here and there because we understand players, cards, position, stacks and tells, but we cannot prevail in the higher no limit games with only this knowledge. The reason is because the opponents we meet there will also understand much of what we know. We must make good bluffs and catch bad bluffs in order to win.

Understanding bluffing will also be a key to expanding our mix of play.

Does bluffing throw more gamble into the game? It does in the sense of being more active with more money. But, as we pointed out in prior Discussions, the rewards are much greater.

Repeating, in small blind no limit games, so much more of the difference in what we win will be found in bluffing, compared to the higher blinds games. The reason for this difference is because we will be doing far more effective bluffing than the opponents do who are typically found in the low blinds games. We will also catch more of our opponents' poor bluffing.

A different thought about image. In a balanced game, the tight players will consider the Dominator to be loose and the loose players will consider us tight.

What kind of bluffer do you want to be?

When playing no limit small blinds poker, we can often look back at the end of the day and attribute our win, or our loss, to three or four hands. Those hands are the ones we're either proud of or ashamed of and, in either case, we wish we could play them once again. The big hands stay with us awhile.

This bluffing category, making the bluff and catching the bluff, depends more on playing the players than anything else in poker. Again, in big play, whether cash or tournament, it largely becomes the game itself.

We'll divide the kinds of bluffs made by us, and by our opponents, into three major categories. They are:

- The Desperation Bluff.
- The Strategic Bluff.
- The Tactical Bluff.

Not all these bluffs will be performed by us. For instance, we will try to never make the Desperation Bluff or any of its cousins; they are for our opponents to try and for us to catch.

The other two broad categories of bluffs, the Strategic Bluff and the Tactical Bluff will be exercised by us with great regularity and with good reward.

The Bluffing Attitude.

The Dominator is always looking for a place to bluff. This does not mean he necessarily does a lot of bluffing. It does not mean he bluffs willy nilly. It certainly does not mean he is a compulsive or indiscriminant bluffer.

It does, however, mean he is constantly looking for the situation and the opponent that gives him the opportunity to bluff and take the pot.

Anyone can be bluffed, including us. Some opponents are easier to bluff than others. For instance, in general, tight players are more easily bluffed than loose players.

It follows, then, that tight games are better for the Dominator than loose games. But the reader may decide the best game of all consists of a combination of tight and loose players so that he can dance among them, showing hands and bluffing intermittently in the right spots.

Curiously, most knowledgeable players at the table see us bluff and never understand we seldom try to bluff them. That attitude brings us some good calls.

A bonus arrives when the loose player helps build a pot that we will ultimately win by bluffing the tight player after the loose player has dropped out.

If we do not bluff, we lose the opportunity to double our winnings, or more. Often the earnings in $1 and $2 blinds from bluffing are a very high percentage of our winnings. Bluffing, obviously, is a big part of what makes us the Dominator.

Definition. The bluff consists of betting and taking the pot when we have the inferior hand.

Of course, sometimes we think we've bluffed when we have the best hand. We'll never know we had the best hand and we usually chalk it up to a good bluff. It makes us feel good.

Taking the pot with the worst hand consists of at least two broad considerations:

- We must convince the opponent we have the better hand. This means we have to be in a situation where we *likely* have the better hand and the opponent thinks we do.

- We must also believe the opponent doesn't have a far superior hand with which he will call automatically. He must have only a good hand in which he has little confidence in the face of our image and our bluffing bet or our bluffing raise.

During the bluff, those of us who do not have the Brunson gift of patter must remain quiet. Anything we say will affect our opponent's decision to fold, call, or raise. We don't know for sure what he's thinking. Therefore, what we say may influence him in a way we do not intend and is not to our advantage.

Sometimes the opponent will try to get us to enter conversation. "Do you want a call? Or maybe you don't want a call. Which is it?" is a common opener to try to pry something from us. In these situations we can't be a statue, so we can simply say without expression, "Your choice." Or something similar.

When we bluff, we must be decisive. We must know that if the flop is garbage and doesn't help the opponents, this time we will bluff. We've made the decision before the flop and we execute our bluff with the same rhythm and demeanor that we always use when it is our turn to act. If we are confused by the flop and we hesitate, we cannot, must not bluff, because players from the next table may come over just to call our weak performance.

Opportunities to bluff will appear more frequently with some players than with others. For instance, the tight player will believe we have the best hand because he's looking for an excuse to throw his hand away. But we must be careful he doesn't have a hand that cannot be thrown away. And we must always ask ourselves what the opponent's attitude toward us is at the moment we want to bluff. Will he call because we have been caught bluffing lately? Will he call because we have lost a couple of pots lately and he believes we can't make a hand? Maybe he will call because he believes he has the best hand. Or maybe he will call because he's on tilt.

The bluff we make must tell a story that isn't true. Of course, that's what a bluff is. But it must deliver a clear story, not a confusing one. If the opponent is confused, he may call in order to search the answer to something he doesn't understand.

Do we ever show our bluffs? Almost never. The exception occurs when we want to change our image to the rest of the table. Then, of course, we shift gears into the game we want to play in this particular company. We'll be careful; not everyone will believe us.

Which brings us to being caught bluffing.

We must not have an overwhelming fear to be caught. (A healthy caution is good.) Once caught, our failure to bluff successfully can be used to our advantage later when we actually have the best hand. After the surprise of being caught happens, we'll change gears and mix our play well. We've lost our tight image and we are viewed as a player. What's more, we will recognize the opponent who caught us, saw us in that manner.

The real game is now afoot. We will explore the various kinds of bluffs in the coming pages.

Discussion 441

The Desperation Bluff

It is recommended that the reader begin this series with Part 101.

Poker is not a card game played by people.

Poker is a people game played with cards.

In review, the three categories of bluffs are:

- The Desperation Bluff
- The Strategic Bluff
- The Tactical Bluff

Fantasy Bluffs. (A type of Desperation Bluff.)

The Fantasy Bluffer assaults the game with more exuberance than common sense.

We don't do the Fantasy Bluff. It is delusional. We are more in touch with reality than those who attempt it. The player who makes the Fantasy Bluff is a real piece of work. He may actually believe he isn't bluffing.

Ever watch several hands go to the turn with one of the players making a big bet to take the pot? I mean <u>several</u> pots in a row taken by a big bet? Those bet-and-take-it pots can accompany a long period of not seeing anyone's pocket cards. During that period, we sometimes start to think, "Oh, so that's all there is to it. Whoever bets can take it." Someone at the table thinking along those lines may actually make such a remark.

Now the Fantasy Bluffer decides that he'll actually, just for this one hand, try the Fantasy Bluff. He'll believe he has the hand he's been waiting for, and he'll bet it that way. He may not even look at his cards. If he actually believes he has the hand, he reasons, it'll show in his positive manner and his opponents will be convinced he has the nuts. There can be no tells, he says to himself, because this fantasy hand will actually exist in his mind and he's going to play it that way. The troublesome opponents with the weaker hands will have to fold. And so it goes.

344

The fantasy player may make his bluff work, maybe once, or even twice. If he does, he's not only lucky, he's in trouble because he'll try it again and he'll lose the farm when he runs up against a good slow played hand.

He'll be detected soon, of course, because he doesn't realize his image at the table. This type is commonly a loose cannon and people will be suspicious about what he's representing. He's normally the type of player who pays little attention to what the other players might be holding. He'll be mainly interested in representing his hand and buying the pot. Consequently, he's bound to run into an opponent's strong hand, maybe the first time he tries it. We hope we are holding that hand.

But Fantasy Bluffing happens. The Fantasy Bluffer is out there among us. He's fun. We like him at our table because of his wild bluffs, and those wild bluffs aren't the only way he's losing.

The Desperation Bluff. (The most common type.)

The Desperation Bluff is made by Paco's fool.

It's more common than its cousin, the Fantasy Bluff, and it's also one we like to see our opponents try.

Once more, the Desperation Bluff is one we never use. We like it because we catch others attempting it. And they do attempt it often in small games.

The Desperation Bluff is trite, empty and is strictly for our novice opponents. It is so named by us because players use it in desperation. They believe it is the only way they can win a lost pot and they make the pathetic bet in feeble desperation.

As bluffs go, it is the easiest to detect and it is used in small blinds games by amateurs much more than it is used in the larger games by knowledgeable players. It feeds us and is, therefore, part of the Dominator's meat and sustenance.

Desperation Bluffs are seldom planned by the opponents. They are, therefore, poorly chosen and poorly executed. They often are made by a player we have determined to be a weak calling station, a player who is much too active and likes to draw to a hand and never give up on it.

Desperation Bluffs are also made by the aggressive player who is drawing to a hand and hasn't been able to make it. The only way he can win is to try a bluff in impulsive desperation.

Desperation Bluffs, therefore, are made by all kinds of weak players. That's why they are made so often.

The easily detected Desperation Bluff usually occurs in an unlikely circumstance. That's the key to detection.

The bluffer thinks to himself, "Whoops, this hand is getting out of control. My power player adversary has a better hand. I've seen him throw a lot of hands away and maybe he'll throw one away for me. It's the only way I can win this hand." Such desperation.

Such opportunity. Such a clear signal for us to call.

The good player has only to determine whether he has the best hand against the desperation bluffer. Many of these pots are called and won by us with a single pair because the Desperation bluffer has missed his draw.

If we think we don't have the best hand, i.e., the desperation bluffer is bluffing with the best hand, we can raise the bluffer and take the pot. We can do it because of the desperation we read in him. That kind of raise or check/raise bluff on our part can happen frequently, but it takes confidence.

Remember to place the opponent on a hand and be able to believe in the decision. It's hard to catch the bluff without that information.

Bluffing the bluffer is our counter to the player who is bluffing with the best hand. However, it will place our stack at risk and so the situation of our raising the bluffer with our own bluff must be chosen well.

Sometimes, but not often, we read the desperation in our opponent after the flop or the turn, and we call or raise him at that time. But the most frequent, most easily detected and the most lucrative impulse bets by our opponents are made after the river cards have missed their hands and, in frustration, they try to buy the pot.

If our opponent has checked his hand to us and we've checked along or, if we're in the lead and he has checked along with us or called us, we often detect the desperate look on his face long before the river. Then, when we check to him on the river, he bets with a desperate prayer to Paco the poker god. We're there to deny him any reward for his desperate prayer.

Often the Desperation bluffer will be bluffing with the best hand and think he is bluffing. On those occasions, we have to come back with an even bigger bluff. Needless to say, it is no time to be short stacked. But then, the Dominator is never short stacked.

We will notice, when we are betting and our opponent is calling with a drawing hand, he can't find a way to raise and we know he is not a slow hand player. He, therefore, is trying to make a hand. Also, this type of weak player can't find a way to raise after the river when he hasn't made his hand. But, we can check to him after the river as an invitation to him to try to buy the pot. When he tries, we have just doubled our win.

More on the invitation to bluff in the next Discussion.

Discussion 442

Inviting the Desperation Bluff

It is recommended that the reader begin this series with Part 101.

Poker is not a card game played by people.

Poker is a people game played with cards.

Inviting the Desperation Bluff.

This is the trap that beats the over aggressive and weak player. This is the trap that beats the bully who doesn't play well. This is the trap in small no limit games that helps make the power player the Dominator.

When the no limit beginner sits at the table, his knees are likely to grow weak when the new guy or gal sits down with a playing bankroll that's three, four or twenty times the amount as the next highest stack at the table.

To experienced players, the new guy is the one we've been waiting for. We're not afraid of him and he's gambling a lot of money that can be won.

Of course, there is the player who places a huge roll on the table and plays the tightest passive game we may ever see. This tight player is simply a money show off and relatively harmless. He can be handled by simply refusing to bet his hand for him and playing nothing but strong hands against him. Plus, he usually is easily bluffed. Because he offers little action, we don't mind when he leaves and he nearly always leaves the table soon after he's impressed everybody with his bankroll.

Never mind him.

We're talking now about the opponent who wants to dominate the table with his money, with his bets and raises. He is inclined to dink in with hands that he can't raise with and later raise at the slightest provocation. He loves to play and he passes up far fewer hands than most of us.

We should recognize he's not usually stupid. In fact, he may have a good understanding of the game. But he loves to play and he is over active, the true recreational player with an ego to chase. If he thinks he can bully the hand, he won't hesitate to try it.

We've discussed many times how we like to have strong players to our right at the table for easier handling and the weaker players to our left. This is not one of those times.

Now understand this: The charger we're talking about is not a strong player, he is a recreational player who may have some understanding of the game and who wants to buy some pots now and then. He's like a maniac, but he hasn't lost his senses.

Our opponent in this discussion is not the hard charging Phil Ivey or Danny Negreanu; our man is someone who doesn't utilize the winning discretion of those famously superior players. So we want our hard charger on our left, if we can arrange it, because he isn't all that good and we want him there for reasons which we will now illustrate.

In this setting, our charger is sitting immediately to our left. He is on the button.

We hold pocket tens.

Because we are next to the button we raise three limping callers.

Mr. Charger, next to act, doesn't like his button action taken from him and he won't be relegated to a junior role, so he re-raises.

We know he wouldn't re-raise without some kind of reasonable hand but, because he is in the habit of trying to occasionally bully the table, we haven't learned much from his raise. We don't really know anything from his raise except that he has a chip on his shoulder and enough chips in his hand to create some action.

We are tempted to re-re-raise at this point, but that would start a raising contest to little avail; we would learn next to nothing from the heated over action. We'll find out much more after the flop than we will with a re-re-raise before the flop. Besides, our tens don't deserve all that much action and he could have a good hand; good hands can happen to anybody, anytime.

The limpers fold and we call our charger's re-raise.

The flop brings us a deuce, a six, and a seven.

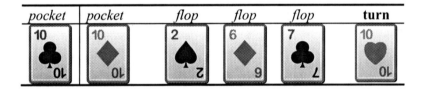

pocket	pocket	flop	flop	flop
10♣	10♦	2♠	6♦	7♣

We bet the size of the pot. The bully calls.

We now have valuable information. Because he didn't raise our flop bet, we can now place our opponent on high cards and no pair and, certainly, no set, flush or straight draw.

The turn is the ten of hearts.

pocket	pocket	flop	flop	flop	turn
10♣	10♦	2♠	6♦	7♣	10♥

Now that we have Mr. Charger on a hand and we have the nuts on the turn, we check our hand so he can take the lead. We know he will; he thinks we haven't helped our hand and he has those big over cards, whatever they are.

We have shown weakness with our check after the turn and now he's going to teach us a lesson.

Mr. Bully makes a sizable bet.

We take an extra moment or two to "think" about what we will do. My, he has a lot of money and he's awfully intimidating. Gee whiz.

Okay, now we're ready. We hesitatingly call.

The river is the eight of diamonds.

pocket	pocket	flop	flop	flop	turn	river
10♣	10♦	2♠	6♦	7♣	10♥	8♦

We check our hand. We aren't afraid of a straight, even though it is possible. It barely enters our mind because we've placed our opponent on big cards with no pair.

Because of our weak check and hesitant call on the turn, our check on the river has given the bully an **invitation to bluff**. And we are quite confidant he will make that bluff.

Mr. Charger promptly tells us he's putting us all-in.

We hesitate a few moments for effect and then say that we call. We don't leap to a call because our egos aren't wanting and we have no reason to rub in our decision. We take our time so we won't insult Mr. Charger (we don't do those things in any situation) and, especially in this case, we want him to stay at the table and try it again at a later time.

The opponent shows us Big Slick and says in a very nice way, "Good call, sir." After all, he is a gentleman. And we are too. We say, "Thank you." We compliment him. "You really had us thinking." "Nice hand," he says. It's his nature to want the last word and so we leave things that way.

Mr. Charger is quite sure we won because we were lucky enough to make three tens. If we hadn't made the set, he rationalizes, we wouldn't have called.

Would we have played the hand the same if we didn't have a set?

You betcha! Although the opponent might not have tried the Desperation Bluff if there weren't a ten on the board to encourage him to represent a straight.

We were fairly sure our pocket pair was the winning hand, but our set of tens was much more comfortable, just in case we were wrong about the no pair which might have given the opponent a small set.

351

We were quite sure he didn't have a pair of aces or kings because he didn't play that kind of hand in the big pocket pair manner. Pocket jacks could have been a possibility, but not likely because Mr. Charger also would have played them stronger; he'd have raised our bet post flop, if not preflop, if he had had jacks or any painted pair in the pocket.

Here's the key. If we had bet our hand on the turn or after the river card hit, it would have given our opponent no room to make his bully Desperation Bluff and he would have had to throw his hand away. There would have been no invitation. If we are to get value for our play, we must give the hard charger lots of room to make a charge.

What if he had pocket nines?

Ouch! Pocket nines would have been a narrow mathematical possibility, considering the broad spectrum of hands that Mr. Charger plays. But, in this case, we had to take the chance of no nines and we were glad to see the eight on the river because it gave our man further excuse, in the form of a possible straight, to make the Desperation Bluff.

Lesson learned: We like the poor playing hard chargers to our left so we can show weakness and invite them to bully and bluff.

When it comes to tells, we can usually find a tell or two with the bully or any recreational player. The most frequent tell will be his fingers around his players' checks when he's eager to enter the pot.

Incidentally, our opponent doesn't have to be the hard charger for us to send the invitation to bluff. Many times we are quite certain we have the best hand and, if we bet the hand, we're sure the adversary will fold. When we sense some desperation in this adversary, we can check the best hand and let him discover the opportunity of trying to bluff us.

Sometimes we can watch him as he slowly tumbles to the idea of bluffing; that's always fun. On those occasions, he's surprised by our check and sees it as weakness.

Discussion 443

The Button Bluff and the Blind Man's Bluff

It is recommended that the reader begin this series with Part 101.

Poker is not a card game played by people.

Poker is a people game played with cards.

Strategic Bluff. At this point, we introduce the Strategic Bluff. It is so called because it is often planned before the cards are dealt. Because it is a long range plan, it is strategic.

Tactical Bluffs will be considered later. They are the ones we decide to use as the hand is played, usually as a result of cards flopped or opponents' maneuvers.

The **Strategic Bluff** is not your spur of the moment bluff or your semi-bluff. It is pure bluff with whatever cards you may be dealt and is plotted without regard to most opponents who could be involved. We are playing a table of players in which the entire assembly is ready to lay down to a good bet from a strong player with a good image.

First Strategic Bluff. The Button Bluff. When the time is right, the easiest planned bluff is accomplished when we are on the button. We decide when the blinds and/or opening bets are ripe for the steal. It will probably be at a time when the game has slowed slightly. As always, to make this maneuver, we need a good image.

We'll do the Button Bluff Phil Helmuth style. In other words, the cards we hold make no difference in our action. They could be good cards (it is better), or they could be rags (it doesn't matter).

When there is a raise before it's our time to act, we re-raise on the button, or when we're near it. We get one or two callers, but no re-re-raise from the opponents. So we place them on high cards, but not paired. The flop comes ten, jack and eight.

When the action is checked to us, we bet more than the size of the pot. In most cases, we'll move the pot to our stacks at that time. The only interruption to our success would be a tremendous flop that helps one of our opponents.

When there are high board cards, our plan may sour. We wouldn't call an after flop bet from the first pre-flop raiser under those conditions. For the same reason we wouldn't bet into that kind of flop if it were checked to us.

We'll also be aware of any slow player in the action.

In the Button Bluff action, we simply are betting the opponents won't help. We are betting they will check to us (we were the last raiser), and they won't care to finance a search to see if we're bluffing. We're in last position with the last raise, and we're getting two to one for our money.

The down side occurs when we are called holding nothing. It happens when a player has a lucky flop and is slow playing to our previous raise. In that case, we have no trouble in throwing our hand away.

The Second Strategic Bluff. The Blind Man's Bluff. This is closely related to the Button Bluff, above, except it comes from the blind. And it is one of our favorites.

We play it from one of the blinds and we like it because, as in the case above, we are rooting for low and middle cards on the flop instead of high cards. It doesn't matter what cards we are holding; we simply want the opponents to be holding high cards.

Again, we must have the proper image and have shown strength recently in a showdown hand or similar impressive action. Whatever the circumstance, in the small blinds game there should be some indication that we are a player to be reckoned with.

The Blind Man's Bluff is a little more edgy than the Button Bluff because of position. Because we are not the last to act after the flop, some math is required.

The math is fairly simple. We divide the thirteen ranks of the suits into thirds. (That's a trick!) We'll do that by placing five ranks in the middle section.

It's a given that we have a more than two to one advantage of generally catching middle and low cards on the flop than we do high cards, jack through ace. These odds are enhanced slightly by placing our two opponents on high cards, taking those cards out of the remaining deck and making them unavailable for the flop. And, if we also have a high card, it eliminates one more possible high card that might otherwise appear in the flop.

In a three handed pot, we have more than a two to one advantage of catching mostly middle or low cards and we have two callers. Therefore, our collective opponents are laying us two to one in money and saying we can't get those slightly better than two to one middle and low cards. It's hard to be in a better pot odds-to-card draw situation.

The down side is there will be three cards in the flop that will have to miss the opponents and we will have to act first. But the situation is good, considering the odds.

Well placed, the Blind Man's Bluff is the Dominator's advantage, if we have chosen the right opponents at the right time. If the flop doesn't work out, we don't bet and we didn't have much invested. But it works much of the time.

The big pay-off lies in getting a lucky flop and making the good hand we hadn't counted on. We'll be laying a good trap.

The big pots in hold 'em are in the surprises. The Blind Man's Bluff gives a good shot at either a small pot with good odds, or that occasional rewarding surprise.

Example:

We are in one of the blinds and the pot is opened with a raise. There is a caller and we call from the blind. It is important here that we call and not raise; we do not want to represent a high card hand, although a raise from one of the opponents would be welcome. It's best if the opponents think we are merely "protecting" our blind and playing middle cards. Actually, what we have in the pocket matters not.

Because of the raise, and a call from another opponent, we place both opponents on high cards. In our action, we are simply betting the flop will not be an impressive high card flop.

Our scheme, the odds, and our play are good and we need only to get the garbage flop. Even one queen or jack is not particularly threatening to us.

In our example, the flop brings us a nine, a ten and a seven. We come out betting the size of the pot or more. With the bet, we almost always bring the pot promptly home to our stacks.

Again, to do this, our image must be good. Also, unlike the Button Bluff, we can't do the Blind Man's Bluff very often because the players with the big card hands will become quickly skeptical and eventually suspicious. We don't want to blow our win for the day by making a series of bad bluffs.

The Blind Man's Bluff, used judiciously, is powerful because the opponents expect blinds to hold middle cards and because the flop hasn't touched anything they hold, especially if there has been a raise. Additionally, the size of our wager is something they don't want to mess with without flop help.

If we are called by one of our opponents, we can usually place him on a pocket pair and, often, a pair which is an overpair to the cards in the flop. In that case, the turn card will tell us what to do next.

If we have to give up the hand, we've lost some checks, but didn't have to show our hand. And we've created action that will give us a playing advantage in the near future.

Discussion 444

The Free Draw Bluff

It is recommended that the reader begin this series with Part 101.

Poker is not a card game played by people.

Poker is a people game played with cards.

Tactical Bluffs.

In a prior discussion, we talked about the Button Bluff and the Blind Man's Bluff. Both are Strategic Bluffs. We'll now move on to Tactical Bluffs.

In review, bluffing is something that has to be done if we are to dominate the small no limit games and win substantial amounts. Taking advantage of the bluff is essential to winning more than our share, which is what Dominators do.

We'll introduce Tactical Bluffs by discussing the Free Draw Bluff.

The Free Draw Bluff.

In this situation, we are near the button holding Big Slick, suited. We have raised the pot and we have two callers. The flop brings us a four flush and an inside straight draw. Now we plan our bluff. We plan it long before the action gets to us.

Pocket	*Pocket*	*Flop*	*Flop*	**Flop**
A♦	K♦	Q♠	J♦	4♦

The action is checked to us. It should be; we were in last position, we were the raiser and the flop is fairly strong. This makes the semi-bluff easy (not a pure bluff).

357

We bet more than the size of the pot. Maybe we'll take the pot, then and there. If we don't take the pot at this juncture and we are called, we are set up for two free draws to big slick, to a flush, and to a straight. The easier semi-bluff has just graduated to the more opportune Free Draw Bluff. It's tactical because it wasn't planned from the beginning.

After the turn, the opponents don't usually bet, because we took the lead the last time around. Now we can check along with them and look at the river card for nothing. Our last bluff after the flop has just gotten us two free cards, the turn and the river with a good chance of making a hand.

If we get and ace or king or make a complete hand on the turn, we may want to bet and take it. And, if it's the nuts, we may want for the river to bet.

If the opponents do take the lead at any time and make a bet, it is likely the board has helped them, maybe even given them two pair. We might throw our hand away. It's time to know our players and determine whether or not they would call our pre-flop raise to draw to jack/queen or slow play what is probably now a set.

But, unless the turn has helped one of the opponents in a big way (or sometimes even if it has), the action will probably be checked to us after the flop, and that is the main feature of The Free Draw Bluff. We can now make our bet in order to get two free draws.

If one of the opponents bets after the turn, we play the hand according to what we know about the opponent, how the card he caught might have affected his hand, how the same card affected our hand, and we take into consideration the amount he bet. In other words, it could get complicated. After some thought, we might throw the hand away.

Often, an inexperienced no limit player will still give us good pot odds with a small bet after the turn. The pot odds often make it advantageous for us to try for a complete hand on the river.

In review, we've had a chance to take the pot before the flop, after the flop, after the turn, and after the river. That computes to four opportunities with only two bets. And that, power players, is the advantage of the Free Draw Bluff.

If we haven't helped our hand by the time we're looking at five board cards the opponents likely suspect we are on a drawing hand. We must not, will not, shall not, make the easy-to-read Desperation Bluff. That's for those other guys. In our case, the hand just didn't work out.

If the above flop had given us an open ended straight draw along with the four card flush, we might have played the hand differently.

Let's say we raised with the king / queen of diamonds and the flop came four, jack, ten.

Pocket	Pocket	Flop	Flop	Flop
K♦	Q♦	4♦	J♠	10♦

Our easy chart shows us the draw is around three to one for the turn and about the same odds for the river. This makes the odds 1.5 to 1 when we can get the two draws for the price of one. Because we have two callers in the hand we have three to one money odds for any pot sized bet we make, or about double the amount of money odds to drawing odds.

At this point, we can bet the size of the pot and be optimistic about any call. This time the bet is not just a bluff for a two card draw, it is also a bet for value.

Here's another angle. We'll look at the stacks of the other players (we should already have done that) and decide whether an all-in bet would be appropriate.

If we have the shortest stack, it will ensure that we will get two cards for the price of one bet and we'll have the drawing advantage – if we are called.

If one of the other players has the shortest stack, or both of them have stacks shorter than ours, it is our religious duty to put them all in and take the draw.

The gamble lies in someone drawing to a nut diamond flush, but that's the chance we take. The best part: It could all be academic; we probably won't get a call.

Discussion 445

The Ambush Bluff and the Delayed Bluff

It is recommended that the reader begin this series with Part 101.

Poker is not a card game played by people.

Poker is a people game played with cards.

Continuing with the Tactical Bluff.

Perhaps The Ambush Bluff should be called the hidden bluff. But we can't call it that because we would like all our bluffs to be hidden; that is, we would like them all effectively to represent false value, win us money, and go undetected.

If we're successful in all our bluffs, we never have to show them and they are all hidden. That's hard to do and it's absurd to think we might be able do it over a long period of time. But bluffing in general can go mostly undetected in small no limit games when properly executed. And the Ambush Bluffer will come closest to keeping his secret the longest.

What kind of bluffer are you?

The Ambush Bluff.

We can only bluff before and after the flop and before and after the river; those are the only four times to bet in hold 'em. One of those times can spring an ambush.

The First Stage. Just as the Free Draw Bluff is made by the thinking player and the Desperation Bluff is made by the novice, the Ambush Bluff is also different because of the type of player who uses it. He doesn't have a bold image. He's the player that lies in wait.

He's not the simplistic hard rock player we see so often, but he has that image. He's the seemingly tight player looking for the perfect bluff. He's good.

360

The Ambush Bluff, then, is made by the quiet, systematic player. He's hiding and he doesn't bluff often. When he does bluff, he's usually a successful bluffer because he seldom bluffs and therefore he is believable and he hasn't been caught. (He also doesn't win many big pots.) When we are the ones springing the Ambush Bluff, we do it at the right time and the opponents believe us.

Many Dominators use the Ambush Bluff early in the game more than later and that's a good idea. We use it after we've been there only a few minutes and we have shown nothing but tight play. We have everybody pretty much lined up into types. We haven't been active because we've been working on the details and waiting for a good rhythm in the cards.

The Ambush Bluff is used on or near the button and it is frequently a semi-bluff. We make the bluff to take the pot but, if we're called, we have a fair hand and something to draw to. (We've covered this technique before.)

When we take the pot, the simple Ambush has worked. We're happy and we haven't shown our hand. It's a perfect half bluff.

When our half bluff is called and we have to make a second bluff after the turn, we have won a larger pot, which is good, and we still haven't shown our hand. The Ambush strikes again.

However, let's consider this. We didn't make a perfect bluff because it didn't work the first time and it took two bets to get the money.

But we have new information. We have learned that our opponent suspects our bluffing but didn't develop a hand he could call with. We know that soon we will be called all the way to the river by an observant player. That brings us to the advanced stage of the Ambush Bluff strategy.

The Second Stage. Sooner or later, our first stage Ambush will be called. We can throw the hand away and not be harmed. Or sometimes we are called and we make the hand or help it on the draw, show the hand and take the pot. Either way our Ambush Bluff has been revealed and it will bring our strategy to the second stage.

The Ambush Bluff in the second stage is really a fake bluff. We have the goods. We're saying in effect, "See? I'm bluffing again." It's a reverse bluff and it is beautiful.

It's important to have a feel for the exact time when we will be called and when we will not be called. We're flirting with danger and the right timing with the right opponent is important.

We will be playing the players and the table. It's even better when we not only get called, but a good player raises us because he thinks we're bluffing and thinks he can come over the top. That's a premium Ambush for us. And it can happen now and then at small no limit tables.

We'll let Murphy play the Ambush hand.

Murphy has been playing in a nine handed game with four good players and four novices, the Dominator's favorite arrangement.

Murphy has raised a few times on the button and stolen a few pots after the flop, and he's made a couple of Ambushes. Players are beginning to get suspicious.

The beginner player to his left has said to Murphy, "I'm going to clip you off." The vernacular in itself is revealing.

Now Murphy is sitting on the button with an ace and an eight. A middle player calls the blind and Murphy raises from the button.

The small blind to his left, Mr. Clip Off, calls the raise. The big blind folds and the middle player calls.

The flop is a jack and two eights.

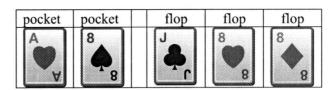

pocket	pocket		flop	flop	flop
A♥	8♠		J♣	8♥	8♦

The two opponents check. Murphy bets the size of the pot.

Mr. Clip Off, in the blind, raises Murphy the size of Murphy's bet and looks at Murphy tentatively. (This would be a good place for a Dominator's Blind Man's Bluff on the part of the raiser, but we're talking about a novice opponent here who is looking for a reason to call and bluffing is not on his mind. Also, an experienced bluffer would have made a bigger raise.)

The middle player throws his pocket cards into the muck. It's up to Murphy.

Could Mr. Clip Off have a jack eight? Not likely, thinks Murphy. He's wants to "clip" Murphy "off" and holding jack / eight is not the way of the novice. He'll do his "clip off" with a bigger hand.

How about two jacks? No way, thinks Murphy. Mr. Clip Off with a chip on his shoulder would have raised before the flop if he'd had a pair of jacks.

Murphy knows if Mr. Clip Off has three eights, Murphy has the best three eights, or at least a tie, because of his ace kicker. Murphy thinks about the novice, the chip on his shoulder, the tentative look when he raised Murphy's flop bet.

Murphy re-re-raises, a bet four times the last raise.

Mr. Clip Off thinks long and hard. Actually, he isn't doing much thinking; he's delaying in order to gain more courage. At last, he calls the raise.

The turn is the five of spades.

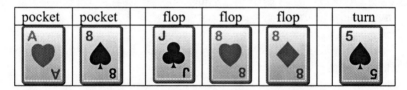

pocket	pocket		flop	flop	flop		turn
A♥	8♠		J♣	8♥	8♦		5♠

When Mr. Clip Off checks, Murphy knows his hand is golden. Murphy moves all-in.

Mr. Clip Off promptly calls because the chip on his shoulder has grown considerably during the last few seconds. He hopes Murphy is on a bluff.

The river is the three of hearts. Mr. Clip Off shows an ace / jack and Murphy takes the pot. The Ambush Bluff, second stage, strikes again.

Besides a good pot, the second stage Ambush has a bonus. After its execution and hands are shown, the Dominator has regained his full tight image and has added some strong play to that image.

363

Those players at the table who were thinking about calling the first stage semi-bluff Ambush are re-thinking their intentions. The real game is now afoot.

The Ambush Bluff, in all its stages, is related to a planned Button Bluff in that it is meant to be played as planned, strategically. But it is subject to change during play, sometimes turning into a Delayed Bluff (below).

The Ambush venture often involves more money, and must be played against certain type players. When we use it in an early or middle position, we must have, not just a tight image, but an extra tight image. With all those requirements, we don't do it often, but it is especially rewarding when it shows itself and it works.

The biggest risk is starting the Ambush Bluff in the first place. We are calling a raise when we have a marginal hand and we have nothing invested. It could be damaging to our power image. That is one reason we play it more often when we first sit down when a tight image is more available.

An additional risk, like some other bluffs, lies in relying on the flop to determine our course of action.

If the Ambush Bluff is tried by us and it doesn't work, we must be ready to instantly shift gears.

The Ambush Bluff can be used at any time, in any no limit game, but it is best used with a very tight image.

The Delayed Bluff.

The Delayed Bluff is yet another cousin of the Ambush Bluff. (All bluffs are related and similar in that they tell a false story and someone believes it.) The Delayed Bluff is unusual and it goes like this:

Once again, we break the "don't ever call" rule. We begin the Delayed Bluff when we don't have a good enough hand to re-raise before the flop and we suspect the very active player who made the first raise doesn't have all that much either.

We think there are two weak hands in this pot, us and the other guy, so we call before the flop when we know the very active player will bet after the flop with only the slightest provocation. We do this instead of raising before the flop and making the opener throw his hand away. We delay in order to win a bigger pot. For us to make this initial call, the opponent has to be the kind of player we know will bet after the flop.

The bluff begins with calling the opponent's raise before the flop. When his raise is called by the power player, the thinking raiser should be immediately on alert and a little afraid. For this bluff, as usual, we need that image advantage.

We hold jack / ten suited, in a late position.

The flop arrives with a king, a five and a deuce, rainbow.

Pocket	Pocket	Flop	Flop	**Flop**
J♦	10♦	K♠	5♥	2♦

The very active opponent comes out firing like we thought he would. His wager is a big bet, made with gusto.

We don't break our rhythm; he must think we have a hand. But we appear serious and deep thinking. We call.

The call is designed to make the opponent think. We have already called his raise before the flop and now we're calling him again. If our image is right, these calls are powerful. (At this point, the "don't ever call" prime directive is really fractured.) The opponent is thinking, "Is the Dominator slow playing me for a sucker?"

The opponent has placed us on high cards, he doesn't know what they are and he feels like he's swimming aimlessly with this hand. Maybe we have ace / king. Maybe we have a face card pocket pair or middle pocket pair. Whatever it is, it appears to him we're committed to this hand for a reason.

When the turn is another rag, he will check; he has to. We will then bluff and take the pot. Many players miss this. We're not trying to best his hand; we're waiting for a time to bluff. Don't forget to.

This opportunity is missed time after time by the average small blinds player. Most players aren't experienced enough to know the advantage of a strong image or how to use it. It is ours to build and to take advantage of. And it can be done against any player we are not afraid of.

The Delayed Bluff is risky because it is delayed and the flop and turn may not favor our planned bluff. We are setting the bluff and we have to draw a lucky board. We must have a garbage flop, some cards the opponent does not have, and a garbage turn to make it work. Meanwhile, we're risking our stacks.

Sometimes the situation arrives accidentally. That is why it is called a tactical maneuver. It is also why it is sometimes hard for us to spot and often hard to take advantage of because it's so far into the play of the hand, we haven't been thinking along those lines.

In our illustration, we started with something good to draw to. If we had gotten two diamonds on the flop or an eight and nine or other connectors, we could still make an Ambush Bluff. So the hand can develop toward one of two bluffs, Ambush or Delayed.

The point of the Ambush Bluff and the Delayed Bluff is to demonstrate that pots can be won with poor flops. To do it, we have to play our players and have a good idea of what kind of hand they have. We have to be very aware of our image to those players. Our bluffs have to be mixed with some good hands and a good image.

366

Discussion 446

Catching Bluffs

It is recommended that the reader begin this series with Part 101.

Poker is not a card game played by people.

Poker is a people game played with cards.

Ah, a metaphor opportunity.

Every football season, the team's offense out-scores the defense. (Really?) We, as the most offensive power players there are, know this. But what a thrill for the football defense when they intercept a pass and run all the way back for a touchdown! That's the same thrill we get when intercepting the Desperation Bluff, or any bluff, and dragging the score all the way back to our stack. It's the ultimate thrill of a good defense. And even better when it's the game winning score.

How do you defend yourself from another player who's deploying a maneuver you have learned so well? The answer is that you can defend against bluffs because you know how bluffs work.

Tells are important. We pick up a lot of bluffs because of tells. Catching a tell on a frequent bluffer is worth our stack weight in pure gold.

Patterns of play are very important. But does the departure from the opponent's usual pattern mean he has an accidental hand? Or does it mean he has a bluff? Answer: Play the player. Here is the key question: Is he a player who would likely bluff in this situation?

One more admonition in this area: Don't be afraid to be bluffed. We all bluff and we are all bluffed. The trick is to bluff more than be bluffed and to catch more bluffs. We must come out on the plus side of the ledger in this bluffing game.

367

Poker is not a card game played by people; it is a people game played with cards. It's not just a slogan. We're concentrating on playing the people, and baby, we're playing poker.

And it's all about bluffing.

Catching Bluffs.

We are constantly on the watch for a place to successfully bluff. So are some of our opponents. We use bluffs often but with discretion. We can get a win without bluffs, but we won't often get a day's good win without them. A rule of thumb at the lower blinds games: If we don't bluff successfully, we lose at least 50% of our potential win.

A bluff is sometimes made with the best hand. Sometimes we don't know whether we bluffed or not. Sometimes we don't whether the opponent bluffed or not.

There is a new two word comment often used these days, other than "nice hand". The new two worder is "good bet". Or "nice bet". It's a compliment from the opponents. It means "we know you didn't have much, but neither did we and it was the proper time to bet and take the pot." Sometimes we have to get our share of these compliments, just to keep our stacks up.

Catching the Desperation Bluff.

We stay away from, watch out for, and catch the Desperation Bluff and the Fantasy Bluff. There is serious money to be made in those catches.

We like the Desperation Bluff. We look forward to it. We reap its harvest. We exploit it. We revel in it. We wallow in its bounty. And the reason we like it so much is we never use it and we almost always catch it when someone tries it.

Desperations aren't planned and are, therefore, poorly chosen, poorly executed and easily caught. They often are made by a player we have determined to be a weak calling station, or a player who is much too active and likes to draw to a hand and never give up on it.

The subject of the Desperation Bluff is covered extensively in Discussion 441.

The Button Bluff.

The Button Bluff is the most common bluff in hold 'em. It is used by us and by our opponents. It's an invitation, sometimes, to simply bet and take the pot. It's a trade we make with the others players. (Whose turn is it this time?) Many times, when we bluff from the button, we are bluffing with the best hand. So are our opponents. But it was their turn and we'll let them have the little pot.

We have seen something like this: In a no limit game, a raise on the button with pocket nines gets calls from the small blind and two middle players. The pocket nines get two nines on the flop, making quads. Everybody checks and our quads player checks along. After all, it's common for the button to bet and take it. But, in this case, the button player wants a call and knows he won't get one, so he checks along.

After the turn, everybody checks and the quads again check along. After the river, some tired person says, "Somebody bet and take this pot!" So the button with quads bets the size of the pot and the small blind calls. "Nice bet." Bad call.

The caller had almost nothing at stake but had made some kind of small hand. As far as we're concerned, in that circumstance we'll let the button take the pot; it's part of the game.

The Blind Man's Bluff.

This bluff represents strength born of weakness. When the flop is weak and we come out betting, we, in effect, announce it hit our blind where it counts. We're saying, "If you don't believe me, call this!" If it didn't help the others, we have a pot no matter what we're holding.

Like the Button Bluff, the blind man got a good garbage flop and we'll let him have the pot. It should take a good hand on our part to raise him, although there are times when we might raise him for so audaciously making a bad bluff. Calling is out of the question.

The Free Draw Bluff.

The strategy in this bluff after the flop is to get two more draws without betting before the showdown. It's used against the tight opponent, when we have a marginal hand and a nut hand to draw to.

We defend against it when we think it is being used against us. We can raise the bettor after the flop. Or, when he checks to us after the turn, we can bet a large amount; he obviously needs a draw and usually can't afford a big price for one. We need only to see him get his free draws once in a prior hand in order to place him on a being a practitioner of the Free Draw Bluff. But don't forget to bet a large amount.

The cards are right for his draw - and maybe for our draw, too. But we are the ones who will raise him if he bets and we are the ones who will bet if he checks.

The Free Draw Bluff is obvious to us practitioners and often we know this opponent well. When we think we have the edge, he won't get his two free draws.

The Ambush Bluff and Delayed Bluff.

Now we're playing poker. The planned bluffs, with their variations, are well executed by us and they could be well executed by our opponents. When they are, they are hard to read and hard to catch.

We're playing our players to the zenith when we defend the Ambush Bluff and the Delayed Bluff. We have to be having an exceptional day to do it often.

In the meantime, we won't be afraid to be bluffed by those we don't catch. It happens all the time.

Summary.

We will bluff and be bluffed. The Dominator will win more of these contests than he will lose. He knows the situations and the bluffing maneuvers.

Discussion 447

The Check and Raise Bluff

It is recommended that the reader begin this series with Part 101.

Poker is not a card game played by people.

Poker is a people game played with cards.

The Check and Raise Bluff.

Most experienced professional players count this category of bluffing as separating the Dominators from the wannabees.

While the Check and Raise is not as complicated as the Ambush Bluff and the Delayed Bluff, it requires pure skill in reading a player and it requires much more money.

The Dominator must know the situation. Moreover, it's done often with almost no previous investment to protect; its reward is based almost entirely on opportunity.

The Check and Raise bluff is not a semi-bluff where we can perhaps recoup with a lucky draw if we're caught semi-bluffing. Nor is it a bluff to rescue our claim on a pot in which we have invested heavily. And we certainly don't do it because it is the only way left to keep from losing. We do it because of a pure and holy opportunity for profit.

In the Check and Raise bluff, we usually have little invested and we have no hope of showing the best hand, whether in a draw out or otherwise. We're not rescuing anything. We are, in fact, manufacturing an opportunity which has no business existing in the realm of objective probability. It takes nerve. It takes money. And it takes skill.

The Check and Raise Bluff is pure action and bluff. It lives in a class by itself.

If we choose not to make the bluff, we haven't lost a thing because we have next to nothing invested. Most low blinds players will opt for that decision every time. However, if we choose not to make the bluff, an expert player may point out that we have just lost a golden opportunity.

The Check and Raise Bluff is especially effective from the blinds where we are expected to sand bag. We simply check after the flop before we make our raise. Relatively speaking, that's the easy one. It's a much easier decision to make than from a later position.

When we are in the blind, many opponents we check to will make the "continuation bet" of simply following through with their betting after the flop because our check shows weakness. This makes them easy prey. A raise against their continuation bet gives us the pot. That said, we'll move forward to yet another level of difficulty and required finesse.

Here, in general, is what we look for in any Check and Raise Bluff situation:

We look for a player who fears us as an opponent. The situation requires at least a little fear on our opponent's part, something players are in the habit of calling "respect" but what we know is really fear. Fear at the table is easy for the true Dominator to detect. A lot of the prevailing fear will be fear of him.

Not many players at the small no limit levels are willing to make the Check and Raise Bluff. But once the reader makes this beautiful move, he'll be very pleased with himself and will have moved to a higher level of play.

All we have to do is check our nothing hand to a scared player who likes to bet (the common button bluffer?) and then raise him when he bets. He can be tight or loose, aggressive or passive; it doesn't matter so long as we have his "respect".

Many small no limit beginners are transparent enough that their bet from last position is almost laughable. Those players belong to us.

Because the Check and Raise Bluff is used so little in the small games, it has a high success rate in those games. That success rate is drastically reduced as we advance through the bigger games.

The bluff must be made against a well chosen adversary and, like all strategic bluffs, it must be planned and then executed with the proper rhythm and in our usual style.

Using the Check and Raise Bluff too frequently is disastrous. A simple counter raise destroys the maneuver and depletes our stacks unnecessarily. Hence, the necessity of the well chosen opponent and circumstance.

Bluffs in general are most successful against good players or, better yet, players who think they are good.

The final payoff.

So far, we have addressed the easiest Check and Raise Bluff, the one from the blinds when there is a garbage flop. Making the move from middle position is a bit harder, especially when a player to our right has checked to us.

It's time for Murphy to play a hand.

Murphy has been watching all the players at the table. He is sitting in seat five and has noticed seat nine has been doing a lot of betting from the button.

The set-up: Number Nine has noticed that Murphy can be taken off a hand fairly easily. (All good players can.) But Number Nine has also seen Murphy win some large pots that were played well. Murphy knows that Number Nine is both active in the game and afraid of Murphy.

Number Nine is on the button. The pot has been opened with a small raise by a player on Murphy's right. Murphy is holding jack / three and has this player set for a first stage Ambush Bluff, so Murphy calls.

The action goes to the button who re-raises. This action has just ruined Murphy's Ambush but, because it is Number Nine raising, a new opportunity has presented itself.

The blinds fold. The player to Murphy's right, the raising opener, calls. Murphy calls. There are three players in the pot.

The flop arrives with a ten of diamonds, a four of clubs, and a seven of diamonds.

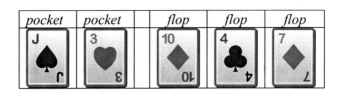

pocket	pocket		flop	flop	flop
J♠	3♥		10♦	4♣	7♦

This garbage flop has helped nobody. And Number Nine may be the longest way from being helped.

The opener checks. Murphy checks. Number Nine checks.

The turn brings the deuce of diamonds.

pocket	pocket		flop	flop	flop		turn
J♠	3♥		10♦	4♣	7♦		2♦

The opener checks. Murphy checks. Number Nine bets.

The opener mucks his hand. Murphy raises the size of the pot, including the bet just made by Number Nine.

"You made your flush, did you?" This question from Number Nine helps the situation; it announces to all the novices at the table that the active player thinks the power player has made a flush. In the image game, table talk counts; it is valuable.

Number Nine, not a bad actor, slowly throws his hand away.

In review, any bluff depends on having the worst hand, but having the best story.

What if the turn or the river hadn't been a diamond or other card to tell Murphy's story for him? We know Murphy would NOT make the Desperation Bluff. No story, no believer – no bluff.

How about just betting the hand when the diamond appeared instead of waiting for Number Nine to bet? The action would be a bluff, but it would be in the Desperation category.

If Murphy bet right out, there would be more danger of a call from Number Nine. The Check and Raise is much more powerful and it wins more money.

What went through Murphy's mind through the play of the hand?

First, Murphy, with a questionable hand, called the opener's raise. He did this because the opener was ripe for an Ambush Bluff and Murphy hoped the flop would favor such a bluff.

But Number Nine fouled the Ambush with his raise. These things happen. But, in raising, Number Nine presented another opportunity. Having called one raise, Murphy called the second raise - not because of the size of the pot, not because of the size of his hand, but because there were two players involved who could be maneuvered if the flop was favorable. There's that "respect" again.

The flop was not wonderful and everybody checked. This confirmed Murphy's placement of big cards for the opponents with no set in sight.

Number Nine did the betting after the turn. Murphy read this as an "I guess nobody wants the pot so I'll try a Desperation Bluff" kind of bet.

The rest was easy.

Murphy never showed his hand and retained his good image. Most of the players placed him on Big Slick in diamonds.

Don't waste the Check and Raise.

Of course, if we check and raise with a good hand, it is not a bluff and occasionally a small no limit player will check and raise just to win a bigger pot. The experienced check and raiser doesn't usually do that because it's a spent maneuver that could be a waste of a future bluff situation.

The Dominator with the good flop waits until he feels an opponent is suspecting him of the Check and Raise Bluff and, not until then does he check and raise with a good hand. At that point, he usually gets a humongous call.

Discussion 448

Defending Against the Check and Raise Bluff

It is recommended that the reader begin this series with Part 101.

Poker is not a card game played by people.

Poker is a people game played with cards.

Defending Against the Check and Raise Bluff.

We won't run into this bluff often in the small blinds games. It will remain mostly in the Dominator's arsenal, but check and raise as a bluff will happen occasionally with a more sophisticated player at the table and so it should be discussed.

We start finding it more frequently in $5 and $10 blinds games. And we will nearly always find it in the higher than $5 and $10 games. Furthermore, in heads up cash games and final table tournaments it often will determine who wins and who loses.

The Dominator should have good command of the check and raise procedure before advancing to the bigger games.

So, now we're into more sophisticated bluffing. We have two players who will make the check and raise bluff and we have to be aware of this kind of bluffer. Few players in the small games can make the bluff convincingly. Few of those players who can make the bluff are ready to risk their stacks in order to try.

Let's say Doyle Brunson is sitting across from us in the big blind and, after the flop, checks to us on the button. We have raised the pot before the flop and he has called us.

We got big cards on the flop, but none of them gave us a pair. We've placed the Texas Dolly on middle cards, at least for the time being. The flop is mixed and we are prepared to take the pot with a continuation bet, which is a planned bluff.

Brunson checks the flop to us. We bet the size of the pot. Our physical movements are normal. Our bet is a usual amount for us. We are measured in our timing. We make the bet with our normal, cool, methodical action.

We'll turn this hand over to you.

Brunson raises you three times your bet! What do you do?

Okay, let's say it isn't Doyle Brunson. (What are you doing in his game, anyway?) Let's say it's your brother-in-law. Now what do you do?

You're playing hard poker here. Is he bluffing or does he have the goods? If it were one of us Dominators, we might be bluffing.

With either player, The Dolly or the brother-in-law, it's a fuzzy decision when you don't have a tell. Maybe there isn't a lot of poker history with your brother-in-law. Then your decision will be an intuitive decision at best.

Here is something interesting: You would more likely call Doyle than the brother-in-law because the Dolly is the more likely player of the two to make the bluff.

But should you make the call?

Whoever the opponent is, your decision will depend on your opinion of the player. It will depend on the opponent's image to you and your image to the opponent. After all, your bother-in-law wouldn't just check and raise anybody. But he might check and raise you.

And what *is* your image? Would you make this bluff if you were in his place?

Our first instinct is very important. We won't quit making other considerations but, in our final decision, we must give a lot of weight to our first instinct. (See Discussion 430 on Intuition.) On the other hand, if your first instinct is defensive (he can't do that to me!), then your second instinct might be better. Your intuitive reads should be well practiced by you at this stage because this is where they are needed most.

Our "other considerations" will include play at the table over the last hour or so. Our considerations will include whether the opponent might be desperate or whether he's the type who will capitalize on his recent image. Or is he the lay-and-wait type who hasn't done much lately and is sand bagging with the goods? (This type was reviewed in Discussion 445 on the Ambush Bluff.) Has he done this before; is the pattern familiar?

He can make this check and raise when he has a good hand. If he's done it before, we'll know that. But what does our opponent have this time? If he hasn't made a check and raise with a good hand, he isn't likely to make a check and raise as a bluff. (Just the opposite is likely with the Dominator – if we haven't check and raised as a bluff, we probably won't be checking and raising with the goods.)

Now it is more important than ever to be able to play the players. These kinds of decisions bring the results that produce tournament champions or send champion wannabees to the side games. Or, in the case of the Dominator's cash games, they are the decisions that can make us bigger winners for the day - or can turn us into one of the day's losers.

The reader can readily see why the Check and Raise Bluff is so effective; it is hard to read when executed properly in the proper situation. And, in big games, it is often the day's deciding strategy.

A Stronger Situation.

Let's make the situation more complicated. Let's say The Dolly, or your brother-in-law, has checked to you after the flop. You have made your bet, and he has called you. He checks again after the turn and you check along with your weak hand. After the river he checks to you once more. You bet because he's shown some weakness and you've made a little hand that you believe has the edge. In response to your bet, he moves all-in. What do you do?

If this is a planned bluff, it is one of the most sophisticated of bluffs. And your decision and what you do, will depend on what you think of your opponent and, in this case, what you think of your hand. Remember, you thought you had an edge and that's why you made your bet.

Sidebar.

Many experienced and knowledgeable players make the Check and Raise Bluff the benchmark in deciding whether or not a player is a sophisticated player.

Many say no one has reached the upper level of play without honing to perfection the Check and Raise Bluff after the river.

Summary.

Bluffing IS poker to the pros. They've stopped concentrating on playing the cards because playing the cards is now second nature. The game now centers entirely around the players.

Playing the players is the biggest part of the bluff game. It IS the game.

Discussion 449

A Review of Bluffing

It is recommended that the reader begin this series with Part 101.

Poker is not a card game played by people.

Poker is a people game played with cards.

When do we finish with our lessons?

"When you can snatch the pebbles from my hand . . . . ."

The solid truth is that we never stop learning. Every time we play, no matter how experienced we are, we learn something. Every pro player learns each time he plays.

To paraphrase Sir Isaac Walton, poker may be said to be so like the sciences, that it can never be fully learned. (I wonder if Sir Isaac would have appreciated the plagiarism.)

If we don't stop learning, we become stale. If we become stale, we lose. The Dominating power player doesn't show a loss on the bottom line of his accounting. He keeps on learning and he learns something every time he's at the table.

The guidelines in these pages are pegs on which to hang good play. But winning comes from the player, not the pegs. And most good players have a coach.

At the final table in tournaments, emphasis is on the bluff. <u>In a cash game we are always at the final table</u>. Our play starts and ends there.

Provided the bluffer knows the game, the only factor that can throw the good bluffer off balance is a lucky streak by an opponent. As long as the cards are in balance among pro players, the contest is decided by bluffing and the best combination of bluffer and bluff catcher will win the day.

Here we go again.

We're in a no limit cash game. We've won a few pots with good hands, mixed our play, and won a few bluffs. Then suddenly the cards stop coming; they don't even arrive occasionally.

A dry spell is bound to come in a cash game for any of us. When that happens, we can't mix our play, we can't even win an honest hand, and we can't make a lucrative bluff because we get no action.

Trying to mix our play without an occasional good hand is simply giving our money away.

We can stay, maybe a long time, and wait for another fair share of cards. That's one way. But, if we've been there awhile, we could deny Paco further pleasure in giving us no cards, and go to dinner. Sometimes it's the only thing to do.

The point is we have a choice of leaving and saving our money. We do not have that choice in tournament play.

All no limit games.

Nevertheless, the margin of play in any no limit game at the higher level is in the ability to make and catch bluffs. In the small blinds games, there is even more opportunity than in the bigger games because we're easily best at it.

Learn the bluff patterns well. Use them well and catch them well. It's how we win.

Bookkeeping.

It is easy to focus on the battle, but it is necessary to deliberate on the war. An easy bookkeeping page can be set up with Microsoft Excel to fit the individual's needs.

See you around the green felt jungle.

Players' Glossary

By: Sam O'Connor

The masculine references in the definitions below are intended to include both genders and are not in any way or manner intended to offend, promote or diminish either gender.

A B C	Ace, deuce, three. Mostly used as razz jargon. A player with starting cards of ace, deuce, three, has an **A B C** hand.
Action	Betting at the table. Includes all bets, checks, raises and other undertakings in the course of the game.
Afraid of His Money	An expression describing a player who is much too aware of the value of his playing chips and is afraid to lose to the point it adversely affects his game.
All In	A player who is all in has all his chips in the pot.
Ante	A small amount of money from each player before the hand is dealt. It's an incentive to play because each player has something at risk from the outset.
B R	The **Bankroll** for playing poker.
Back Door	**Drawing out**. The back door occurs on the **turn** and/or the **river**. A player beaten in this way is said to be **back doored**.
Bad Beat	Occurs when a **made hand** is beaten by a lucky draw, or a large and therefore apparent winning hand is beaten by a better hand.
Bankroll	The money set aside for gambling that is not a part of the daily living budget. A true capital venture. The **BR**.
Barking Dog	The appearance of an open pair on the **board**. The pair loudly signifies a possible **set,** full house or four of a kind. Also, the nick name, in Hold 'em, of the **pocket** cards, king and nine.
Bet	The wager made at the appropriate time at the table.
Bets	A term used in highly **structured limit** poker to designate the original bet and the number of raises. "Three bets" would mean a bet and two raises.

Big Blind	The largest posting in lieu of antes before the dealing starts. Usually there are two blinds, **big blind** and **small blind**.
Big Slick	**Pocket** cards consisting of an ace and a king.
Blank	A board card of little or no value. Also known as a "**rag**".
Blind	Used instead of an **ante**, sometimes in addition to antes, especially in Hold 'em type games. The act of the first, and usually the second, player beginning the betting before the hand is dealt.
Blind Raise or Bet	A **raise** or **bet** made by a player before he sees his cards or any card not yet seen during the hand.
Bluff	To bet a losing hand hoping the opponent will **fold**.
Bluff	A weak hand represented by its owner as a strong hand.
Board	The **community** cards in the center of the table.
Board Cards	In Texas Hold 'em and related games, the exposed cards in the middle of the table which are used by all players at the table. The board begins with the **flop** and is followed, after betting, by the **turn** card and the **river** card making a total of five **board cards**.
Bottom Pair	A card in a player's hand, matching in **rank** the lowest **board card** after the **flop** constitutes the **bottom pair**.
Bounty	A prize paid in some Texas Hold 'Em tournaments to a player for knocking an opponent out of the tournament.
Bowed Neck	Determination to extreme. A player off balance. (See **Tilt**.)
Box Man	The man who sits at the craps table to watch over the dealers and players. He helps keep the dealers and players honest and to referee any alleged mistakes. May be sitting next to you at the poker table.
Bringing the Pot in	Beginning the action in the hand. Starting the betting. Starting the pot.
Broadway	An ace high straight.
Brown Bagging	Bringing one's own lunch from home to the table. Looked down on by veteran players as a symbol of being ordinary.

Buddy Show	Occurs when two buddies are at the table and in the same pot. After a strong bet by one buddy, the other folds. The winning buddy then shows his hand to let the loser know he really did have the stronger hand. In most rooms, the **buddy show** must then be shared with the rest of the table.
Bullets	Two aces. Applied primarily to **pocket** cards. "I had *bullets* in the pocket."
Bully	A player who tries to dominate the table by betting more than the other players. The bully is usually a garrulous type. Wait for him.
Burn	The removal of the top card of the deck before dealing. Helps maintain the integrity of the game. It is customary among gentlemen and necessary among thieves.
Burn Card	The top card of the deck which is discarded sight unseen before dealing.
Button	An indicator showing which player is designated the dealer and the player to act last in the betting sequence, the blinds having already acted. The blinds, however, have the choice of acting again. The designated dealer position may also be referred to as The Button.
Button Round	The number of hands it takes for everybody at the table to play the **Button**.
Buy In	The amount of money a player starts with at the table.
Buy the Button	The act of buying the dealer designation to gain position in coming hands. Designed for those poor at math.
Call	To accept the amount bet. To match the amount bet in order to stay in the hand.
Calling Station	The position occupied by a player who calls many bets, seldom raises and is reluctant to fold.
Cap	The maximum amount of **buy-in** allowed by some casinos for some poker games.
Capping the Raises	To make the last raise permissible in a **structured** game.
Case Card	The last card of a given **rank** in the deck. If three jacks have been accounted for, then the last jack is cased or in the deck. Also, the last card of a given **rank** that has not appeared anywhere is sometimes called the case card.

Cash Game	A game played for cash or true valued **checks** as opposed to tournament play.
Cat Hop	Drawing to a **four flush** or **country straight**.
Center Deal	In casino games, a professional dealer deals for all players and sits at the center of the table.
Check	If there has been no bet, a player may decline to bet and remain in the hand by **checking**.
Check	A casino or poker room betting unit which represents true money value and is redeemable at the cashier's cage. Often incorrectly referred to as a **chip**.
Check and Raise	Or check/raise, is accomplished by first checking a hand and, after an opponent has bet, raising the bet.
Chip	The unit of value used in tournament play. Chips do not represent true value, but only the betting value in the tournament being played. (See **check**.)
Chopping	Dividing the pot. Usually, after no action in the hand, the two players playing the blinds, by agreement, take their money back rather than play the hand.
Chopping the Bet	Raising a player knowing, because of position, he can't call.
Cold Call	A call after two preceding players have acted, the first in the action betting and the second in the action raising. Also known as **jumping the fence**.
Community	The cards that are shared by all players.
Community Card	A **board card**. Part of the **community**.
Company	The group of players at a table. Commonly used in sentences such as, "He was playing in easy **company**" or "She was playing in good **company**."
Complete Hand	A hand using all five cards for value. A straight, flush or full house. Four of a kind is also considered a **complete hand**.
Connectors	Two cards which are one unit of value apart. Example: a four and a five, the Moneymaker lucky hand.
Continuation Bet	When a player has raised before the flop and bets after the flop, continuing to represent a good hand, he has made a **continuation bet**.

Counterfeit	The elimination of the strength of the lesser pair of two pair by a superior pair on the board. Example: The strength of a player's aces and fives can be eliminated by a pair of sixes on the board giving the opponent an equal hand.
Country Straight	A four card straight looking for the fifth card.
Cut	The act of transferring a portion of the deck from the top of the deck to the bottom of the deck. In a center deal game, the professional dealer **cuts** the deck. In a ring game where everybody deals, the player to the right of the dealer **cuts** the deck. It is customary among gentlemen and necessary among thieves.
Cut Card	A blank card placed on the bottom of the deck, when the deck is **cut**, so the bottom card that's part of the deck will not show if the deck is tipped, turned or slanted.
Cutting Checks	The method used by most dealers and most experienced players to count casino checks or tournament chips. The cutting act is performed by placing the hands over a stack of standing checks or chips and moving the forefinger through the stack in the desired place in the stack repeatedly to create smaller stacks, usually in divisions of five, four or three, for counting.
Dead Game	A game just starting with house players present in the game. Sometimes used to describe any game with little action.
Dead Man's Hand	Aces and eights, the hand Wild Bill Hickok held when Jack McCall shot him in the back in Deadwood. Some say the fifth card was the queen of spades, but we really don't know.
Deuce	Any card with the **rank** of two.
Dick Smith	**Dick Smith** never picks up the tab.
Dink	To bet a very small bet when there is a very large pot. The reasons for implementing this procedure are obscure.
Dominated Cards	A hand or hole cards that will usually lose to a lesser like-kind hand or hole cards. For instance, ace / deuce will usually lose to **big slick,** in which case ace / deuce would be **dominated**.
Dominator	The best player at the table who takes huge advantage of it.

Draw Out	To receive a card or cards during play that convert a losing hand to a winning hand.
Drawing Dead	Trying to make a hand that, if made, would still lose to the opponent.
Equity Value	If a pot is $1,000 and a player judges that he has a forty percent chance of winning the pot, he is said to have an equity value of $400. It is usually a symbolic number since the winning player will have either all or none of the pot.
Exposed Card	A card that has inadvertently been rendered face up. Sometimes caused by an **orangutan**, sometimes by a careless player.
Family Pot	A pot in which all players are participating at the outset.
Fast Play	Playing a hand very aggressively. (See **Speeding**.)
Feeding the Table	An expression introduced by the ineluctable **Silver Dollar Sam** in describing the habitual losses of players who make playing poker profitable for the rest.
Filler	The cards which convert three of a kind into a **full house**. Three aces and two kings would be aces full with the kings as the **filler**, aces full of kings.
Flat Call	Calling without raising.
Flop	After the initial betting, the first three **board cards**, dealt face up and used by all players in the **hand**.
Fold	To throw in (**muck**) a hand in the face of a bet. To quit the hand.
Forced High	In stud poker, when the high card is required to open the betting.
Fouled Hand	A hand out of play because of a violation of procedure or other action. Usually, a player's hole cards which have touched another player's cards or touched the **muck** are declared **foul**.
Four Flush	A four card **flush** looking for the fifth suited card.
Freeze Out	The time when no more alternates are allowed in the tournament.
Grinder	A player who concentrates on small pots, those he is sure he can win, in order to make a slow, more certain profit. But it doesn't always work that way.
Hand	The cards a player plays during the **action**.

Hand	The **action** from start to finish of one deal From shuffle to shuffle.
Harness	The money given a **shill** to play at tables where a player is needed. **Shills** were, at one time, called **mules** and the money supplied by the house were their **harnesses**.
Heads Up	A hand being played between two players only.
High Stacked	(See **Tall Stacked**.)
Hole Cards	The first two cards received by a player in Hold 'em. The two cards are dealt down, remain down, and are the player's alone to use until **mucked** or shown at the end of the hand.
Hot and Cold	Showdown. Because of an **all-in**, the betting has stopped and the remaining cards in the hand are dealt, **hot and cold**.
House	The casino, the premises and the representations controlled by management.
Hustler	Anyone who is a competent player who is in it strictly for the money.
Image	The apparent quality of play and character represented by any individual at the table.
Jackpot	An unusually large pot for the size of the game.
Jackpot	In casinos, a bonus paid a player for getting a large hand beaten or for beating a large hand. Typically, aces full must be beaten by four of a kind or a straight flush.
Jamming	In limit poker, making many raises or raising the maximum number of raises allowed.
Jumping the Fence	See **Cold Call**.
Kicker	A card used to determine the winner of a hand which would otherwise be tied, limited to five cards per hand. Also, the smaller of two cards held in the **pocket**.
Kill Pot	A practice in some limit games in some casinos whereby a winner of two hands in a row must **straddle** the next hand. The betting limits for that hand are then doubled.
Knave	The jack of any suit. Look out; he'll steal your tarts.
LA	A Loose Aggressive player.
Limit Game	(See **No Limit**.)

Limp In	To call the **blind**. To enter the pot without a raise.
Limper	One who **limps in**.
Live Game	In casinos, a game in which real money is used as opposed to tournament money. May be chips and/or currency.
Live Game	A game with no **shills** or **proposition players.**
Lock	A **lock** is the **nuts**.
LP	A Loose Passive player.
Luck	The force that <u>seems</u> to operate for good or ill in a person's play at the table in shaping events, circumstances and opportunities, especially in the random arrangement of cards in the deck and their subsequent fall attributed to an element of chance in the play of a hand. Hmmm Got it? (Sometimes said to be a lady.)
Made Hand	A hand that needs no improvement to win at a given time during the **action**, especially a **complete hand**.
Maniac	A player who tries to **bully** the table by entering more than the usual amount of pots with extreme overbets and bluffs.
Mechanic	A cheating player who manipulates the deck to his advantage.
Mechanic's Grip	The very best way to hold a deck of cards! The deck is held flat in the hand with a corner tight against the base of the drumstick of the thumb. The tip of the thumb lightly pressures the top of the deck. The forefinger is in front of the deck to ensure that only one card is dealt at a time. The remaining three fingers hold the side of the deck. The card is dealt by either the thumb on the deck hand pushing the card forward (not sideward) or the dealing hand pulling the card forward off the deck. This method assures control – no two cards at a time, no dancing cards, no soaring cards overturning, etc. Unfortunately, this best method of legitimate dealing is named after less than 1% of those using the grip. See **mechanic**.
Middle Pair	(See **Second Pair**.)
Move In	(See **All In**)
Muck	The pile of discards during a hand.
Mule	(See **Shill**.)
Mustache	A competent, experienced dealer. (We haven't heard it lately.)

389

Neutral Flop	In Texas Hold 'Em, a **flop** which doesn't improve any of the players' hands.
Nice Hand	Common expression made by a loser to a winner after losing a large pot, especially if the loser was **drawn out** on. Common return: thanks. Does not necessarily convey true feelings.
Nits and Lice	Twos and threes.
No Limit	No ceiling on the amount of money that can be **bet** or the amount of the **buy in**. No limit games are usually **table stakes** games.
Nuts	The best possible hand when viewing the board. The origin of the expression supposedly lies in the Old West. When a player had the best possible hand and was out of money he would go to the street, take the nuts off his wagon and place them in the pot, thereby betting the wagon. Obviously, not all games in the Old West were **table stakes** games.
Off Suit	Hole cards not of the same suit.
One Gap	Hole cards that are two values apart such as nine / seven.
Onsuit	Cards of the same suit. See **suited**.
Orangutan	An incompetent, bumbling, awareness-challenged dealer.
Outrun	To **draw out** on a **made hand**.
Outs	The number of cards or combinations of cards which could help a hand.
Over Card	A **pocket** card that is higher than any of the **board** cards.
Over Pair	A higher pocket pair than the highest pair made possible by the **board cards**.
Over the Top	An aggressive play made after an opponent's aggressive play. Example: Opponents bet and raise; another raise by a third player would be a play **over the top**.
Overcall	To call a bet after several others have called the same bet.
Paint	Any face card.
Pay Off	Occurs when a player knows he's beat but calls a bet because of the size of the pot, hoping the poker gods will rescue him, or there must, somehow, be some mistake.

Picked Up	The act of removing, by management, a player's **chips** from the table.
Play	More than just being in the game. **Silver Dollar Sam's** word for knowledgeable and sophisticated action in a poker game.
Play the Board	Something a player chooses to do when the player's hole cards can't improve the **board**.
Playable Hand	A **hand** which is not dependent solely on the cards held, but is also a contestant because of player **image**, **position**, and the quality and demeanor of the opponent.
Players' Checks	(See **Chips**.)
Plunging	The manner of play of a poker player on **tilt**.
Pocket	The two **hole cards** held by a player in Texas Hold 'Em. Usually used to describe a **pair** as in "pocket aces".
Pocket	The **hole cards** in Hold 'em, face down; the player's cards alone.
Poker	A name applied to the wagering on the outcome of playing cards. Some believe the word was coined in the nineteenth century from the French *poque*, and that may be correct. But the true derivation lies in a Latin verb meaning "to lay waste a man's pride and take his riches on the river".
Poker Chips	(See **Chips**.)
Position	The physical place we have in the **hand** that is being played. If we are third to act in a hand, we are in third **position**.
Post	To place money into play before the cards are dealt. Used for **blinds, blind raises, straddles** and penalties for moving to a position of better advantage or missing **blinds** because of absence.
Pot Committed	Occurs when a player has so much in the pot and the amount in the pot is so high, he will call all bets hoping for help from the poker gods.
Pot Limit	Limits the size of bet a player may make. The bet limit is calculated to be the size of the pot.
Pot Odds	The ratio of the size of the pot to the size of the bet required to stay in the hand. Often, the resulting percentage is calculated against the percentage of chance of improving the player's hand.

391

Proposition Player	A player **staked** by the **house** to play in poker games. The **prop player** splits his winnings with the **house**. (See **Shill**.) Or, a player being paid to play his own money in games designated by the **house**.
Protect a Blind	A player playing weak beginning **hole cards** in order to try to get the money back that he has placed in the blind.
Protect a Hand	To bet a large amount with the intent of driving out the opponents thereby ensuring a good hand will not be drawn out on or, if the opponent calls the large amount, making him pay to draw to his weaker hand.
Protect Cards	To place the pocket cards in a secure position on the table so that other players cannot foul the hand or so that the dealer won't muck the hand accidentally.
Push	A small pot that is negotiated to be split by the players. Usually done when no one is in the hand but the blinds. A **chop.**
Put on	Making an educated guess concerning an opponent's hole card. "**I put** you **on** a pair of aces."
Quad or Quads	Four of a kind.
Rabbit Hunting	Not calling a **bet**, thereby ending the **action**, and then asking the dealer what the next card is. The card unpaid for is sometimes called the "rabbit".
Rack Up	The act of a player placing his chips in a rack in order to carry them away from the table. It's usually the winners that **rack up**.
Rag	A card on the board that is useless to a given player.
Rag	(See **Blank**.)
Rainbow	A **board** showing a variety of suits.
Rake	In casinos, the amount of money removed by the dealer from nearly every pot. Reasons for not **raking** could be very small pots or pots in **short handed** games.
Rank	The numerical value of a card. Also, the drunk sitting next to you.
Read	The observance by a player of another player, the cards and the hand being played.
Representing	Playing as if the hand you are playing is better than the one you'll have to show if called. A **bluff**.

Ring Game	A game in which every player deals his own cards. Lately, used synonymously, however erroneously, with **live game** or **cash game**.
River	The seventh card in Hold 'em. It is the fifth board card and therefore is sometimes called "fifth street". The **river** expression comes from seven card stud in which the seventh card is dealt down and the strongest hand in six cards was often washed "down the river".
River Rat	A player with the reputation of drawing out on the **river**.
Rock	A player who plays very tight with no mix or exceptions to his solid play. This type loses, but slowly, unless novice players "pay him off".
Rolled Up	Three starting cards of equal **rank** in seven card stud. **Rolled up** aces, **rolled up** kings, etc.
Rope	Casino **checks** or tournament **chips,** numbering less than five, laid one partially upon another to resemble a chain or rope.
Rounder	A sophisticated card player. He knows all the angles.
Runners	The draw cards on the **turn** and **river.** Used most often to describe **draw outs** or **bad beats**. Originally, one hand *out-ran* another hand on the draw, hence **runners.** Making a hand on the **back door.**
Sandbag	To **slow play** a good hand with the intention of setting a trap.
Scare Card	Any board card that threatens a **made hand**.
Scramble	Sometimes center dealers will place all the cards face down and mix them in a circling motion to demonstrate that any chance of repeating patterns of shuffling and dealt cards have been broken. After **scrambling** the deck, a **shuffle** is still necessary.
Scream	The unnecessarily loud complaint of an irregularity at the table. Made mostly by inexperienced players. This type has a hard time acting like an adult.
Search Out	Calling a bet to make sure it isn't a **bluff**. Finding out, by calling, how a player plays. **Searching** an opponent's pocket cards.

Second Hand Low	The art of inducing a player to raise instead of you doing the raising with your superior hand. It usually involves three players. The first player bets, the second player with the **nuts** calls so that the third, aggressive player, will do the raising.
Second Pair	A card in a player's hand that matches in **rank** the second highest **board card** after the **flop** constitutes the **second pair**.
Semi Bluff	A bet that is made as a **bluff** on a hand that has possibilities. The bettor hopes the opponent will **fold**, but the bettor has a few **outs** if the opponent doesn't fold thereby rescuing the bettor.
Set	Originally, "**set** of threes" from draw poker. Loosely, any three of a kind of equal value, but more specifically, three of a kind in Hold 'em with two of the cards as pocket cards. (See **trips**)
Seven Toed Pete	Seven card stud played in the south, where the game was born.
Shill	A paid house player who appears to be playing his own money but, in fact, is playing a **harness**.
Short Call	A **call** made by a player who does not have enough money to match the bet. He plays only for the existing pot and the amount of his **short call**.
Short Handed	A game usually is said to be **short handed** when there are five players or less.
Short Stack	A small amount of money compared to the amount of money in front of most or all of the opponents.
Short Stacked	Short on **players' checks**. Will likely go all in the next marginal hand.
Showdown	Poker without betting or poker without any more betting. Time to show the hands.
Shuffle	The act of mixing the cards before the cut and deal.
Side Pot	After a player or players are **all in**, a pot created among those players who still have money to bet during the hand. If one or more players are **all in**, the remaining players with money can win the **side pot** they create by subsequent betting and/or a show of hands, even if they don't win the main pot.
Slow Play	Playing a strong hand as if it were a weak hand so players will remain in the action and will build a large pot.

Slow Roll	The despicable, low life practice of ever so slowly showing a cinch hand as the winner. An additional insult: "I have two pair. Jacks and jacks." Tempers have flared. People have been hurt.
Small Blind	The least **posting** in lieu of **antes** before the dealing starts. Usually there are two **blinds, small blind** and **large blind**.
Smooth Call	(See **Flat Call**.)
Smooth Call	Simply calling either a bet or a raise.
Speeding	Playing in a manner that is an obvious overplay of the hand.
Splash	The act of tossing chips for a bet, call, or raise, directly into the pot. Considered bad form because it could be disguising the actual amount submitted for the bet, call, or raise.
Split Pot	A pot divided equally between two or more players having winning hands of equal value.
Spread Limit	A **limit** poker game in which the betting is structured to allow a range of betting as, say, in units from two to six or four to twelve.
Stack	A group of casino **checks** or tournament chips one on top of the other. A proper stack is either a group of five or twenty; stacks of less than twenty are properly divided into groups of five and the number of less than five **roped**.
Stake	The money a player has for playing poker and usually money supplied by someone else. (See **Stake Horse**.)
Stake Horse	Someone who makes a practice of **staking** players. Stake horses usually get half the winnings but all the losings.
Steam	Irritation after a **Bad Beat**.
Steam Raise	An ill advised raise made under a **steam** condition.
Straddle	A form of **blind raise**. In most games, any player can straddle before the cards are dealt, but the straddle is usually made by the player situated after the **big blind**. The **stradddler** will then be the last to act.

String Bet	The act of placing money in the pot in more than one motion. Unless the player has verbally announced a raise, he will be limited to the money he has placed in the pot in his first motion. However, in a limit **structured** game, if he has placed more money in the pot than the original bet, he must make more trips to his stack to complete the **raise, bet** or **call**.
Structured	The schedule of bets allowed to be made in some limit games. There is usually one level of betting before and after the **flop** and another level before and after the **river**. Sometimes, but rarely, there are three levels which create another level before the **river**.
Suck Out	**Drawing out** on a winning hand.
Suited	Two cards of the same suit in Hold 'em. Usually refers to **hole cards**.
Swimming	If a player has no idea of his position or value in a hand, he is not on solid ground and is said to be **swimming**. He's a fish.
TA	A Tight Aggressive player.
Table Captain	A well seasoned player who knows more about running the game than the fledgling dealer and who sometimes must take charge. However, the <u>self appointed</u> type **table captain** may sometimes be just a loudmouth.
Table Stakes	Applied to all professionally run poker games. Under **table stakes** rules, a player may not increase his playing money during a hand, remove playing money from the table without exiting the game, or withhold any playing money from a bet he wishes to call if it renders his call a **short call**.
Tall Stacked	Having more **checks** or **chips** than most players at the table. **High Stacked.**
Tap City	See **All In.**
Tell	A mannerism which inadvertently conveys to the observant player the value of an opponent's hand or the intention of the opponent. An expression derived from days of yore when it was said that a player *telegraphed* his hand before he bet.
Tilt	A manner of play by a player who has lost discipline or control.

Time	A request by a player to take a little more time than usual. The time request is in deference to the other players and to the dealer and is considered good form.
Time	The **vigorish** timely collected by casinos in some games, for house costs and profit.
To Muck	To throw in a hand upon leaving the **action**.
Toke	A small amount of money given to the dealer, floor man, chip runner or cashier by players, usually the winners. Originally, "token of appreciation".
Top Pair	The card in a player's hand that matches in **rank** the highest **board card** after the **flop**.
TP	A Tight Passive player.
Tres	(Pronounced "tray") Any card with the **rank** of three.
Trips or Triplets	Loosely, any three of a kind. But, specifically, three of a kind in Hold 'em with two of the cards on the **board**. (See **Set**.)
Turn Card	The card following the completion of betting after the **flop**. The card is dealt face up and placed with the flop and is sometimes called "fourth street".
Under the Gun	The first player to act is considered **under the gun**. Usually refers to the player after the **big blind** before the **flop** and is the **small blind** after the **flop,** but can simply mean the first player to act. Sometimes shortened to **UTG.**
UTG	The player who is first to act after the blinds is **Under The Gun**.
Value	The **rank** of a card. Also, the **rank** of a hand if all hands were shown.
Vig or Vigorish	The **rake**, fee or margin collected by management to pay for costs and provide profit for the **house**. If a tournament has a $230 entry fee with $200 for the tournament winners, then $30 is the **vig**.
Wheel	The smallest straight, ace to the five.
Window Card	The **hole card** or **pocket card** some players are willing to show an opponent during play or after the hand.

Cheaters' Glossary

By: Sam O'Connor

The following descriptions are not intended to be inclusive nor are they intended to adequately instruct. They are, however, presented to underscore the fact that irregularities in poker are with us everyday. Because a few of the methods of cheating at cards are presented here does not make the reader immune to the methods of cheaters nor does it allow the reader to detect, necessarily, the presence of cheating. The reader is cautioned that, if he suspects irregularities at the poker table, he should leave the game.

Copyright © 2005 by I T Solutions, Inc.

Basements	(See **Bottom**.)
Bender	A player with the bad habit of bending certain cards so that he can spot them in or on the deck or in another player's hand. Benders cause the deck to be changed frequently. They never grow up.
Bottom	The act of dealing from the bottom of the deck. The deck is held flat in the hand. The ring finger moves the bottom card while the thumb moves the top card to hide the bottom card coming out of the deck. With a slight dip of the deck, the bottom card can be dealt without being seen. There are variations of this procedure.
Burning	The act of a cheater watching another cheater to see how he operates. It's considered bad form among cheaters.
Bust Out Game	A game devised by one or more players to take all the money on the table. There are many, many ways.

Capping	Capping the deck is done by a dealer who knows what the top card is and prefers a different top card. He may want another card because he likes the top card and doesn't want it to be the burn card or for many other possible reasons. The dealer finds a card in the muck and palms it. He then appears to adjust the deck thereby depositing the palmed card on top the deck. This kind eventually falls into bad hands.
Catcher	The player at the table who receives the **run up** hand from the dealer. This scam is prevalent in ring games where everybody deals and it has made the rounds in center deal games in casinos. Watch for the cheating dealer, not the **catcher**.
Check Cop	The art of stealing checks (chips) from a poker pot. A product called "check cop" has been marketed from time to time but the same effect can be gained from holding a match under adhesive tape until it liquefies the adhesive and then placing a dab of the stuff on the palm of the hand. However, a skillful check copper much prefers to palm the checks without adhesive; adhesive can leave tracks on the checks and can make it awkward to handle cards. In a ring game, watch the player who has a habit of organizing the chips in and around the pot.
Clean Up	The act of getting rid of a **hold out** card or **copped check**. The cheater must occasionally show a clean hand. He throws the extra card into the muck, or **swings** the chip into his pocket or stack.
Cold Deck	A pre-arranged deck of cards designed to **bust out** a table's **mark**. The pre-arranged deck is introduced surreptitiously into the game after the **mark** has warmed and is less wary. The **cold deck** name comes from the new deck being a cooler temperature than the **front** deck which has been warmed by the players' hands. The cold deck is placed on a handkerchief in the lap of the cheater. The **front** disappears for only a split second, falls into the handkerchief and, in that same short time, the new deck appears in the cheater's hands, ready to be dealt. (Done nicely in the movie *The Sting*.)

Collusion	Two players playing the **same money**. Such cheaters usually situate themselves at opposite ends of the table in order to place players between them as evenly as possible. As one player enters the action he traditionally will bet his checks to the right for a strong hand and to the left for a weak hand, although there are many other ways of signaling the partner. The weak hand then raises for the strong hand thereby building a pot. This simple **sandwiching** is happening today and every day in Internet games and can only be detected by the pattern of play. Is somebody raising a lot and never showing his hand? Are two people (there have been instances of more than two) in the same pot more often than is usual? When those two are in the pot do they seldom show both hands? Is one, or both, a huge winner? Internet hosts are attempting to preempt collusion through registration. But there seems to be no sure way to counter such Internet cheating and, so far, the only remedy is to leave the game.
Cooler	(See **Cold Deck**.)
Crimp	A gap in the deck, placed there by a **run up** man so his partner, who is to cut the deck, will cut it in the right place. (See **Thumb Brace**.)
Cut In	A player recognizing a cheater's maneuvers at the table and signifying he wants a part of the action. The **cut in** signal is crossed fingers on the table. If both are cheaters, the **cut in** could signify that they will share their spoils. More likely, they will not signal the **cut in**, but will signal a **George**, stay out of each other's way at the table, each keeping his individual take.
Deuce	(See **Second**.)
Double	The skill of dealing two **run up** or **cold deck** hands to two players in the same hand at the table. One, of course, is the **catcher** for the **run up** artist or **cold decker** and will receive the best hand. The other hand will be a close second and lose a big pot.

Eye in the Sky	The people and apparatus behind the mirrors and cameras that can see everything and everybody in the casino. If you're in a casino, smile, you're definitely on candid camera.
False Cut	A maneuver that appears to cut the deck but, in fact, does not. The false cut can be accomplished by a **pop**, **jogging** a card, **gap** or **thumb brace** and many other methods. Beware the smiling dealer.
False Shuffle	An apparent shuffle that is no shuffle at all, leaving the entire deck undisturbed or at least that part of the deck that has **run up**, **cold deck** or a **pick up** hand or hands.
Front	(See **Cold Deck**.)
Gap	A space left in the deck so that an accomplice can **false cut** the cards.
George	A code word between cheaters used in a sentence signifying everything is okay. ("I hear George is coming to town".) **Georg**e can also be signified by an open hand with fingers extended on the table. (See **Tom**.)
Going South	(See **Swinging**.)
Grab Game	(See **Snatch Game**.)
Handkerchief Trick	(See **Cold Deck**.)
Hanger	Evidence of a **mechanic's** maneuver gone awry, such as a second card which didn't quite make it out of the deck or a **hold out** card not quite hidden. Very embarrassing.
Hindu Shuffle	The art of shuffling a deck keeping two cards together and located, usually on the bottom of the deck.
Hold Out	Holding a card in the palm of the hand instead of **mucking** the card at the end of play. The **hold out** player will then have the advantage of an additional card in the next hand. And there are many other reasons for a cheater to hold out.
Inside	All those recognized by the clan of cheaters to be fellow cheaters or those knowledgeable about cheaters. It's a tight group.

Jogging	Handling the deck in a way that one card is slightly out of place thereby marking a **located** place in the deck. It is also useful in **false cutting**. The jog is common among **mechanics** and is a favorite tool of magicians.
Knocking	A method of dealing the second card in the deck. Using the **mechanic's grip**, the thumb of the deck hand presses the top card of the deck. The dealing hand then "knocks" the thumbnail of the deck hand forcing the top card backward slightly with just enough exposure to allow the dealing thumb to catch the end of the second card. With only the slightest dip of the deck, the second card is dealt without being seen. The knock can be detected only by the motion. "He *knocked* a few seconds tonight."
Locating	A dealer knowing where a card or cards are before and/or after the shuffle. Locators can't be trusted.
Luck	Luck? In cheating, **luck** is not a factor.
Machine	A metal spring-loaded rack that fits in the sleeve where cards can be stored and called upon at will by the cheater. It originated on river boats when players wore frilly shirts and coats. Machines haven't been seen or squeakily heard in decades. For one thing, today's sleeves can't hide one. Common remark by one sharp eared river boat gambler to another: "Either learn to play poker or get that machine oiled."
Mark	The player at the table who is the target of a **bust out game**. "This sure is a friendly game."
Marking the Cards	There are many ways. One of oldest is to tamper with the diamonds on the back of Bee decks. Another is to modify the wheels on Bicycle decks. Or **shading**. Markings can be many, various and very hard to detect. Bring your own cards.
Mechanic	A cheater who can manipulate a deck to his advantage. Includes **run-ups, seconds, pick-ups, deuces, bottoms, doubles, locating, peeks, spilling, capping** and much, much more.

Mechanic's Grip	The very best way to hold a deck of cards! The deck is held flat in the hand with a corner tight against the base of the drumstick of the thumb. The tip of the thumb lightly pressures the top of the deck. The forefinger is in front of the deck to assure that only one card is dealt at a time. The remaining three fingers hold the side of the deck. The card is dealt by either the thumb on the deck hand pushing the card forward (not sideward) or the dealing hand pulling the card forward off the deck. This method assures control – no two cards at a time, no dancing cards, no soaring cards overturning, etc. Unfortunately, this best method of dealing is named for less than 1% of those using the grip. Nearly all **mechanics** use the **mechanic's grip**.
Outside	All those who are not knowledgeable about cheating. All those outside the cheater clan are fair game. Even the cheaters' cousins.
Over the Top	To turn a cheater's game against him. Example: When a cheater marks cards and a player has discovered it, the player uses the information to know what's in the cheater's hand or to falsely represent what in his own hand by making it difficult to read some of the marked cards.
Palming	The act of secretly holding a card, a poker chip or other item in the palm of the hand. As with so many other practices in cheating, misdirection is key in palming. Works even easier with today's bridge sized cards. Dealers, box men and floor men must all show their palms upon leaving a gambling table or transferring checks to a table. Clap hands, you're on camera.
Peeking	The act by a dealer of looking at the top or bottom card during the deal of the hand. There are many ways. Some involve slanting the deck slightly and pinching the top card, some moving the bottom card slightly and bending it. Some peekers ride the top card up the drumstick of the thumb. There have even been reflective rings worn by some dealers so the deck can remain still.

Pick Up	Picking up the cards in a manner to enable **locating**. In a loose ring game, the cards even can be picked up to make a complete hand or hands that only require a **false shuffle** and/or **false cut**.
Pigeon	A player who is easily beaten and returns to be beaten again. Games have been built around this type.
Poker	A name applied to the wagering on the outcome of playing cards. Some believe the word was coined in the nineteenth century from the French *poque*, and that may be correct. But the true derivation lies in a Latin verb meaning "to lay waste a man's pride and take his riches on the river".
Popping	A method of **false cutting**. The cheater cutting the cards divides the deck into two sections and places them back the way he found them so quickly that we cannot see the **false cut**. The maneuver is usually accompanied by a loud **pop** of the cards.
Pull Thru	A form of **false shuffle**. The dealer appears to be shuffling but, in fact, is pulling one portion of the deck through the other portion leaving the order of the cards undisturbed.
Rail Thief	A person who roams casinos looking for a craps table with lots of action where he can steal checks from his rail neighbor during heavy betting. As he reaches forward and down to the table to make his bet, his other hand goes under his armpit and takes the neighbor's checks from the rail rack. The **rail thief** usually isn't betting much.
Readers	Glasses engineered to see colors on cards that cannot be seen with the naked eye. The numbers and suits of cards can be written on the backs of cards in colors which can only be seen through the *readers*. The colors are sometimes placed there with the thumb or finger during play.

Run Up	Building a hand or hands in the act of shuffling the cards. The cards must be **located** and placed in a known spot in the deck. Then the cards are moved during the shuffle to the desired spot for dealing the prepared hand. A single hand, a **double**, or more hands can be run up by an accomplished **run up** artist. Detect the **run up** by noticing that there are too many shuffles or that the shuffles aren't very finely dividing the cards. However, a dealer with a good **pick up** need only shuffle a few times to get the cards in the desired place for dealing the **run up** hand.
Same Money	(See **Collusion**).
Sandwiching	The act of two players in **collusion** raising a player caught between them. One player has the nuts; otherwise they could lose two hands to the one being **sandwiched**.
Scratch Out	A player caught cheating in a casino is directed to leave the game by the simple scratch across the cheater's back by a floor man as he passes behind the cheater's chair. Cheaters know the sign and are relieved at the offer to leave the game without fuss or embarrassment. The cheater is then dealt with in private after he leaves the game. This practice helps keep a peaceful atmosphere at the poker table.
Scream	The unnecessarily loud exposure of an irregularity at a casino poker table. It's a performance made by some inexperienced players and is absolutely the worst way to expose a cheater. The best way to extricate a cheater is to leave the table quietly and inform the shift manager. The manager will observe the cheater, tell the **eye in the sky**, and deal with the infraction when it occurs once again, without fuss. Old saw: "If you're going to be a sucker, be a quiet one".
Second	The second card from the top of the deck is called a **second** and can be dealt at will as if it were the first card by an accomplished **mechanic**. The second card, or **deuce**, is dealt either by **slipping** or by **knocking** the second card from the deck and neither procedure can be seen when skillfully performed. Only the familiar tell tale motion can be detected.

Send Over	The act of informing a co-conspirator about an opponent's hand, usually by a person standing or sitting behind the opponent. (Done nicely in the movie *Goldfinger*.) Information about the cards the opponent is holding is **sent over** to the co-conspirator player at the table.
Shading	The practice of placing valued cards in the sun for a short time to slightly change the shade of color on the backs of the selected cards. Works well with plastic cards. But don't let mother know.
Shiner	A type of ring which, when worn by a dealer, reflects the bottom card or the top card when slightly moved and can be read by the dealer to help in dealing **seconds** and **bottoms**.
Shirt Man	A method of **holding out**. A pocket is sewn into the inside of the front of a shirt, just behind a false middle button. A player, holding his cards close to his chest, can slip cards in and out of the concealed pocket. Does not work well for polo players.
Slipping	The best method of dealing the second card in the deck. Using the **mechanic's grip**, the deck is held loosely using the deck hand thumb to slide the top card thereby exposing the corner of the second card. With only the slightest dip of the deck, the second card is **slipped** out of the deck without being seen. Only the familiar tell tale motion can be detected.
Snatch Game	A center deal game in which the dealer is taking way too much rake from a pot, usually by palming the chips and placing them in the rack. Prevalent in the 1950s and 1960s in Las Vegas casinos, some dealers specialized in snatch games and were paid a percentage of the excessive rake. A common practice during a black period of the Las Vegas poker industry.
Spilling	The act of a dealer moving the deck over the **muck** and **spilling** the top cards which are not favorable to his **catcher**. The cheating dealer misdirects with his dealing hand while the deck hand **spills** the top card or cards.

Spread	Executed by two players sitting side by side in a draw poker ring game. The two players signal to each other what each has, what each needs to make a hand, and whether the partner has what is needed. (Knees are used a lot.) After the last bet and call the playing partner lays his hand face down on the table, **holding out** the one unneeded card. The partner supplying the needed card (**palmed** before he mucks his hand) picks up the hand and spreads the complete and winning hand for all to see. Each partner then proceeds to **clean up** while the pot is pulled in by the winner and the cards are gathered by the partner.
Steer Man	The man who urges a **mark** to play in his **bust out** game. Many times it's a steer lady. Beware the winning smile and the trim ankle.
Sucker	The weakest player at the table and doesn't know it.
Swinging	The covert removal of chips from the table, usually by **palming**.
Thumb Brace	A gap in the back of the deck held open by the dealer's thumb so that a **false cut** can be made. Very effective in center dealing where the center dealer does both the shuffling and the cutting. Watch for a revealing line in the front of the deck caused by the gap in the back of the deck when the gap is not held open just right. Also, the deck must be cut from the middle of the back of the deck. (See **crimp**.)
Tom	A code word between cheaters used in a sentence signifying that there is a problem. ("How's your brother, Tom?".) **Tom** can also be signified by a closed hand on the table. (See **George**.)

Printed in the United States
104720LV00003B/36/A

9 781434 302892